SCHOOLED AND SORTED

HOW EDUCATIONAL CATEGORIES CREATE INEQUALITY

Thurston Domina, Andrew M. Penner, and Emily K. Penner

The Russell Sage Foundation NEW YORK

LIBRARY OF CONGRESS CATALOGING-IN-PUBLICATION DATA

Names: Domina, Thurston, 1975- author. | Penner, Andrew M., author. | Penner, Emily K., author.
Title: Schooled and sorted : how educational categories create inequality / Thurston Domina, Andrew M. Penner, and Emily K. Penner.
Description: New York : Russell Sage Foundation, [2023] | Includes bibliographical references and index. | Summary: "The popular imagination views education primarily in terms of teaching and learning. Schools matter, in most tellings, because they give students skills that they draw upon as they move into the labor market, the public sphere, and other areas of their adult lives. But teaching and learning are only a part of what happens in schools. In this book, we want to advance a view of schools as category construction machines. We do not want to discount the importance of the skills and knowledge that students gain at school. But we argue that educational organizations are always and everywhere engaged in the production, manipulation, adaptation, and enactment of categories. This category work necessarily creates inequalities and is essential to the operation and social significance of educational systems in contemporary schooled societies. Schools construct social categories—kindergartener, English language learner, honor roll student, cheerleader, Ivy League material—that shape students' identities and their access to resources. In the process, schools also reflect, adapt, and reify powerful social categories—including categories related to race, ethnicity, class, gender, sexuality, disability, and religion—that organize and divide the societies in which they operate. The categories that schools create, enforce, and even on occasion reimagine have far-reaching consequences for people's lives. At the most basic level, we argue that exposure to any form of formal schooling marks a person's potential to be a full member of contemporary communities. Becoming a student, we argue, is a crucial step on the way toward becoming a citizen. Furthermore, we argue that the credentials that schools confer to students at the end of their educational careers play a central role as young adults move out of school and into a complex and highly specialized adult society. In the contemporary world, educational categories don't just influence where we work or what we earn. They influence where we live, who we live with, our civic participation, and even our longevity"—Provided by publisher.
Identifiers: LCCN 2022058298 (print) | LCCN 2022058299 (ebook) | ISBN 9780871540003 (paperback) | ISBN 9781610449021 (ebook)
Subjects: LCSH: Track system (Education)—United States. | Educational equalization—United States. | Educational sociology—United States.
Classification: LCC LB3061.8 .P46 2023 (print) | LCC LB3061.8 (ebook) | DDC 371.2/54—dc23/eng/20230215
LC record available at https://lccn.loc.gov/2022058298
LC ebook record available at https://lccn.loc.gov/2022058299

The paper used in this publication meets the minimum requirements of American National Standard for Information Sciences—Permanence of Paper for Printed Library Materials. ANSI Z39.48-1992.

Text design by Matthew T. Avery.

RUSSELL SAGE FOUNDATION
112 East 64th Street, New York, New York 10065
10 9 8 7 6 5 4 3 2 1

SCHOOLED AND SORTED

To Kathryn, Cyndi, and Marilyn, who modeled how to build paths through the limits people put on them because they were girls—EKP

To Daniel, who highlights the perils of categorical definitions—AMP

To Lincoln and Willa, who are determined to be their full selves, categories be damned—TD

CONTENTS

ILLUSTRATIONS

ABOUT THE AUTHORS

THURSTON DOMINA is Robert W. Eaves Distinguished Professor of Education at the University of North Carolina, Chapel Hill.

ANDREW M. PENNER is professor of sociology at the University of California, Irvine.

EMILY K. PENNER is associate professor of education at the University of California, Irvine.

PREFACE

This book began when a local reporter happened to call while we were having an informal lunch meeting. The reporter wanted a quote for a story about the use of color-coded ID cards in a school. He never really got it. But his request for comment started a conversation between the three of us that has spanned nearly a decade. The conversation meandered through student center food courts in Irvine, cafés in DC, conferences in Europe, library basements in Durham, state parks in California, and home offices in the midst of a pandemic. And given the longevity of the conversation so far, it seems unlikely that it is finished. After some encouragement from Suzanne Nichols at the Russell Sage Foundation, however, we were convinced to share these thoughts in a more formal context. The result is this book.

If this book summarizes our ongoing conversation, it is important to note that the three of us disagree on many points. For example, while we are all troubled by the level of inequality present in contemporary society, we have different perspectives on how to bring about a more egalitarian society. As a result, our policy prescriptions here are, for the most part, less specific and more general. We have tried to pull together the points on which we agree, provide a sense of the framework that informs our discussion, and invite you, the reader, into our conversation.

We write this from an interesting position, as people who have excelled at meeting the sometimes bizarre requests of the Western educational system. We are all currently employed at institutions of higher education, whose revenue benefits from education's unique role as an arbiter of social mobility. And we are all employed by public universities, where education is understood to be a public good and increasing access to social mobility is a central aspect of the institutional ethos. In addition, much of our teaching involves preparing students to be educators and much of our research involves working with educators to confront the challenges facing schools.

We are writing this at a time when the public conversation around education is bifurcating: on the one hand there is a strong movement for the provision of universal free access to early and higher education, while on the other there is a movement away from education as a public enterprise and toward a greater focus on individuals. Although we are firm believers in—and beneficiaries of—the expansion of public education, and view higher education as an essential public good, we are also troubled by education's increasing monopoly over social mobility and the ratcheting up of the stakes of this status competition (even though it likely benefits our employers). We suspect that many of you will struggle with a similar tension. In the following pages, we invite you to share our discomfort and reflect on how we might make productive changes.

ACKNOWLEDGMENTS

We are grateful to Priyanka Agarwal, Brenda Cervantes, Ariel (Hong) Chan, Daniel Chen, Jomar Lopes, and Joyce Ni for research assistance. Our thoughts have also benefited immensely from conversations with and comments from Geof Bowker, Patricia Bromley, Miles Davison, Wang Feng, Eric Grodsky, Paul Hanselman, Lenore Katz, L'Heureux Lewis-McCoy, Andrew McEachin, John Meyer (whose encouragement resulted in part I), Chiqui Ramirez, Catherine Riegle-Crumb, Evan Schofer, Sarah Soule, Shoufu Yin, and countless others. We are especially grateful to Emily Katz, who lived with this book as long as any of us, gave us invaluable writing advice at several key moments, and introduced us to Katherine Anne Porter's Stephen.

CATEGORIZATION: HOW SCHOOLS ENACT INEQUALITY 1

Stan Sitwell had a problem. The principal of Horace Mann High School in Sudden Valley, California, Sitwell knew that people everywhere—from the real estate agent down the street to his bosses on the district board of education and the policymakers in Sacramento and Washington—were judging him based on his students' scores on the annual California Standards Test (CST). But he also knew that his students didn't care about the test:

> It means everything to the school, but nothing to the students. The SAT, the high school exit exam, professional licensure exams—all have incentives for test takers, but the CST does not. A pop quiz in home economics has more incentives for students. I have had teachers work incredibly hard to prepare their students only to watch them bubble in pictures on their answer sheet or take a nap.

Sitwell had to find a strategy to make his kids care about those scores.

Thinking about how students gave their best to earn varsity letters in sports and other extracurriculars, Sitwell hatched a plan. Together with the principal at a neighboring school, he created color-coded student IDs and distributed them to students based on their performance on their prior-year CSTs. Students who performed in the top proficiency bracket on all their CSTs got "platinum" ID cards.[1] Students who scored in the top two brackets got "gold" ID cards, and all other students were given plain white ID cards. The principals required their students to wear their IDs at all times and carry matching homework planners, in the hope that they'd give students a social incentive to take the CSTs seriously. They printed banners to hang around campus with catchy slogans like "The Platinum Card: Membership Has Its Privileges" and "The Gold Card: Don't Leave Home without It." To sweeten the deal, they provided a series of token rewards for students with platinum and gold ID cards, including free admission to athletic and other school events, the opportunity to enter lotteries for items such as class rings and school yearbooks, and access to specially demarcated "express lines" in the high school cafeteria.

In Sitwell's telling, the plan worked like a charm. The school's test scores shot up and students who might have once randomly bubbled in the multiple-choice Scantron forms suddenly started boasting about their excellent scores. What's more, the color-coded ID cards shaped social life at Mann. Platinum-card students raised their eyebrows when a white-card student showed up in an honors class, and white-card students expressed frustration that the cafeteria ran out of "the good food" before they were served.

But two years later, a local newspaper reporter found out about the program. The story landed on the paper's front page (eventually making a cameo appearance on cable news), and a raging controversy erupted. Sitwell was shocked when a local professor described the program—above the fold in the community's largest newspaper—as "the worst idea ever." Community groups threatened to sue. Sitwell's bosses at the district office said that they had never heard of the program and eventually denounced it. Within days, the state department of education ordered the program discontinued, citing concerns about student privacy.

It's tempting to dismiss Sitwell's color-coded ID card program as a curio or a symptom of a test-obsessed American educational system. But the program, we argue, is emblematic of something much deeper. We think the color-coded ID cards illustrate one of the most powerful—and vexing—roles that schools play in contemporary societies. Although we don't often like to admit it, schools are social sorting machines. When Sitwell built the color-coded ID card program, he drew upon the school's power to create social categories and invest them with social meaning.[2] Sitwell and the ID card program created new social categories by drawing categorical distinctions between students based on their achievement on end-of-course tests and reinforced these categorical distinctions by marking students with ID cards. Doing so motivated some students. But it also created inequality among students as it produced new gaps in achievement, behavior, and educational experiences between students with platinum, gold, and white ID cards. Though perhaps more visible in students' daily lives, the categories created by the ID cards had much in common with the categories generated when schools give students grades or offer admissions to honors programs. School categories shape identities and assign labels that carry over into nearly every facet of students' lives.

This is not to say that schools try to create inequality. Nor is it to say that all of the inequalities that schools and their categories create are equally problematic. In fact, contemporary mass education systems are founded on the egalitarian notion that all people are educable and deserve an opportunity to learn. And indeed, schools often intentionally construct categories in the pursuit of entirely justifiable—and even laudable—educational goals.

Consider, for example, the remarkable curriculum that a third-grade teacher, Jane Elliott, created in her Riceville, Iowa, classroom on April 5, 1968. The night before, Jane and her family had spent the evening glued to their television, shocked and heartbroken by the news of Martin Luther King Jr.'s assassination. Aiming to help the students in her all-White class "find out for themselves, personally, deeply, what discrimination was really like, how it felt, what it could do to you," Elliott divided her classroom by students' eye colors.[3] On that Friday morning, Elliott announced to the class, "Today the blue-eyed people will be on the bottom and the brown-eyed people on top."[4] As the day progressed, Elliott watched the brown-eyed students turn on their former friends as they created and came to believe in stereotypes about the blue-eyed students. Meanwhile, the blue-eyed children withdrew from their classroom work and their attitudes regressed as they became increasingly angry over their treatment.

The next Monday, Elliott reversed the roles. Suddenly, despite having been through the exercise in reverse just a few days prior, the blue-eyed kids claimed the mantle of superiority, while the brown-eyed children became the disadvantaged group. Confident that the experience, though painful for all involved, had made a lasting impression, Elliott repeated the exercise over the next several years. Year after year, the same patterns kept emerging. Even though Elliott made no secret about the fact that students were participating in a role-playing exercise, virtually all of them seemed to take on and enact group identities almost immediately. Once the experience was over, many were able to understand discrimination with a new level of empathy and concern.[5]

Both Sitwell and Elliott used their power as educators to construct categorical inequalities. But they did so with different goals and consequences. Sitwell designed the color-coded ID program to create lasting identities and encourage academic engagement. By contrast, Elliott sought to create temporary categories in the hope that they could help her White students better understand American racism and its consequences. Like all educational categories, however, both shaped student experiences and defined the social order.

Categories and the Grammar of Schooling

The popular imagination views education primarily in terms of teaching and learning. Schools matter, in most tellings, because they give students skills to draw upon as they move into the labor market, the public sphere, and other areas of their adult lives. But teaching and learning are only a part of what happens in schools.

In this book, we want to advance a view of schools as category construction machines. We do not want to discount the importance of the skills and knowledge that students gain at school. But we argue that, just as Sitwell and Elliott drew upon categories—distinct groupings of individuals with one or more shared characteristics imbued with different social meanings—to pursue their educational goals, educational organizations are always and everywhere engaged in the production, manipulation, adaptation, and enactment of categories. This category work necessarily creates inequalities and is essential to the operation and social significance of educational systems in contemporary schooled societies.

Schools construct social categories—kindergartener, English-language learner, honor roll student, cheerleader, Ivy League material—that shape students' identities and their access to resources. In the process, schools also reflect, adapt, and reify powerful social categories—including categories related to race, ethnicity, class, gender, sexuality, disability, and religion—that organize and divide the societies in which they operate.[6] The categories that schools create, enforce, and even on occasion reimagine, have far-reaching consequences for people's lives. At the most basic level, we argue that exposure to any form of formal schooling marks a person's potential to be a full member of contemporary communities, in other words, a citizen.[7] Furthermore, the credentials that schools confer on students at the end of their educational careers play a central role as they move out of school and into a complex and highly specialized adult society.[8] In the contemporary world, educational categories influence not just where we work or what we earn, but also where and with whom we live, our civic participation, and even when we die.[9]

We simply cannot understand the wide-ranging consequences of education without coming to terms with the social category construction processes that occur in and around schools. In this book we highlight the many ways in which schools construct and maintain social categories as well as the indelible link between these categorization processes and social inequality. In doing so, we use ideas about categorical inequality to make sense of the complex relationship between education and inequality.[10] This framework, developed most extensively in the work of Charles Tilly and Douglas Massey, provides a set of conceptual tools for understanding the common social processes that underpin race, gender, sexuality, social class, disability, and other axes of inequality.[11] A categorical inequality perspective on education provides a framework for organizing the insights that emerge from a diverse and interdisciplinary body of recent scholarship on education and inequality. It also provides an account of the ways in which particular educational practices interact with and contribute to the persistent chasms that divide our society. Although this framework suggests that categorization—and therefore inequality—is at some level an inevitable component of social life, it also suggests that the size and shape of social inequalities can vary dramatically across social contexts and times. As such, we argue, a categorical inequality framework suggests how we might collectively work to build systems of education that contribute to a more just and egalitarian society.

Categories: Origins and Implications

Categorical inequality scholarship proceeds from the observation that people are frighteningly good at creating distinct social groups based on seemingly trivial differences and then acting on those distinctions. As work on the origins and implications of categorical thinking in philosophy and psychology documents, these social groups might be completely arbitrary at their inception.[12] Indeed, Jane Elliott's students adopted fierce identities around their eye colors despite the fact that she explicitly told them that she was drawing distinctions between blue-eyed and brown-eyed children to teach them about discrimination—and then arbitrarily switched the roles in the middle of the experiment! Elliott was surprised by her students' eagerness to enact these categorical roles. But a rich research literature in social psychology and behavioral economics suggests that we shouldn't be. Study after study, whether conducted in the lab, in the classroom, or in the community, has demonstrated that people identify with their own group and define themselves in opposition to other groups even when they know that group assignments are random.[13]

These group memberships are the germs of durable social inequalities. Stan Sitwell's decision to require his high school students to wear white, gold, or platinum ID cards based on their prior test scores changed the social and academic structure of his school. Platinum card holders, already concentrated in high-track classes, began to think of themselves as the school's undisputed academic superstars. White card holders, meanwhile, increasingly felt that they were academic failures. In time, as the white card holders' class attendance, behavior, and grades suffered, the achievement inequalities between these social groups began to widen. This basic social process—in which schools help to construct social groups, define the boundaries between them, and distribute valuable social resources across them—is repeated at every stage in the educational system.

In fact, we argue that sorting students is a central task for virtually all schools, and this sorting influences the shape of inequality in the societies in which they operate. Sometimes (as in the color-coded ID program) schools sort to honor some students and position them as models for others to emulate. Virtually every high school in the United States has an honor roll; virtually every elementary school hosts recognition ceremonies for students with perfect attendance or exemplary behavior records. At other times—as in Elliott's brown eyes–blue eyes intervention—educators sort students to facilitate their pedagogy. Regardless of why schools create categories, their categorization processes separate people. And because separate is not equal, categorization inevitably leads to some form of social inequality.

The Paradox of Education and Inequality

We thus believe that education is inexorably implicated in the construction and maintenance of categories that inevitably contribute to social inequalities. In light of this, we harbor a deep skepticism toward the idea, taken almost as an article of faith by many of our relatively highly educated friends and colleagues, that simply expanding educational opportunity is an effective strategy for countering the forces that drive social inequality. Indeed, from our perch in the United States—where the last several generations have witnessed a dramatic expansion of educational opportunity along with persistent social inequalities and widening economic inequality—it sometimes seems like the opposite is true.

Our skepticism that educational equality will flow from educational expansion as a matter of course is informed by a rich body of critical educational scholarship from scholars like bell hooks and Henry A. Giroux that highlights and critiques how political, social, and historical forces heighten the salience of social boundaries in educational spaces and create and maintain inequalities along race,[14] gender,[15] sexuality,[16] class,[17] disability,[18] and other socially constructed and fluidly drawn axes. Critical scholars have chronicled how schools formally enforce categorical distinctions and power differentials, such as through school segregation, as well as how educators seemingly accidentally replicate racialized and gendered hierarchies.[19] Scholarship in these traditions increasingly takes an intersectional perspective, highlighting how these different axes combine to change the meanings of different categories and shape people's experiences.

At the same time, scholarship that takes a more internationally comparative perspective documents that the spread of mass education has corresponded with the development of democratic systems of government and the expansion of human rights protections.[20] This occurs in part because the most fundamental educational category is the one that divides people who can access formal education from those who cannot. Since this line between the schooled and the unschooled often corresponds to distinctions between rights-bearing individuals and members of permanent underclasses, we see education as a fundamentally egalitarian institution that is inevitably implicated in the production of social inequality. We grapple with this paradox throughout the book: How can it be that education is both a source of human rights, democratization, and liberalization and also a driver of profound inequalities?

The work of the sociologist John Meyer helps to explain how both aspects of this paradox can be true. In his 1977 article "The Effects of Education as an Institution," Meyer conceptualized education as "a set of institutional rules which legitimately classify and authoritatively allocate individuals to positions in society."[21] It is useful to unpack some of the major ideas embedded in this sentence. We have already highlighted classification and allocation as key tasks for education. But what does it mean to describe education as a "set of institutional rules"? And what does "legitimacy" have to do with anything?

We take the word "institutional" as a reminder that education is a social project that draws upon the efforts of people working in a broad range of capacities all over the world. Some of the "rules" that organize this project are formal educational policies. But many others are shared expectations, norms, and beliefs that shape our behavior even if nobody ever bothers to write them down. These institutional rules define the taken-for-granted "grammar of schooling."[22] This grammar dictates, for example, that any organization that wants to be understood as a "school" should separate students into classrooms and put at least one trained and credentialed teacher in charge of making sure that the students in each classroom are exposed to the set of learning opportunities that constitutes their curriculum.

When young people interact with the set of institutional rules that we call education, they become students—people who are capable of growing, learning, and flourishing. In this sense, education acts as a "great equalizer," as it steps into social systems defined around statuses such as race or caste and asserts a fundamental

Figure 1.1 *Earnings Distribution for U.S. Adults Ages Thirty-Eight to Forty-Two, 2015–2019*

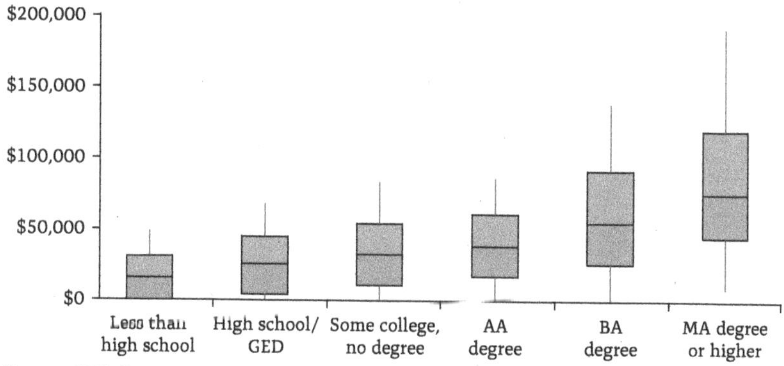

Source: U.S. Census Bureau, American Community Survey (ACS) Five-Year Data; Ruggles et al. 2021.

Notes: The boxes represent the twenty-fifth and seventy-fifth percentiles of the earnings distribution of individuals with that education level, with medians marked by the horizontal lines. The lines above and below the boxes represent the tenth and ninetieth percentiles.

commonality. This equality is often fictional. Drawing on the work of generations of critical educational scholars and historians of education, we will document profound inequalities in the opportunities within educational systems. But the fiction of equal educational opportunity is extremely powerful, because it implies that the inequalities that emerge from educational systems accurately reflect differences in people's abilities and merit. The legitimacy that Meyer attributes to education as an institution hinges on its ability to maintain this fiction.

The Long Arm of Educational Inequality

The inequalities associated with categorical differences in education are large, persistent, and thoroughly documented. A graphical illustration of one of the best known of these inequalities can be seen in figure 1.1, which represents the earnings distribution for U.S. adults ages thirty-eight to forty-two, by educational attainment category. These categories are blunt and thus obscure important categorical distinctions among members at various degree levels. For example, these data would place Harvard dropout and billionaire Bill Gates in the same category ("some college, no degree") as a student who left Northeast Nebraska Community College after struggling through remedial math. Still, they provide an easy way to look at the economic inequalities that emerge at the culmination of a sorting process that bestows differentiated credentials on students. The line at the middle of each of these plots represents the median earnings for any given category. For workers who never earned a high school diploma, that median is approximately $15,600 per year. Put differently, a forty-year-old high school dropout who earns $15,600 is earning more than approximately 50 percent of forty-year-old high school dropouts and less than the other 50 percent of these dropouts.

Not surprisingly, as educational attainment increases, so do median earnings. Also not surprisingly, these earnings gaps are remarkably large—those with a graduate education earn nearly five times more than those who never finished high school.

Some social scientists explain the premium in terms of human capital. Reasoning that education makes workers more productive by increasing their store of job-relevant skills, this theory—which dates back at least to Adam Smith and remains highly influential—suggests that education improves worker productivity. Employers are thus happy to pay highly educated workers more, just as they make other investments to improve their firm's efficiency. Others take a more skeptical view, however, and argue that instead of indicating skills or capacities, credentials simply signal social group membership and legitimate the advantages that come with it.

There is evidence that each of these theories explains a portion of the education premium.[23] For our purposes, it is sufficient to note that regardless of the mechanism at work, categories play a central role in the production of the education premium. Schools may produce human capital inequalities by deciding which educational opportunities to offer to which children. Alternatively, they may simply communicate information about these inequalities by constructing categorical frontiers between graduates and nongraduates. Either way, school categories are clearly implicated in producing the inequalities between students who have different levels of educational attainment.

This is not to say, of course, that educational attainment categories are the only factors relevant to the production of earnings inequality in the contemporary American labor force. Indeed, figure 1.1 also reveals a striking degree of variation in earnings among adults with the same level of educational attainment. One way to conceptualize this variation is to think about the fact that approximately 5 percent of adults with no high school diploma earn more annually than the median adult with a graduate degree.

But education is often also implicated in earnings inequality among people with similar levels of degree attainment. We know, for example, that young adults who earn BAs from highly selective and prestigious colleges tend to make more than graduates from non-selective colleges. And the categories that education helps to create may even play a role in producing inequalities that seem, at first glance, to be unrelated to education. We know, for example, that women earn approximately four-fifths as much as similarly educated men.[24] Schools might not create gender categories on their own, but they certainly play an active role in policing gender boundaries and defining the nature of gender roles. Virtually all schools operate gender-specific bathroom facilities, a practice that reinforces a conception of gender as a binary by teaching children that a child can use a boys' bathroom or a girls' bathroom because they can only be a boy or a girl. Countless other school practices help children learn what it means to be a boy or a girl in ways that may contribute to gendered earnings inequalities. Curricula may disproportionately feature men in typically male occupations and women in typically female occupations. And given the fact that high school mathematics teachers are disproportionately male while early elementary grade teachers are disproportionately female, schools often provide students with gendered role models.[25]

What Lies Ahead

This book provides an account of the relationship between school and inequality, using the framework of categorical inequality to synthesize evidence from multiple strands of scholarship. We focus our attention on the categories that schools and other educational organizations interact with directly. In some cases, these are categories that schools are thought to create out of whole cloth (such as the category of the bachelor's degree recipient); in other cases, they are categories that schools co-create with other institutions (such as gender.) A key insight of the categorical inequality framework is that all categories are inherently unequal. Our discussions focus on the educational inequalities that strike us as most deeply unjust, including those that sort children on the basis of their race, gender, and other ascriptive characteristics.

We see educational categories as the direct result of educational practices that are malleable. But because education is a supremely complex global institution, it is often difficult to change educational practices in ways that remake educational categorical inequalities. Difficult, however, is not impossible. And because the first step in changing educational categories is recognizing them and understanding how they work, we have attempted throughout this book to write for a broad audience that includes educational practitioners—scholars, teachers, school leaders, and policymakers—as well as students, families, and other stakeholders who are engaged with education. We hope this book will help readers trace the connections between educational categories and social inequalities and think about how education might work differently. We also hope the chapters that follow inspire efforts to reform some of the most troublesome inequality-producing educational practices in our current system.

The remainder of the book is separated into four parts, each of which consists of two chapters. We argue in part I that schools create citizens, teaching students that they belong to a category of individuals who can make claims on the collective. In part II, we discuss some of the specific ways in which schools sort students into categories, and we underscore the surprising amount of agency educators have in making specific categorizations. Part III focuses on how the categories created by schools signal that some students are more or less valued by society and the implications of being categorized as more or less meritorious. Finally, in part IV we show that understanding schools in terms of the categories they create can help us categorize our way toward a different world.

It might be tempting to draw a sharp distinction between the way education creates citizens (part I) and how it sorts students within schools and into stratified positions in an unequal society (parts II and III). We argue, however, that these categorical processes are deeply interconnected, because even the most broadly inclusive citizenship category is nonetheless defined by its boundary and by those it excludes. And perhaps less obviously, these processes are also connected because education's role in making citizens bolsters its legitimacy to sort students—and vice versa. That is, because education is understood as broadly inclusive in defining people as educable and therefore valuable, we are willing to accept the ways in which schools categorize people as being more or less valuable. And because education marks some individuals as more valuable than others, people living in contemporary society find it easier to accept education's broadly egalitarian ethos.

Understanding that both of these seemingly contradictory roles are foundational to the institution of education is key, we think, to finding paths for productively engaging with educational categories to create a more equitable future.

Part I: Sorting into School

Part I introduces the active role that schools play in creating the categories that shape students' identities and placing them into community with others. Schools are among the few institutions in which all children in the United States participate, and they are also places where children spend a large proportion of their waking hours. As a result, school experiences help children and youth understand themselves as learners and individuals who have rights and responsibilities vis-à-vis others. At their best, schools cultivate passions, skills, and career interests that shape children's understanding of their individual identity, build their solidarity with peers, and guide them into adult roles.

In the contemporary United States, all people who are schooled are expected to complete a progression of thirteen grades and acquire basic skills in order to attain membership in the category of "high school graduate." This category often serves as a baseline for entry into full membership in society and comes with opportunities and privileges that are unavailable to individuals who have not been credentialed with a high school diploma. Chapter 2 describes how school—the institution that creates this boundary and defines what it means to be educated—came to play such a central role in American society. It details how schools bestow the identity of "schooled" upon individuals by forging a collective identity that draws them into the society of the schooled.

Schools' formative influence on individual and collective identities also makes them important sites for expanding and contesting the boundaries around full societal membership. Chapter 3 examines several historical and contemporaneous cases that demonstrate the primacy of schools in these boundary-enforcing and -extending processes. In some cases, as when school access was extended to women, elites allowed boundaries to expand with limited opposition. By contrast, as exemplified in the case of the Jim Crow South, the powerful have often blocked access to school as a way to deny Black and other racially minoritized individuals full citizenship rights and equal participation in society. Other cases, like Native American boarding schools, provide examples of coerced schooling. Time and again in the United States, leaders who are typically powerful, White, male, and abled have created laws, policies, and budgets that support the learning needs of some while hindering and excluding others, particularly those from historically marginalized and minoritized groups.[26] As our country has grown and evolved, fights over school access, participation, and resources continue to be fights over who is entitled to full personhood and on what terms.

In the contemporary United States, debates about the boundaries of school participation have shifted to conflicts over the experiences and content of schooling. We see debates around who has access to adequate, culturally relevant, and rigorous coursework; to what degree of literacy individuals are entitled; and in which facilities and sports transgender youth are permitted as debates that are fundamentally about whose lives matter. These issues highlight how schools serve as vehicles both to unite individuals from disparate backgrounds under a common identity of "schooled" and to maintain division between those with and without power in society.

Part II: Sorting within School

Even as schools pull children together into a community of citizens, they also divide students into separate and unequal categories for instruction. In part II, we turn our attention to the categorization processes that shape how students navigate their school days. School-based category construction processes are so pervasive in contemporary schooling that it is difficult to imagine a school that does not sort students into categories for instruction. In this sense, we describe instructional categories as essential elements of the grammar of formal schooling. In chapter 4, we argue that, like grammatical rules, these categorization processes so thoroughly pattern organizational behavior and define expectations that we come to take them for granted. We have become so used to sorting students into age-based grades that we often forget that there are other ways to organize schools. But of course, a wide range of alternatives are available, from the mixed-age one-room schoolhouse to systems that organize students strictly on the basis of their demonstrated skills rather than their age.

When we stop taking school-based categorization processes for granted, we realize that the people who live, work, and learn in and around schools have a great deal of power over the categories that schools enact and, as a result, over the social inequalities that schools help to construct. In chapter 5, we explore educators' use of that power, looking in particular at the many ways in which math teachers think about sorting students for accelerated instruction in the middle school grades. We draw attention to four important dimensions on which sorting systems differ and their likely implications for educational inequality: (1) the timing of sorting decisions; (2) the stakes associated with these decisions; (3) the criteria that are used to make these decisions and to rationalize their use; and (4) how the resulting inequalities differ by features like category quantity and exclusivity.

Schools are complex organizations that must navigate the interests of multiple stakeholders, work within externally imposed constraints, and ensure that they maintain social legitimacy. As such, educational leaders and practitioners are often constrained in their capacity to alter educational practices and change categorical inequalities. However, educational systems change over time and vary across places. By critically assessing their practices and contexts, educational stakeholders can cultivate the agency necessary to influence the scope and shape of the inequalities produced by their educational organizations.

Part III: Sorting into the World

Although mass education is predicated on each child's educability and worth, in part III we argue that the categorization processes described in part II sort students into value-laden, status-conferring hierarchies. Schools force students to compete for categorical distinctions that mark their merit and worth. These categorical distinctions are at the heart of educational meritocracy, a social structure that grants educational systems a near-monopoly on the creation of merit in contemporary societies.

In chapter 6, we argue that education's legitimacy as an arbiter of merit in contemporary societies hinges on several central myths: that all children come into school with equal chances at success; that the educational system affords students reasonable opportunities to acquire merit; and that educational sorting processes actually identify merit. Educational organizations enact elaborate rituals to perpetuate these myths and continuously adapt category creation processes in order to maintain the system's legitimacy. As we examine the strategies that educational organizations adopt to maintain their legitimacy as creators of merit, we draw on examples from contemporary American higher education, as well as historical examples such as the civil service examinations in Imperial China, to show how educational categories convey worth by creating merit.

Because educational categories matter for nearly every aspect of adult well-being, educational categorization is constantly contested. In chapter 7, we consider three broad forms of this contestation: individual cheating, collective resistance, and efforts to formally change the rules. Despite the differences between college students buying homework answers on the internet, community groups broadcasting exam answers outside of testing facilities, and mayors advocating to end test-based admissions to selective high schools, we argue that people contesting the creation and allocation of merit recognize this process as fundamentally a political project and seek to intervene in it. We dwell particularly on cheating because it illuminates the boundaries around merit-based educational categories as well as the social and political work required to maintain them.

Regardless of how merit-based categories are allocated, they inevitably create not only winners but also losers. Merit is inherently positional—that is, it only makes sense to think about somebody as having merit if somebody else does not have merit (or has less merit). Although the meritocratic paradigm dominates the contemporary American education system, other futures are possible. We argue that society should invest in absolute goods—where the gains experienced by one individual are not achieved at the expense of others. In part IV, we describe a path to a more equitable educational future.

Part IV: Sorting toward a Better Future

We conclude this book by asking how understanding schools through a lens of category creation can help us create an educational system that contributes to a more just world. Because category construction is an essential feature of contemporary formal education, questions about how to make our schools more just are questions about how to change categories. By attending carefully to school sorting processes and the dimensions of the categorical inequalities they create, educators with egalitarian goals can identify and develop strategies to build educational organizations that better reflect these goals.

In chapter 8, we take a step back and reflect on how the categories created by schools reflect the divergent visions that different stakeholders have for schools. Contemporary schools are simultaneously engines of solidarity, self-actualization, and efficiency, and the categories schools create reflect tensions between these logics.[27] We posit that re-forming the categories created by schools should be done with an eye toward achieving a more desirable balance among these mutually incompatible logics, particularly given what we see as a contemporary tendency to overemphasize efficiency and self-actualization logics and to underemphasize solidarity logics. Chapter 8 provides a series of examples aimed at illustrating how the categories embedded in our education system reflect tensions among these three logics of schooling. We hope this framework will help readers critique contemporary schools but also imagine a better school system.

Our discussion in chapter 9 takes a more prescriptive approach: we provide ten concrete principles and suggestions for how to make a more equitable educational system. We recognize that, because categorization depends on exclusion and creates inequality, any system of educational categorization will be definitionally unequal and likely problematic. Thus, we focus on the creation of incrementally better categories rather than the quixotic realization of completely unproblematic categories.

To create better categories, we believe that it is important to (1) strike a balance among the educational paradigms discussed in chapter 8. As we seek to balance these competing goals, it is also important to (2) recognize that all categories and categorical allocation processes are political, and that the current categories are not neutral but reflect the interests of decision-makers in the past and present. Therefore, it is important to (3) create inclusive processes for category construction and revision so that the rules governing educational categories incorporate the perspectives of a wide array of stakeholders.

Although category meanings are notoriously difficult to change, we believe that it is nonetheless crucial to (4) engage in the long, important process of redefining category meanings. We believe that the rules governing the allocation of students into categories represent a key site for change, so that we should (5) redesign category assignment processes to change category meanings. In particular, we believe that educational systems should move away from winner-take-all tournaments and (6) lower the scope of educational categories so that multiple dimensions of excellence are celebrated. At the very least, schools ought to (7) avoid manufacturing scarcity and creating bottlenecks.

To the degree that some parts of our educational system help individuals gain advantages that come primarily at the expense of others, these parts are just picking different winners and losers and providing little societal benefit. We thus argue that society should (8) divest from institutions that focus on positional aspects of education and invest in educational institutions that focus on education as an absolute good, where educational benefits help students thrive by providing advances that do not come at the expense of others. In doing so, it is important that we (9) expand educational standards, so that our definitions of school quality are based on a broad understanding of how schools contribute to the common good, not simply on whether they boost students' test scores. Finally, we argue that schools too often dehumanize students. If we want schools to be contexts that foster healthy communities and prepare students to contribute to their world, schools need to (10) cultivate caring, trusting relationships between all students and school personnel.

We see these ten suggestions as preliminary steps to a more equitable educational system.

Schools Can Build Better—and More Equitable—Categories

We wrote this book because we believe that a better understanding of the ways in which schools build categories that reinforce social inequality is central to building better schools and a more just society. To be clear, our aim is emphatically *not* to assign blame for contemporary American inequalities to educational institutions and practitioners. In fact, we view mass education as one of recent history's great global success stories.

But we also believe that education can—and should—do more to realize its egalitarian goals. Approaching education and inequality from a categorical inequality perspective draws our attention to the mutability of social inequality. We hope this perspective serves as an antidote to the determinism or political pessimism that infuses many accounts of education and inequality.[28] We often think about Malcolm X's aphorism: "Racism is like a Cadillac: they bring out a new model every year." The same can be said of sexism, class inequality, ableism, and other inequalities stemming from categorical distinctions. But we believe that a categorical inequality perspective highlights a streak of radical hope embedded in Malcolm X's "new model every year." Educational practices—what students, teachers, families, administrators, employers, legislators, and others do every day as we interact with our schools—create categories and give them meaning. Changing educational practices thus has the potential to fundamentally reshape categorical inequalities. The forces that perpetuate inequality are strong, both because current arrangements limit our ability to imagine the many ways in which the world could be different and because the winners in our contemporary education system have considerable power. But with imagination and a clear sense of how educational practices build categories and how categories build inequality, it is possible to work toward a future in which each "new model" better matches our collective values than the one that came before.

We hope this book cultivates this sense of radical hope and empowers each of us to work together to build a more just educational system and world. By analyzing how our actions contribute to the construction of educational categories and adjusting our actions accordingly, we each have the power to reshape the categories that define our social world—if only in small, local ways. Because education is such an important nexus of inequality in the contemporary world, and because a commitment to egalitarianism is so deeply embedded in contemporary educational ideologies, those of us who think of ourselves as educators have a particular responsibility to interrogate our power and carefully develop our educational practices in order to more effectively confront the educational systems that build unjust and persistent inequalities.

PART I
SORTING INTO SCHOOL

I pledge allegiance
To the flag
Of the United States of America
And to the Republic
For which it stands
One nation
Under God
Indivisible
With liberty
And justice
For all.

If you came of age in an American public school, you probably remember standing in a neat line of classmates, hand over your heart, reciting the familiar words of the Pledge of Allegiance at the start of every school day. For us, the Pledge's words are so familiar and well-worn as to be almost without meaning—more a collection of syllables than a statement of patriotism or collective commitment.

But where did the Pledge come from? How and why did it come to be a centerpiece of American educational practice? And what does it have to do with educational inequality?

The Pledge's history begins in the early 1890s, a period of rapid immigration, industrialization, and urbanization in the United States. One-term president Benjamin Harrison was facing an uphill battle in his bid for reelection. In an attempt to shore up a defecting base, Harrison picked up the mantle of "Americanism" and barnstormed with patriotic fervor. Sensing rising anxiety and xenophobia among White Protestant Americans, Harrison sought to rekindle American civil religion. Education, to Harrison, was a central part of this patriotic project.

Describing schools as "nurseries of citizenship," Harrison argued that the American flag should be flown over every schoolhouse in the country. He campaigned—ultimately unsuccessfully—for a dramatic expansion in federal support for primary, secondary, and higher education, arguing that "our educational institutions, beginning with the primary common schools and culminating in the great universities of the land, are the instrumentalities by which the future citizens of this country are to be trained in the principles of morality and in the intellectual culture which will fit them to maintain, develop, and perpetuate what their fathers have begun." Countering campaigns to use public funds to support Catholic schools, Harrison argued that teaching English to the children of immigrants should be a central educational task.

But Harrison carefully made room for immigrant communities in his "Americanist" vision. Allying himself with the Knights of Columbus and other Catholic groups, Harrison played an active role in incorporating Christopher Columbus—a Catholic hero—into the nation's founding myth. Harrison designated October 21, 1892, as a national holiday marking the four-hundredth anniversary of Columbus's "discovery of America." Harrison, along with Congress, launched the Pledge of Allegiance to the World's Columbian Exposition, choreographing an event in which schoolchildren across the country were to recite the pledge and salute the flag at the same time. The coordinated Columbus Day celebrations were not enough to save Harrison's presidency. But the Pledge of Allegiance was clearly a political success. It continues to be widely used and is now a ubiquitous demonstration of American national identity. In 1942, on its fiftieth anniversary, Congress adopted the Pledge as part of a national flag code, and state legislatures across the United States passed laws requiring public school students to recite the Pledge daily. In 1954, following a lobbying campaign by the Knights of Columbus, President Dwight Eisenhower revised the Pledge, adding the phrase, "under God."[1] Eisenhower also replaced the customary flag salute, which closely resembled the Nazi salute, with the now-familiar right hand over heart. Although the U.S.

Supreme Court has ruled that individual students may abstain from participation in Pledge recitation, forty-six states require that schools make time for the Pledge.[2]

The Pledge—and its shared history with Columbus Day—is a poignant example of how schools fashion national, common, collective identities. At its inception, Americans used the Pledge as a common "American" civic ritual to heal a rift between Catholics and Protestants. Today it continues to bind American youth to a common identity. When students say the Pledge, they learn that they are citizens of a particular country ("The United States of America") and that their citizenship makes particular claims upon them ("one nation, indivisible, with liberty and justice for all"). Further, when students stand together to recite the Pledge, they are becoming the public in which they are citizens. Looking around and seeing other children also pledge their allegiance to the American flag, children get a sense of the broader community they are joining.

The Pledge's lesson extends beyond the United States. As we will argue in part I, civic identity construction is a key purpose of formal education in all modern societies. By defining young people as educable and worth investing in, exposing them to shared bodies of knowledge, and putting them into contact with one another, schools construct the category of the citizen. This citizenship represents a national identity, but as the conception of education as a universal human right increasingly takes hold, education has come to confer global citizenship too. Citizenship is a central social category in contemporary life, since it defines a group of people who are entitled to participate in and make claims on the state and other collective entities. Understanding the important role that schools play in defining that category—and how access to schooling helps to determine who is included in the category of citizenship and who is excluded—makes it clear why the stakes in many battles over schooling seem so high.

Educational history is full of battles by excluded groups for fuller access to schooling and the opportunities it provides. But schooling is not always a force for liberation. As schools define collective identities, they impose particular tenets on children in exchange for the opportunity to participate in schooling, and at times they force students to ignore or erase their own cultures, histories, and current circumstances in order to participate in civic life. When the Knights of

Columbus lobbied for the addition of the phrase "under God" to the Pledge, they were fighting for explicit inclusion of a particular set of beliefs in American identity. But this phrase forces students who do not come from a Judeo-Christian background to either proclaim a set of beliefs they may not hold or to leave the classroom and thus opt out of a collective educational experience. Further, over the years, the Pledge has forced many students to identify with a nation that they experienced as oppressive and exclusionary. In the 1940s, Japanese children in incarceration camps were required to recite the Pledge. In 2018, the *Washington Post* reported that asylum-seeking children who had been separated from their parents at the country's southern border were required to say the Pledge while in detainment. "We tell them, 'It's out of respect,'" said one employee of the facility, known as Casa Padre.[3] While the process of learning categories and identities—that is, being schooled—is affirming and empowering for some, it is thoroughly humiliating and dehumanizing for others.

Regardless of the type of welcome they receive, students learn the grammar of categories through a series of rituals that begin the moment they enter formal schooling. These rituals have what the sociologist Pierre Bourdieu describes as "social magic," in that they both express an individual's identity and impose that identity on the individual by making the expression public. Bourdieu offers the dubbing ceremony for knights as an example of this social magic: the pomp and solemnity of the ceremony is designed to bring about a change in both the way newly knighted individuals think of themselves and the way others think of them. Similarly, we argue that schools simultaneously express youth identities and impose them on children by creating rituals that train students in the social myths that our society has developed around the school-based categories that the rest of us take for granted.

In part I, we highlight cases from the history of public education in the United States that illustrate how schools construct and define social, political, and economic boundaries. Schools turn children into students and students into individuals with social rights and obligations. We foreground how schools create and reinforce American identities in children and thus create the boundaries around citizenship that define who is fully human. Because schools create citizens, struggles for educational access become crucial sites for women, people of color, and other marginalized groups seeking full inclusion in society.

Part I also tells the story of how schools construct categories and train students to occupy them. We describe how schools introduce students to the logic of specific categories by teaching them what categories are, which categories matter, how they relate to one another, and what this means for the educational experiences and opportunities they and their peers will encounter. We examine how schools teach students to think in categorical terms by training them to use discrete, often arbitrary categories in place of the rich and complex diversity of human experience. We discuss how schools help students understand what it means to occupy some categories and be excluded from others. And we consider critical moments when practices and laws around schooling access, quality, and content redrew, reinforced, and reinscribed categorical boundaries between different social groups. We draw primarily upon cases that focus on three social categories that schools are active in creating and maintaining: citizenship, gender, and race. In interrogating distinctions between the schooled and the unschooled, distinctions between schools, and distinctions within schools, part I highlights that categorical distinctions, and the inequalities they create, are fundamental to American education.

MAKING STUDENTS CITIZENS 2

Benjamin Harrison was by no means the first American to use education and educational rituals to build a sense of shared civic identity. Indeed, education has played this important role throughout the nation's history.

In the early Republican period, the nation's founders realized that education had a contribution to make in the forging of the nation. "The nation's character is not yet formed," observed Noah Webster, the dictionary writer whose spelling books helped to document the emergence of a distinctively "American" English language. To help crystalize that character and instill "an inviolable attachment to their own country," Webster envisioned a national network of schools that would provide four months of foundational mathematics, literacy, and character instruction annually to boys and girls of European descent.[1] Although Webster did not achieve his vision, he was far from the only leader of his day to argue for formal schooling as a way to reinforce the bonds of citizenship in the young nation. Benjamin Rush, Thomas Jefferson, Gideon Hawley, and James Carter, among others, articulated similar ideas about the central role that education was to play in the American experiment.

Webster, Jefferson, and their contemporaries believed that schooling provided an important form of "social glue" that helped to create an "us" where there might not otherwise have been one.[2] In this chapter, we argue that Webster, Jefferson, and their contemporaries were right. Mass formal education is key to the establishment and maintenance of a rights-based and pluralistic society, in no small part because education builds, reinforces, and defines a category that lies at the heart of a liberal social order: the citizen.

Many of these early leaders also set the stage, however, for what we have outlined as one of the fundamental tensions of the U.S. education system: the need for an increasingly educated plurality to have a more educated leadership, and in turn using the training of that leadership as a mechanism for preserving largely inherited privilege. In addition to advocating for a baseline of universal education for citizenship, Webster argued that a republic needed to provide advanced educational opportunities in order to train talented young men to occupy elite social positions. In an aristocracy, determining which students could advance to specialized training was a matter of allowing aristocratic parents to secure educational opportunities for their children. But aristocratic self-selection contradicted early American educational theorists' notions of republican governance. Jefferson was particularly preoccupied with designing educational systems that would "separate the wheat from the chaff." Like the educational system that his nation eventually created, Jefferson's vision was at once strikingly egalitarian and harshly competitive. Much like the systems of meritocracy we discuss in more detail in part III, Jefferson envisioned an educational structure that would operate as a sieve: providing opportunities for all youth to acquire basic skills and demonstrate native talent and then elevating a handful of highly successful youth to advanced opportunities based on their prior performance.

Although the examples in this chapter draw primarily from U.S. educational history, there is nothing distinctively American about the link between education and liberal citizenship. Mass education systems grew symbiotically with the modern nation-state in societies around the world throughout the nineteenth and twentieth centuries, often with the financial and rhetorical support of national elites who viewed the provision of schooling as a tool to build national identity, co-opt political opponents, staff newly rationalizing bureaucracies, stimulate economic development, and legitimate state power.[3] And while the category of "citizen" confers rights vis-à-vis the nation-state, increasingly the globalization of education is linked with a broader notion of universal human rights, in which global citizenship allows individuals to make claims on the international order.

Data collected across the globe consistently point to a strong and robust statistical association between educational attainment and political involvement. Within any given society, more highly educated people are more likely to vote, volunteer, join associations, affiliate with social movements, and communicate with their political representatives.[4] Further, the best available evidence suggests that this relationship is causal.[5] Indeed, as Alexander Wiseman and colleagues demonstrate, the effects of educational attainment on political knowledge and behavior even outweigh the consequences of growing up in a society that offers few opportunities for democratic participation.[6]

But this evidence, as convincing as it is, does not tell us *how* education contributes to the construction of citizenship and the creation of citizenship boundaries in democratic societies. In this chapter, we highlight several ways in which formal schooling helps turn people into citizens. First, we argue, the experience of schooling teaches young people to think of themselves as individuals in a social order. Second, by exposing young people to a common set of developmental experiences, educational systems help to build the collective identities upon which modern nation-states are built. Third, when societies make decisions about who deserves—and who does not deserve—access to formal education, and of what quality, they define the social boundaries between those who deserve rights, self-governance, and elite status and those who do not. Fourth, schools seek to erase many cultural differences as they force young people to alter or even replace the identities of their birth to conform with the expectations associated with the category of citizenship. Fifth, we argue that the content of formal school curricula both explicitly and implicitly communicates a canonical base of knowledge and values that underlies a society's political culture. The multifaceted ways in which education builds citizenship boundaries and gives the category of "citizen" its particular meaning thus draw upon demarcations between the schooled and the unschooled, as well as on the categorical distinctions drawn among those within the same educational systems or within a particular school building.

How Schools Make Selves

First, and most fundamentally, the very process of schooling helps to cultivate *individuals*, by which we mean people who see themselves as having a distinct existence outside of any social relation. Consider, for example, this account of a child's first days of kindergarten in Katherine Anne Porter's short story "The Downward Path into Wisdom":

> School was easy. Teacher was a square-shaped woman with square short hair and short skirts. She got in the way sometimes, but not often. The people around him were his size; he didn't have always to be stretching his neck up to faces bent over him, and he could sit on the chairs without having to climb. All the children had names, like Frances and Evelyn and Agatha and Edward and Martin, and his own name was Stephen. He was not Mama's "Baby," nor Papa's "Old Man"; he was not Uncle David's "Fellow," or Grandma's "Darling," or even Old Janet's "Bad Boy." . . . All the children talked and sang in turn, and then all together. Stephen thought it a fine game.[7]

From Stephen's perspective, navigating the social system of the school requires more than simply learning when to sit, stand, speak up, and be quiet. Before going to school, he saw himself exclusively in relation to others—as Mama's "Baby," Papa's "Old Man," Uncle David's "Fellow," and so on. By contrast, school imposes a conception of self that is entirely new. In the transition to kindergarten, Stephen becomes *Stephen*. As such, he comes to see himself as a self and to understand that this same self is present in each of his social interactions. Stephen is the same Stephen when he struggles to make a clay cat at school as he is when he eats bread and jam with his grandma or blows up balloons with his favorite classmate. In this sense, school quickly transforms him from an ontological state of dependence to one of independence. It makes Stephen into an individual. We argue that this process of individualization, and the concomitant understanding of the self as a holder of interests and rights, occurs to some degree in any child who is exposed to formal schooling. We further assert that this ontological transformation is fundamental to the creation of the citizen.

At the same time as Stephen begins to see himself as "Stephen," he begins to recognize that "all the children had names, like Frances and Evelyn and Agatha and Edward and Martin." In this recognition lies the germ of social responsibility. At school, Stephen learns that all of the people he encounters—his teachers and caretakers as well as his classmates—also have distinct selves. It is a small step from this realization to the realization that he himself has responsibilities and ethical obligations to the other individuals he encounters.

The school places children in social categories even as it facilitates the process of individualization. Stephen begins to grapple with the idea of the self as he realizes that there is a fundamental distinction between "teacher" and "students," the latter being the "his size" people who attend school with him. This co-occurrence may be somewhat surprising, since we often see a tension between the notion of individualism and the process of social categorization. However, it speaks to a second part of the process of creating citizens: in its day-to-day operations, the school draws its newly formed individuals into collectives. As Stephen's school transition continues, he begins to see himself as a part of a social group (students) that is sometimes subject to the power of teachers and other adults and that can sometimes conspire to resist this power. The individualization that occurs in the school is thus not Hobbesian atomism. Rather, it is developing a view of oneself as a discrete unit that is both a whole unto itself and an entity malleable enough to fit into one or more social agglomerations as circumstances require and permit.

We note, however, that the school defines Stephen's individuality in relation to the organizational whole. Although Stephen probably walks away from school with a sense of himself as an individual, the school, in defining the contours of Stephen's individuality, also shapes the content of his self-understanding. For example, the existence of a category of "student with a learning disability" in Stephen's school is likely to shape his sense of self even if the school never places him in that category.

Stephen thinks school is "a fine game." School has turned him into a player and taught him how to join teams. Fortunately, since he is just a kindergartener, Stephen does not appear to grapple with this game's stakes. In time, he will come to realize just how apt the analogy between school and a game is. School creates winners and losers. To progress through the school—from the category of a kindergartener to the category of a first grader, from the category of an elementary school student to the category of a high school student—is to win. To stall in this progression—or to opt out of the game altogether—is to lose.

So at the most basic and fundamental level, the school helps to develop in students an identity as an individual and an understanding of the rights and obligations this status confers, categorizes these individuals as it teaches them that they can form social collectives, and acquaints students with social inequality by moving them among categories that are differentiated in status and privilege. It is important to note that these processes are largely independent of the content of schooling. As we will see later, that content matters as well. But even if students learn no formal skills in school, exposure to what David Tyack and Larry Cuban refer to as the "grammar of schooling"—the distinction between teacher and student, the collection of many students into classrooms, and the status progression of grades and school levels—builds in students an understanding of the self and the social world that is essential for contemporary citizenship.[8] Schools mark their students as educable, as bearers of a fundamental human worth. At the same time, schools judge and sort their students, acculturating these proto-citizens to life in an unequal society.

To be clear, our claim is not that school is the only institution that contributes to the construction of the individual self, either historically or in contemporary societies. But there is strong evidence that individualistic conceptions of the self are on the rise globally, and that this increase correlates closely with the global expansion of formal schooling.[9] Given the fact that school is typically the first institution outside of the family to which children are extensively exposed, as well as the fact that virtually every child in the United States—and indeed elsewhere in the developed world—attends formal schools, our argument is that the school plays a central role in the development of individual selves in contemporary schooled societies.[10]

Indeed, homeschooling may be the exception that proves the rule regarding the profound social power of school and its grammar in contemporary society. As the homeschooling movement continues to grow in the United States, a small but growing number of children are raised and educated without ever stepping foot in a formal school. Homeschooling families typically describe their decision to homeschool as a reaction to formal schools' bureaucratic inflexibility, and homeschooling parents and their students celebrate their educational independence. Although it is difficult to make rigorous empirical claims about these students' developing ontologies, the data that do exist suggest that homeschoolers and their parents are, if anything, more engaged in citizenship activities than their formally schooled peers.[11] It is thus clearly not the case that exposure to formal schooling is in itself essential to the development of an individual self in contemporary societies.

It's worth noting, however, that even homeschooled children are typically exposed not only to a wide array of messages from a broader schooled society but also to many of the institutional roles and structures associated with traditional schooling.[12] Homeschooling parents often band together to provide their children with formal curricula, and many homeschooling families go so far as to replicate the classroom's physical plan—complete with chalkboards and school desks—in their own home.[13] In this way, even the sharpest critics of formal schooling in our society adopt some of the grammar of formal schooling and are likely to reproduce its individualistic consequences.

These rituals shared by traditional public schools, private schools, and even many homeschools represent what scholars sometimes refer to as a "hidden curriculum." This curriculum may not be explicitly designed to teach children to occupy the social role of the student and to interact and identify with diverse others, but it creates structures through which young people learn these lessons—which are, we argue, foundational to citizenship—as if through osmosis.

How Schools Define Communal Identities

Even if homeschooling creates individual selves as effectively as traditional formal schooling does, Michael Apple and others worry that these homeschooled selves are "cocooned" and detached from a broader public.[14] These concerns draw attention to a second way in which we expect schools to contribute to the construction of citizenship in contemporary society: by putting children in contact with diverse others, schools teach them about the broad social groups to which they belong. Once Stephen, Porter's fictional kindergartener, comes to understand that he is a member of a classroom community of students with Frances, Evelyn, Agatha, Edward, Martin, and all of his other classmates, he can soon begin to grasp that he is also a member of a broader category: the many other students who have similar experiences in similar schools.

Noah Webster appreciated education's capacity to build a common identity. His call for a dramatic expansion and universalization of basic education in the United States gained relevance throughout the nineteenth century. The nation experienced dramatic economic growth in the first half of the 1800s as the steam engine, the mechanical lathe, and the industrial organization of labor were adopted by American industry. Rapid population growth accompanied these rapid economic and technological advances. Between 1800 and 1860, the nation's population increased more than sixfold as waves of immigrants arrived on its shores and settled in its new industrial cities. The resulting transformations lent a renewed air of urgency to the early republican calls for universal citizenship education in a young nation that had previously taken its agrarian, Protestant, Anglo-Saxon identity for granted.

Popular fears about linguistic, ethnic, religious, political, and class cleavages bolstered the common school movement in nineteenth-century America. Perhaps the figure most closely associated with this movement was Horace Mann, the Massachusetts secretary of education. Mann's effort to build a broadly accessible, statewide public education system consisted of two threads: First, he helped communities across the state organize to build and fund schools. Second, he worked with universities and educational professional organizations to create an infrastructure for training teachers and developing curricula that could be used across contexts. Mann promised that the resulting unified educational system would serve as a "levelling machine" that could remove artificially created distinctions in society.[15] By replacing urban Americans' patchwork of charity schools, passing child labor laws that brought young children out of the mills and factories, and building state educational agencies to regulate local educational offerings, the common school movement sought to incorporate all American youth into a shared set of educational experiences.

The common school movement dramatically expanded the scope of the American educational enterprise, creating a system of mass education that ultimately incorporated youth from all walks of life. In 1820, approximately 40 percent of children in the United States between the ages of six and eleven were enrolled in some form of formal primary school. That proportion had doubled by 1850 as common school advocates built schools across the nation. By 1870 virtually all children of elementary school age in the United States were enrolled in elementary school.[16] Furthermore, the common school movement dramatically changed the organization of public schools throughout the United States. In the nation's small towns and rural areas, common schools took the form of one-room schoolhouses where students from across a community were educated together under one roof. Although these schools often offered little more than basic literacy instruction, rudimentary mathematics, and moralistic character education, they created a common baseline from which shared identity proceeded. In the nation's cities, the common school movement replaced a patchwork of "poor schools," which had often been incapable of meeting the demand for schooling, with a system of compulsory public education.

As historians Carl Kaestle and David Tyack have documented, the common school movement also established organizational technologies that continue to shape contemporary schooling.[17] In the early nineteenth century, for example, many "poor schools" in urban America were organized on the monitorial system: students of all ages would meet in a large, open schoolroom, where a schoolmaster would oversee the education of one hundred or more students arrayed in rows. A handful of the most academically advanced students served as monitors who policed other students and provided instruction as needed. New students would be seated at the back of the room. As they demonstrated their mastery of the material, they would slowly move up the rows to the front of the room. Or as occurred more often, they would become discouraged and leave the school and formal education.

Common schools replaced this starkly hierarchical model with the age-grading system still used in contemporary schools. Championed by the educational reformer Henry Bernard, age-grading moved away from the unrelentingly fierce competition of the monitorial school. Instead, students in nineteenth-century age-graded schools were assessed annually and progressed to the next grade based on their mastery of materials rather than on their standing relative to their peers. Further, as we argue in chapter 4, in schools organized by age rather than by academic performance, students' attention was drawn to their fundamental similarity to their peers rather than focused on their skill disparities.

This expansion of mass education helped to build a cohesive American public by pulling individuals from a broad swath of the American public into a single, overarching "citizenship" category regardless of their political, ethnic, or religious categorical affiliations. The common schools that Mann and his compatriots created were publicly funded, tuition-free, and available to poor and affluent students alike. Importantly, these schools were also typically coeducational: they provided basic education to both boys and girls, despite the fact that women were largely excluded from nineteenth-century labor markets and civic life. Many common school advocates saw coeducation as an efficient way to provide future mothers with the basic skills that they would need to nurture the next generation of American male citizens. But as we argue in chapter 3, the consequences were far more sweeping, as coeducation paved the way toward women's suffrage in the early twentieth century.

The common school movement helped to build what the anthropologist Benedict Anderson calls "imagined community" in the nineteenth-century United States, and in the process built the United States as a modern nation-state. Since national identities transcend localities, their existence and legitimacy hinge on shared identities among individuals who will never meet and may have little in common. Historically, Anderson notes, the development of shared languages and media played a central role in the creation of national imagined communities. When eighteenth-century Europeans read literature and news in a common language, they developed a national conversation that helped to define new national categories like French, German, and Italian. Something similar occurred in North America as colonists used new printing technologies to share grievances and collectively define themselves against their home countries.

Both for better and for worse, cementing this process of national identification has been a major priority for American public schools since the common school era. It is an important reason why the Pledge of Allegiance—a ritual with dubious merit from the perspective of basic academic skills pedagogy—has long held pride of place in the typical American public school's schedule. As we argued earlier, the classroom recitation of the Pledge is a ritual that enacts a common American community. Just as playing the role of a student among other students helps Stephen understand that he is an individual with rights as well as communal obligations, reciting the Pledge with a roomful of classmates helps Stephen begin to grasp the contours of the broader national civic community to which he belongs.

Considering how schools enact and define this broader community sheds light on the limits of an educational system that provides schooling for all but does not ensure that students enroll in diverse school communities. When homeschoolers say the Pledge, they are likely to be surrounded only by family. When students at religious schools say the Pledge, they do so primarily among co-religionists. And students at racially segregated schools say the Pledge alongside students primarily of their own race or ethnicity. Furthermore, the Pledge is just one of the many rituals in which schools enact a broader public. As students interact with and select their friends from among their classmates, they learn (or fail to learn) important lessons about how to interact and deliberate with their fellow citizens.

Critics of homeschooling—like critics of religious school vouchers or the critics of school segregation we will discuss in chapter 3—worry that surrounding children with relatively homogeneous groups of peers leads them to develop narrow conceptions of the publics to which they belong. This concern is difficult to test empirically. Reassuringly, evidence suggests that homeschooled youth are relatively involved socially, but it does not speak directly to the idea that participation in shared public schooling helps to build that public. Just as mass public schooling incorporated generations of new immigrants into the American fabric, it also provided a mechanism for those new Americans to change the American fabric in their image. Furthermore, we suspect that the globalization of schooling and the emergence of curricula that emphasize global human rights are creating new cosmopolitan identities, particularly among the highly educated elite.[18] Given the strong evidence that exposure to diverse peers encourages students to see themselves as members of a diverse society and enables them to recognize the virtues of that pluralism, we suspect that the ongoing project of civic identity construction and reconstruction is central to the school's role in large, diverse societies.[19]

Recent history provides other examples of certain groups resisting the assimilating forces of American schools to preserve their religious ideology and practices. Harry Brighouse tells the story of *Mozert v. Hawkins*, a 1987 Tennessee case in which fundamentalist Christian parents objected to several secular aspects of elementary school curricula that seemed anodyne, including a textbook picture in which boys are making food for girls and elsewhere an Anne Frank quote about the superiority of unorthodox religious belief versus no belief at all. After the school refused to excuse the kids from the curriculum and the courts agreed, the parents pulled their kids out of public school and created their own (unregulated) sectarian school. Brighouse argues that *Mozert v. Hawkins* was a legal victory for secularism. But was it a victory for citizenship? "A system in which the state collaborates with faith organizations in the provision of schooling," he conjectures, "is more likely to produce autonomy facilitating schools and an autonomy-facilitating culture, other things being equal, than a system in which the state refuses to collaborate with faith organizations, but allows them to run their own schools independently."[20]

How Schools Separate the Educable from the Uneducable

The third way in which education helps to construct the category of "citizen" is by defining the set of people who are capable of benefiting from education and are thus eligible for the rights and responsibilities conveyed by citizenship. When a society extends access to education to a child, it is implicitly asserting that the child has a capacity to benefit from that education. Schooling thus operates as a sort of social contract. Because our schools promise to equip students with the skills, norms, and dispositions that they will need to be citizens, acquiring education strengthens individual and group claims on the rights and responsibilities of citizenship. This is why access to education is closely related to the acquisition of democratic citizenship rights in the United States and elsewhere. As we discuss in chapter 3, the rise of coeducational schools in the early nineteenth century opened a path to women's claims for greater political and economic power.

But the association between education and citizenship is a double-edged sword, since educational exclusion often represents an effort to define the excluded individual or group as uneducable and therefore outside of the category of "citizens." Because schools play a central role in creating young citizens, the restriction of access to formal schooling is a component of a system that excludes some individuals or groups from the rights and privileges of citizenship. Oppressive systems reinforce categorical boundaries to exclude undesired groups and develop new ways to preserve some element of relative privilege even when access is granted to new groups. Likewise, marginalized groups' desire for equal status conflicts with the dominant groups' notions of how these rights should be shared and allocated, producing repeated struggles around education.

Thus, in addition to equipping some children for citizenship, schools also delineate between those who are entitled to full membership in the class of "citizen" and those who are not. This boundary work can take many different forms. Perhaps the most direct way in which schools police the boundary of citizenship eligibility is by deciding who can attend school. But sometimes schools can take a more subtle approach to maintaining civic boundaries, both between and within individual schools. For example, schools can regulate who has full access to educational opportunities or provide some children with substandard educational resources or less rigorous coursework as preparation for a sort of second-class citizenship. Or the school curricula can elevate some identities and personal traits and devalue others, creating cultural barriers to full social inclusion. In each of these cases, decisions about educational inclusion and exclusion have wide-ranging implications for public conceptions of what it means to be a citizen and who deserves to claim the rights and responsibilities associated with full citizenship.

Again, the history of the American common school movement is instructive. Even as the common school introduced children to what it meant to "be American" and welcomed many newcomers into the national fold, the common school movement carefully wrote Whiteness into the new American identity it constructed.[21] As such, we—like many scholars working from a critical race theory perspective—see the expansion of public education in the United States as a racial project that reinforced the exclusion and marginalization of people of color.[22] As the nineteenth-century common school movement labored to expand educational opportunities and forge a unified citizenry in the United States, Whites—especially in the free North—vigorously resisted efforts to build schools for African Americans. Educational opportunities for Black children were more common in the United States during the seventeenth and eighteenth centuries, when the institution of slavery served as a check on African American citizenship claims. However, as Hilary Moss documents in her history of African American education in the nineteenth century, efforts to educate free Black children became increasingly contentious over the course of the century. "The common school movement," Moss writes, "empowered white children, regardless of their religion or ethnicity, to claim citizenship, but it also reinforced white efforts to withhold civil rights from African Americans."[23]

African American activists like Frederick Douglass recognized that formal education pointed "the direct pathway from slavery to freedom," and worked to secure access to the growing public school sector and create private schools and colleges for Black children and youth.[24] Whites, also sensing education's power to induct members of previously disenfranchised groups into the category of "citizen," often worked to block these efforts. In 1835 a mob of White citizens of Canaan, New Hampshire, celebrated Independence Day by demolishing a newly established schoolhouse for free Black children. As abolition neared and the number of freed Black residents in the North increased, many White abolitionists came to argue that education should be provided only to Black people who promised to emigrate to Africa. In the years leading up to the Civil War, Horace Mann, Catharine Beecher, and other committed common school movement advocates remained relatively silent on the question of Black education. Apparently they judged that pushing to educate Black youth endangered their "universal" educational project, as freed Black people were thought of as uneducable and antithetical to the racial project of the common school movement.

Interestingly, in the period prior to the abolition of slavery many Southern Whites were less concerned about Black education than Northern Whites were. While many Southern states had anti-literacy laws on the books and many enslavers carefully restricted enslaved people's access to even the most rudimentary education, vocational schools for free Black children proliferated in many Southern cities. This contrast illustrates both education's power to construct social categories and its limits. The notion of incorporating Black youth into common schools represented a threat to Northern Whites in the antebellum period precisely because educational inclusion was such an important step toward full inclusion in the category of citizenship. In the South, by contrast, where the common school movement was less developed and the institution of slavery stood as a check on free Blacks' citizenship claims, White elites could allow Black residents to enter skilled trades without risking their own privilege.

Black youths were far from the only children to be excluded from the promise of universal schooling in the common school era. Although the American School for the Deaf, established in 1817 as the first school for Deaf children in the Western Hemisphere, predated the common school movement, and Gallaudet University was established in 1864, most Deaf children in this era had limited access to any sort of formal education. Widespread neglect of the educational needs of Deaf students, as well as children with disabilities, remains a pervasive shortcoming of American education more than a century later. Even as late as the 1970s, American schools educated only 20 percent of students with disabilities, and many of those who were enrolled in schools were not receiving an education appropriate to their needs.[25] Moreover, some states had laws that specifically excluded students with certain types of disabilities from any type of schooling.

American educators and policymakers also repeatedly invoked the boundary-drawing power of school access during the nineteenth and twentieth centuries to discourage the presence of low-status noncitizens residing in America. In 1975, Texas enacted a state law that allowed school districts to charge tuition to the parents of undocumented immigrant children. Superintendent James Plyler in the town of Tyler, near Dallas, began charging parents of Tyler's sixty undocumented immigrant children $1,000 in annual tuition to attend Tyler public schools. A group of students and their families contested the policy in court and a U.S. district judge ordered the state to release funds for these children to attend school. In 1978, the same judge found the Plyler policy and the Texas state law in violation of the Fourteenth Amendment's equal protection clause.[26]

The Plyler case, as well as a similar case from Houston, was later heard by the U.S. Supreme Court, in 1982. In a 5–4 decision, the Court majority struck down the Texas law, declaring it unconstitutional because it was "directed against children, and impose[d] its discriminatory burden on the basis of a legal characteristic over which children can have little control"—specifically that they had had no control over their parents' decision to bring them into the country. The majority decision, written by Justice William Brennan, made a pragmatic case for broadening the category of the educable to include undocumented youth. Brennan wrote that denying undocumented immigrant children access to public education when they were "already disadvantaged as a result of poverty, lack of English-speaking ability, and undeniable racial prejudices" would keep them "permanently locked into the lowest socioeconomic class."[27]

Justice Brennan's opinion also reaffirmed the centrality of education in creating an American identity and bringing together disparate members of society under that common identity. He clearly articulated not only the harm to a child's academic and social development from withholding education, but also the harm to American society from denying an entire group of students access to education. He noted that "public education has a pivotal role in maintaining the fabric of our society and in sustaining our political and cultural heritage; the deprivation of education takes an inestimable toll on the social, economic, intellectual, and psychological well-being of the individual, and poses an obstacle to individual achievement."[28]

Although this decision affirmed the right of noncitizens to participate in American education, the decision continues to be contested to this day because education is such an important public domain for reinforcing citizenship boundaries and excluding the "others" who are not entitled to the same benefits. In one of the more notable challenges, California's 1994 Proposition 187, voters approved the exclusion of over three hundred thousand undocumented immigrant children from public schools.[29] The rhetoric of withholding education and other social services was seen as a first step in forestalling an "*illegal alien* invasion."[30] As in the past, schools continue to serve as a primary public setting for negotiating the rights of "others" and defining who those others are. The long-standing and recurring nature of efforts to withhold educational access and full citizenship identities from children highlights how entrenched distinctions of "otherness" are.

An important aspect of the connection between educational access and citizenship is the widespread association between education and worthiness. In the United States, this association has deep religious roots. Education was central for the Puritans, who believed that only those who could read the Bible on their own were capable of resisting the temptations of sin; education was thus an essential step on the path to salvation. Horace Mann articulated a less literal but no less powerful version of this educational theology. He believed that the extension of educational opportunity would create a "cultivated class or caste" and "open a wider area over which the social feelings will expand." Mann argued that by bringing all people into this elevated class, universalized education would help eliminate artificial distinctions in society.[31]

This link between education and virtue remains intact in the contemporary world. In her treatment of the for-profit higher education sector, the sociologist Tressie McMillan Cottom draws attention to the modern "education gospel," which, she argues, holds that schooling is a fail-safe path to advancement in contemporary society and worth pursuing at virtually any cost.[32] In an echo of Weber's Protestant ethic, we now believe that schools are places where people cultivate and demonstrate their basic human worth. To succeed in school is to join the elect. But even to enroll in school is to demonstrate human worth, since only those who are potentially eligible to join the elect can participate in the competition for admission. To be educable, therefore, is to be valuable, and those who are valuable have the right as citizens to make claims on the benefits that membership in society provides.

How Schools Force Conformity and Suppress Difference

In each of the instances described earlier, the *exclusion* of individuals and groups from school served to maintain unjust power imbalances and keep members of the excluded group out of the citizenship category. Although these acts of exclusion strike us as dehumanizing and unjust, we should note that not all educational *inclusion* is just either. History is replete with examples of coercive schooling, in which forced inclusion in formal educational systems interrupted the intergenerational transmission of minoritized cultures, supplanted existing communities, and silenced marginalized voices.

In the United States, we often associate education with assimilation—the process through which communities adopt new habits and norms in order to gain entrée into the American mainstream. But some educational processes can be far more violent than the word "assimilation" implies, as when schools require young people to relinquish their ways of living and conform to the cultural, religious, linguistic, and social norms of White American society. This coercive universalism obligates both willing and unwilling groups to adopt the norms and values of American citizenship. Moreover, since the education imposed on subjects for coercive schooling is often segregated and inferior, these students are ultimately denied full inclusion in the citizenship category despite justifications for their coerced schooling that are rooted in claims of equality. In this way, coercive education often resembles a rigged bargain: required to participate in formal schooling, children lose connection to the communities of their birth without gaining full access to the community of U.S. citizens.

The nineteenth-century creation of a mass system of public education came at a high cost for Catholics and the immigrant groups that were to be assimilated into the common school movement's "educated citizens" category. "Here," the journalist and Irish nationalist Thomas McGee wrote about the nineteenth-century American public school, "is precisely where . . . our children become our opponents."[33] McGee was right to be worried. One textbook of the era opined that immigration would make America "the common sewer of Ireland," and the New York State Assembly, in calling for more public schooling, proclaimed, "We must decompose and clean the impurities which rush into our midst."[34] Educators often faced harsh backlash when they attempted to adapt public schooling to make space for immigrant cultures and allow groups to preserve pieces of their heritage. In 1844, for example, public schools in Philadelphia decided to allow Catholic students to read the Douay Bible during the school day. In response, Protestants rioted, killing thirteen and burning a church.

Education also played a central role in the oppression of Native Americans throughout American history. In the colonial era, Catholic missions worked with the tandem objectives of cultural and religious assimilation. One such mission, built in the current state of Maryland in 1634, worked to "extend civilization and instruction to this ignorant race, and show them the way to heaven."[35] More than two centuries later, in 1865, the U.S. government contracted with missionaries to create schools for teaching citizenship, English, Christian religion, and practical skills to Native American children. Many such schools, designated as "manual labor schools," were designed with the express purpose of "re-educating displaced Indians" for "domesticated" lives.[36] In 1879, Richard Henry Pratt established the nation's first Native American boarding school, Carlisle Indian Industrial School, under a philosophy of "assimilation through total immersion."[37] To ensure the full cultural immersion of its students, the school provided vocational and domestic training and summer employment in local towns and farms in addition to teaching basic academic subjects.

Native communities often faced stiff penalties when they resisted coercive schooling. In 1894, federal troops arrested nineteen Hopi fathers who had refused to send their children to government boarding schools and imprisoned them in Alcatraz for nearly a year. Underscoring the prevailing view that Native Americans were resisting benevolent efforts to "Americanize" their children, a San Francisco newspaper, *The Call*, described the situation in an 1895 article:

> Uncle Sam has summarily arrested nineteen Moqui [Hopi] Indians . . . and taken them to Alcatraz island, all because they would not let their children go to school. But he has not done it unkindly and the life of the burnt-umber natives is one of ease, comparatively speaking. They have not hardship aside from the fact that they have been rudely snatched from the bosom of their families and are prisoners and prisoners they shall stay until they have learned to appreciate the advantage of education.[38]

By 1902, the Bureau of Indian Affairs ran twenty-five federally funded boarding schools. Students at these schools were often relocated far from their home communities, and forced to cut their hair, wear English-American-style uniforms, and use English names. Forbidden to speak their native languages, youth in Native boarding schools were required to engage in Christian religious practices rather than maintain their home cultural practices and beliefs.[39] These boarding schools often featured forced labor and unsanitary conditions, and Native youth frequently contracted unfamiliar diseases and suffered from physical and emotional abuse.[40] Forced relocation and acculturation left many survivors traumatized and disconnected from their birth communities when they returned to reservations as young adults.[41] This model was further expanded into the twentieth century; all told, over one hundred thousand Native American children in states across the country attended more than five hundred boarding schools.[42]

Indian boarding schools and other government-run reservation schools served as a primary vehicle for "schooling" generations of Native American children in the government's White, Western ideals.

Thus, to gain "citizenship," which for many Native Americans remained an unequal status at best, they were forced to hide or abandon their culture, language, and previous way of life. Although many students and their families engaged in brave acts of resistance, the universalizing force of American schools profoundly reshaped Native communities across the country.[43]

Similar efforts to compel other dominated groups to adopt American ideals and values have been made at many points in U.S. history since the Indian boarding schools first flourished. As America took or laid claim to more territory and exploited the work of the enslaved peoples who had been forcibly brought to the country and the laborers who had come voluntarily, education in American practices, norms, and values often stripped the next generation of their families' cultures and languages. For Native Americans, Native Hawaiians, Mexicans, Puerto Ricans, Chinese immigrants, enslaved Africans and their descendants, and many others, an important component of being educated in what it meant to be American was having their previously held identities, values, traditions, and beliefs minimized or removed.[44] Students from these minoritized groups were often obligated to conform to dominant behavioral and social expectations, punished for using their native languages and dialects, and presented with few—and often dehumanizing—depictions of their own cultures and histories in classroom settings.

Although the group identities imposed on many students through schooling contributed to the erasure of their cultural identities, in some cases group educational settings have helped to ignite and sustain the citizenship claims and cultural identity formation of marginalized groups. For example, it was precisely the creation of schools that grouped deaf children together that allowed Deaf culture to emerge. Without schools for children who are deaf, many are unable to access language, with severe neurodevelopmental consequences. Ultimately the development of these language skills and the social communities in schools facilitate both the development of Deaf culture and the ability of deaf children to become Deaf students and obtain the other skills necessary to participate more fully in society. However, even in spaces explicitly designed for Deaf education, such as residential schools, the legacy of eugenicist fears linking a reliance on signed languages to ineducability led to the explicit banning of

American Sign Language (ASL) for many decades; once again, an explicit boundary was drawn between those who could be educated in a native or accessible language and those who could not.[45] The flagship Deaf postsecondary institution, Gallaudet University, resisted this requirement and instead maintained the use of ASL so that "Deaf people could be educated in a manner . . . *coequal* with hearing counterparts"[46] Still, the ongoing debates about campus leadership and climate at Gallaudet and in other Deaf educational settings echo similar contestations of full citizenship rights, as Deaf institutions debate how to fully include individuals with a variety of skills in signed languages (including ASL and related dialects), as well as those with a continuum of oral language skills and from additional marginalized identities.[47]

Horace Mann celebrated the school's capacity to serve as a "levelling machine" and "obliterate" artificial distinctions in American society. We celebrate this egalitarian impulse. The common school movement broadened access to the rights and responsibilities of U.S. citizenship for many, just as mass education has brought about a human rights revolution around the world. But sometimes the educational leveling machine has operated more like a bulldozer that suppresses and obliterates rich cultural traditions and deeply held identities. We see this on full display in U.S. education as schools often enact an exclusionary vision of American citizenship, subjugating youth and community identities in the process of recategorizing youth as *American* citizens—a category defined by rights and responsibilities, but also by creedal, racial, religious, linguistic, and cultural affinities. To recite the Pledge of Allegiance in school settings may force students to deny some other affiliation with or devotion to another nation and its cultures and values. Although many European immigrants heading to America in search of a better life might have gladly welcomed this process, schools forced others to repudiate past skills, cultural knowledge, and heritage.

How Schools Shape Collective Norms and Values

Much of the discussion thus far has focused on how various aspects of educational structure create citizens and define the category of citizenship. By organizing schools into grades and classrooms and organizing classrooms into a hierarchy of teacher and students, education socializes students into a sense of self and an understanding of the relationship between self and other that are foundational to contemporary citizenship. By putting students into relationship with diverse others and enacting widely shared rituals, schools help create national "imagined" communities. And even as schools enforce boundaries around these imagined communities by excluding certain groups of young people from educational experiences, they also bulldoze other categorical identities by forcing youth to participate in educational experiences.

But of course, educational content also matters for the definition of the category of citizenship and the maintenance of citizenship boundaries. Implicit in the patriotic brand of "civic virtue" education that has long been dominant in the United States is a consensus-based conception of citizenship. In this vision, people and groups demonstrate their educability—and thus their eligibility for citizenship—by affirming their identity with the American collective and their allegiance to its founding creeds and organizing culture. It is this educational vision that motivated the Trump era's 1776 Project, as well as the moral panic around critical race theory in schools spread by the American right in the early 2020s. Because these conservative voices believe that the category of citizenship is grounded in a shared patriotism and sense of collective identity, they see curricula that allow students to interrogate the nation's ideological roots and investigate the extent to which it has lived up to its ideals of liberty and equality as a fundamental threat to the nation's social order. For these conservative educators, only curricula that celebrate a United States aligned with their particular values can draw students into a meaningful citizenship category.

But this is not the only vision of education and citizenship available. Throughout American history, educators have worked together to advocate and enact a more skills-based conception of education for citizenship. The vision of citizenship in these curricula is not founded on a consensus around a single set of ideas and values or a unified identity but rather on a set of mutual obligations and responsibilities. Alternatively, advocates for ethnic studies and forms of multicultural education curricula point to a more pluralist conception of citizenship founded not on consensus or similarity but on an understanding of and respect for difference and a recognition of prior and continuing marginalization. These educational approaches are not mutually exclusive. Schools can—and do—simultaneously engage in patriotic celebrations of American values, teach civic skills, and make space for diverse identities. However, because these educational approaches proceed from different understandings of the nature of citizenship, they are in profound tension. Debates among these visions thus represent fundamental disagreements about what it should mean to be a citizen and what it should take to be included in this foundational category.

In the early 1990s, a congressionally mandated commission of prominent historians and educators set out to articulate the critical thinking skills they hoped that schoolchildren would learn in history classrooms and to identify a set of primary sources that teachers might incorporate into their lesson plans in order to "better allow the student to understand the warp and woof of past ages, peoples, and cultural perspectives."[48] The National History Standards Commission demurely described their effort to write up a set of national history standards as a modest undertaking. Mindful of the nation's tradition of local control in education, the authors of the commission's report took pains to describe their report as a set of "guidelines" that sought less to direct the content of K-12 history instruction than to inform its goals.

If the authors had hoped that their disclaimers would head off controversy around the standards, they were surely disappointed. In October 1994, former second lady Lynne Cheney, the chair of the National Endowment for the Humanities (which provided partial funding for the National History Standards Commission), took to the editorial pages of the *Wall Street Journal* to decry the standards' "grim and gloomy" portrayal of American history. Arguing that the document neglected the crowning achievements of American history—the Revolution, the Constitution, the Wright Brothers—Cheney argued that in their pursuit of "their revisionist agenda" the commission members "no longer bothered to conceal their great hatred of traditional history." Before the week was out, the commission found itself the target of outrage fueled by AM talk radio host Rush Limbaugh. In one rhetorical flight, Limbaugh attributed the guidelines to a "secret group" that aimed to teach students "that America is a rotten place . . . and they don't have a chance here." Ultimately, he predicted, the standards would turn American students into "a bunch of embittered people growing up, robbing and stealing and turning to crime because they've been told all their young lives that there's no future for them."[49]

Before long, the Senate had rejected the commission's work by a vote of 99–1 and the idea of national history standards receded from public view. As the commission's chairman, historian Gary Nash, reflected:

> The controversy of the 1990s is, in fact, a replay of similar controversies in the 1920s, 1930s, and 1950s. The positions taken by today's adversaries to the history standards are uncannily similar to an acrid exchange in the 1930s involving a new set of textbooks in history and social studies used across the country. The textbook author urged teachers to teach children to pursue "fair mindedness and honesty, to see clearly both sides of an historical controversy." Instill in students "tolerant understanding." Ask over and over: "Why do you think so? Are you open-minded about the matter? What is your authority? Have you considered all sides of the case?" From the other side of the cultural chasm, an outraged patriot flayed this point of view for trying "to give a child an unbiased viewpoint instead of teaching him real Americanism. All the old histories taught my country right or wrong. That's the point of view we want our children to adopt. We can't afford to teach them to be unbiased and let them make up their own minds."[50]

Fast-forwarding to the 2020s, we see this controversy playing out yet again. Just weeks after the insurrection on January 6, 2021, a team led by the Harvard University political theorist Danielle Allen released *A Roadmap for Educating for American Democracy*. With support from the National Endowment for the Humanities and the U.S. Department of Education, the "Educating for American Democracy" project aimed to provide a framework for uniting U.S. history and civics education curricula in order to reinvigorate citizenship education in American K-12 schools.

The Education for American Democracy project took an even more modest tone than the 1990s national history standards project. It emerged out of a carefully curated and politically diverse working group, explicitly avoided the words "standards" and "curriculum," and stuck to a discussion of the broad "themes"—civic participation, geography and demographics, national identity, civic institutions, the nation's place in the world, contemporary debates—that could be woven through and organize K-12 schooling.

Although it has thus far avoided the controversy that spiked the national history standards in the 1990s, the project's *Roadmap to Educating for American Democracy* is by no means out of the woods. Writing in the *National Review*, Stanley Kurtz alleged that the *Roadmap* aims to "force protest civics (leftist political protest and lobbying as a 'civics' requirement) onto every school in the country—with a generous helping of critical race theory to boot."[51] While Kurtz manages to toss in a dog-whistle comment about critical race theory, his critique focuses on the *Roadmap*'s emphasis on civic skills ("leftist political protest and lobbying") rather than patriotism and a belief in American exceptionalism as a foundation for citizenship.

Despite Kurtz's invocation of the critical race theory bogeyman in his critique of the *Roadmap*, this project—like the national history standards project before it—is largely silent on how educators should engage with the nation's racial history. This is in spite of the fact that many civic educators believe that schools must directly confront race and racism in order to build a truly inclusive and diverse citizenship category. It is this belief that motivates the effort to implement ethnic studies courses in K-12 education, a movement that one of us (Emily Penner) has studied extensively. These courses, which grow out of ethnic studies courses in higher education settings, center racially marginalized groups' histories and social movements and lead students in a consideration of the systems that perpetuate the marginalization and discrimination of these groups. Organizers have recently mounted calls in several states for the creation of ethnic studies courses at the K-12 level and even the inclusion of these courses in high school graduation requirements.

The ethnic studies course recently adopted as a graduation requirement in San Francisco and subsequently statewide, for example, examines the histories of racially and ethnically marginalized groups—including instances of both their perseverance and their resistance to persecution and dehumanization—and guides students in discussions of the impact of issues like racism and stereotypes on their own identities and communities. The course also asks students to study and help to address an issue in their own community. For many students, being assigned to take a high school course that provided this content and signaled the academic value of marginalized communities proved transformational and deepened their participation not only in high school but in postsecondary education as well. Thomas Dee and Emily Penner have demonstrated that academically marginalized high school students experience substantial and persistent academic benefits from this course.[52] This ethnic studies course substantially raised attendance rates and academic GPAs, which rose from the equivalent of a D average to a C+. Follow-up work with Sade Bonilla found large effects on high school graduation and postsecondary enrollment.[53]

Critics, however, see ethnic studies as a threat to dominant notions of American identity. For example, Arizona state officials argued that the Tucson Unified School District's Mexican American Studies (MAS, a type of ethnic studies) courses "promote the overthrow of the United States government," "promote resentment toward a race or class of people," and "advocate ethnic solidarity instead of the treatment of pupils as individuals."[54] The MAS program was routinely met with political resistance and efforts to shutter the program eventually succeeded in 2010 with the passage of HB 2281, which banned the teaching of MAS, along with any ethnic studies course in K-12 classrooms across the state. On January 1, 2011, officials who had pushed the legislation also threatened to withhold $15 million from the district—10 percent of its state funding—because, they argued, it had violated the ban the day it went into effect.[55] Program instructors responded with a lawsuit. HB 2281 was ultimately overturned in 2017 by the Ninth Circuit Court of Appeals on the grounds that it had been enacted for political and racial reasons, in violation of the equal protection clause of the Fourteenth Amendment.[56] The court found evidence of racial animus in anonymous blog posts from John Huppenthal, the state superintendent of schools who enforced the MAS ban. He wrote, for example: "The rejection of American values and embracement of the values of Mexico in [MAS] classrooms is the rejection of success and embracement of failure." Such posts made explicit how he and other state officials conceptualized the challenge posed by MAS and ethnic studies courses to both American identity and the academic integration and success of students.

Similar controversies have erupted in California, where the University of California and California State University systems are moving to implement an ethnic studies component in their recommended college preparatory course sequence and where the legislature has made ethnic studies a high school graduation requirement. Concerns about ethnic studies have taken two forms in California. One critique of the proposed curricula is that it excludes or underemphasizes the experiences of particular groups, including Jewish Americans, Muslim Americans, and South Asian Americans.[57] The other, more fundamental concern comes from opponents of current efforts to institutionalize ethnic studies courses, who see the potential of these courses to shape our definitions of who occupies citizenship categories and fear the consequences for our collective identity. For example, one critic of the model curriculum worries that a strong ethnic or racial identity developed through such a course will come at the "expense of identifying as part of the larger American society."[58]

As this argument makes clear, debates about ethnic studies are fundamentally debates about the definition of citizenship as an educational category. Advocates see ethnic studies as a way to recognize and indeed celebrate ethnic diversity and the resulting plurality of citizenship experiences. Rather than requiring assimilation to a dominant identity, these curricula reflect an understanding of Americanism that is comfortable with difference and responsive to conflict. In this conception, the category of citizenship is broad enough to encompass multiple other citizenship categories. This argument provides a ready explanation for the positive effects of ethnic studies participation observed among students in San Francisco. But it should not be surprising that opponents of ethnic studies remain unconvinced by the success of marginalized students because to them, ethnic studies represents a repudiation of a much more assimilationist and less accommodating vision of American citizenship.

Perhaps it is predictable that people are inclined to argue about the shared knowledge and set of cultural referents established as the content of school curricula. What is taught and whose histories are included and centered in school indubitably have long-lasting consequences for the assumptions and values that students will carry with them as citizens. But as important as those values are, we suspect that schools make an important contribution to the definition of citizenship categories simply by providing a focus for these sorts of arguments. When we argue about what we ought to teach our children, we acknowledge that there is a "we" and that this collective includes people with very different political ideals and values. As such, arguing about the content of schooling is one way in which communities remind themselves that they are communities, even as they debate what it means to be a member of a community and what community itself means. In this sense, education does more than create the category of the citizen: it also provides a venue for negotiating that category's meaning.

Other Models of Education and Citizenship on the Global Stage

So far, our discussion of education and citizenship has emphasized the school's role in the development of the citizenship categories in the American context. Of course, this process is not unique to the United States. In fact, despite the common school movement's deep American roots, the U.S. educational system is arguably less "common" than the educational systems in many liberal democracies. Americans traditionally reserve important decisions around educational finance and governance—including crucial questions about curricular content and design—for local school boards and other local educational actors. The state and federal roles in schooling have intensified over the past fifty years as policies such as the 1965 Elementary and Secondary Education Act (ESEA) created a sizable stream of federal funding for public schools and subsequent revisions of the act (most notably the 2001 No Child Left Behind Act) attached regulatory requirements and accountability mechanisms to the federal funds. Nonetheless, as illustrated by the recent controversies surrounding the Common Core State Standards Initiative—a partnership among several governors, philanthropists, and the Obama administration that aimed to articulate and implement a shared set of curricular goals for schools in all fifty states—the notion of local control over schooling remains a powerful force in American educational politics.[59]

By contrast, many nations have far more highly centralized educational systems, where national educational ministries develop content standards and textbooks, train teachers, and monitor educational offerings nationwide. In France, the saying goes, you can tell the time and date by seeing what page the kids in the nearest elementary school are on in *Babar*. Likewise, South Korea, in an effort to minimize socioeconomic segregation between schools, randomly assigns students to public secondary schools rather than having them attend neighborhood schools. In such systems, the role of the school in the construction of the social category of the citizen is arguably more pronounced.

However, many liberal democracies place much less emphasis than the United States on the use of schools to create inclusive citizenship categories. Indeed, most Western European nations provide considerable public resources to private educational providers, and they often share educational responsibilities with religious denominations or groups of educators with similar pedagogical philosophies.[60] The Dutch constitution, for example, provides private schools the right to receive the same amount of financial support from the state as public schools.[61] Today nearly 65 percent of Dutch students are enrolled in state-supported private schools; though most of them are affiliated with Christian churches, they also include Jewish, Muslim, and Hindu schools, as well as schools organized around Montessori, Waldorf, and other alternative educational models.

Such an approach arguably fosters a more pluralistic educational system and enables families to choose from a more diverse set of educational opportunities in order to educate their children in a way that more closely matches their own values. Although centralized educational systems impose a set of shared educational experiences and values—thereby increasing the salience of membership in the broad and inclusive category of "school systems"—pluralistic educational systems arguably provide more freedom for the members of multicultural societies to develop and reproduce their identities.[62] Arguments for educational pluralism have gained political traction recently in the American context. Since the 1990s, nearly all U.S. states have begun to authorize independently managed but publicly funded charter schools. More recently, dozens of states have implemented school voucher programs, which provide state subsidies for poor students who seek to attend religious or nonreligious private schools.

Debates rage in the United States about the educational consequences of these choice-based school reforms. In the realm of educational evaluation and policy analysis, these debates revolve around the consequences of school choice for choosers' own measurable educational outcomes. This research is frustratingly inconclusive. Some charter schools clearly provide their students—particularly poor students attending schools in educationally underserved communities—with educational opportunities.[63] However, charter schools vary considerably in quality.[64] Similarly, the evidence on the effects of attending private schools via vouchers is mixed. Policy experiments in several contexts across the United States show that giving poor parents a voucher to pay for private school tuition increases their satisfaction with their children's schools. However, results from these relatively small-scale policy experiments, as well as evaluations of statewide educational voucher programs in Louisiana and Indiana, indicate that attending a choice school does little to improve students' educational achievement or attainment and may actually have negative effects.[65]

In addition to being inconclusive, this research on the educational consequences of school choice for students overlooks pressing questions—ones that are much harder to answer empirically—about the effects of educational pluralism on citizenship and the development of a shared public identity. Some studies indicate that charter school participation increases voting behavior, particularly among historically marginalized students.[66] It is still unclear, however, whether choice has broader impacts on the creation of pluralistic identities.

It is relatively clear that youth in systems that prioritize access to common educational opportunities are more likely to come into contact with peers from diverse segments of society, while youth in pluralistic and choice-driven educational systems are more likely to be exposed to peers from similar family backgrounds. In systems in which families choose schools based on religion, children are likely to go to school with their co-religionists. Given the relationship between religion, race/ethnicity, and socioeconomic status in many societies, choice-based educational systems also tend to contribute to school segregation along racial and class lines. In Chile—a nation viewed as a model of market-based school policy based on a national voucher program implemented in the 1980s that allows parents to use public funds to send their children to a private school of their choosing—schools are more segregated by social class than elsewhere in the world, and they are becoming more racially segregated.[67] Levels of school segregation in the Netherlands are also high and are increasing in the face of rising immigration.[68] Likewise, as school choice systems spread and become more entrenched in parts of the United States, racial and class-based segregation appears to be on the rise.[69]

But does the association between educational pluralism and educational segregation necessarily imply that choice undermines education's citizen-creating role? Perhaps so, if contact with diverse others is an active ingredient in the construction of citizenship identities. Or perhaps this association simply reflects a different understanding of what citizenship means and who is a citizen.

Wrapping Up

It may seem like a long conceptual journey from little Stephen's first day of kindergarten to today's fierce battles over the teaching of U.S. history and the soul of American democracy. But viewing education from the perspective of categorical inequality provides a clear roadmap for this conceptual journey.

In this chapter, we have argued that formal schooling turns young people—children, siblings, cousins, and friends—into individuals by socializing them into a sense of self and into a set of rights and obligations that apply in school and beyond. Schools then bring these individuals into community, both by structuring day-to-day classroom interactions and by exposing students to the common knowledge, norms, and expectations that permeate our society. The fact that this shared community forms citizenship boundaries that operate throughout society explains why efforts to exclude young people of color from fully integrated educational opportunities so often maintain racial hierarchies in which people of color have second-class citizenship. It also explains why efforts to force young people from marginalized communities to attend schools that ignore or demean their cultural background can exclude the bearers of diverse traditions from the category of full citizens.

We are struck by how persistent and seemingly intractable the debates about education and citizenship are. To be clear, we are not confident that the theory of categorical inequality provides a resolution to these debates. However, understanding the different ways in which education participates in the construction, maintenance, and enforcement of citizenship categories lays bare the stakes in so many of our educational arguments. When people fight about education, they are often having a fundamental disagreement about who gets to be a citizen and what that citizenship means. In a democracy—particularly one forged through the contradiction of defending inalienable rights for all while depriving many of such rights—these fights have become part of how citizenship is defined.

3 CONTESTING CITIZENSHIP BOUNDARIES

Polities continuously define and redefine the category of citizenship as they debate who can participate in civic life and in what ways. In chapter 2, we considered education's deep engagement in this socially foundational category-building process. In this chapter, we consider the implications of this process for our understanding of educational change.

Because political communities use education to define and reproduce themselves, education is fundamentally political.[1] When we talk about education, we are talking about who "we" are. Who matters and how? Who should govern and who should be governed? Which ideas and stories define our collective identity, and which ideas and stories contradict or undermine it? Which attitudes, values, and dispositions do we take as common in our day-to-day public sphere interactions? What are our social expectations for what categorical belonging means for different people? Which inequalities do we celebrate? Which inequalities do we merely tolerate? And which inequalities do we vow to ameliorate?

In this chapter, we consider how societies—and their schools—continuously work through these big questions as we describe a messy, recursive, and ongoing process in which diverse social actors scramble to make their society's educational enterprise better meet their interests and needs. No part of this process is fixed—the field of actors changes as society's population changes; the balance of power among those actors shifts as social and economic conditions change; ideas about citizenship, representation, and rights develop over time; and the venue and tactics for debating and struggling over these issues evolve. As a result, whenever and wherever formal education occurs, stakeholders continuously contest, suppress, negotiate, and compromise around each of the citizenship category-building processes that we described in chapter 2.

We focus here on moments in American educational history in which minoritized groups sought fuller access to the rights and responsibilities of citizenship by pursuing more equal inclusion in the American education system. The struggles we describe in this chapter challenged the boundaries and terms of the citizenship category in the U.S. context. They are stories about people—primarily people of color—confronting unequal categorical assignments that had consigned them to a subjugated status as well as stories about their resistance and countermobilizations to pursue greater access. We highlight the focused and often collective efforts made by marginalized groups to achieve educational inclusion, as well as the repeated efforts of the powerful to block this inclusion by legal and extralegal means. Although the events discussed in this chapter eventually led to more integrated schools and coeducation, the unequal foundation on which they played out continues to shape inequities in educational quality and access today.

Although many of the examples and events recounted here will be deeply familiar to some readers, an enduring legacy of our decentralized educational system is the unequal and limited inclusion of the histories and perspectives of marginalized communities in school curricula. Because we believe that categorical inequality in the American context cannot be understood without recognizing the long history of schooling being used to reinforce the subjugation of Black, Indigenous, and other racialized minority students, it is important to highlight some of these examples of categorical inequality in these pages. Our work in this chapter benefits from and synthesizes a rich body of scholarship on social movements in education that has emerged over the last several decades, and we take care throughout the chapter to attribute this scholarship and flag sources for further reading. If the stories are new to you, or if you are interested in reading more, we hope this chapter provides a starting point in your exploration of these important histories and the critical traditions that have elevated them.

What we include here from these histories is necessarily incomplete. But viewing several episodes in this history through the lens of categorical inequality reinforces the lesson of chapter 2—education draws citizenship boundaries, and educational inclusion marks the line between people who have the power to fully participate in self-governance and those whose power is limited and whose rights are insecure.

Our review of American efforts to support educational inclusion yields four major insights into education, citizenship as a nexus for categorical inequality in contemporary societies, and social change.

First, we emphasize that citizenship is just one of many foundational social categories that schools help to construct and define. Schools also serve to define social identity categories that play an outsized role in our day-to-day life, such as gender and race, and they help to determine how these categories interact with one another and with other crucial categories (including citizenship categories). This chapter focuses on efforts to bring children of different genders and races together into the same schools and learning environments because we believe that spatial proximity magnifies the salience of the common category of citizenship and reduces the power of gender and racial category boundaries.

Second, we draw attention to the mutability of educational practice and to how changes in educational categories can instigate broad and long-lasting shifts in the definition of citizenship and the social distribution of power. For example, our review of the history of gender in American public education describes how coeducation in eighteenth- and nineteenth-century schools that educated White youth paved the way for (White) women's suffrage and fuller gender equality in American civic life.

Third, our review of key moments in the movement to desegregate American public education shows that educational advances for one marginalized group can lay the groundwork for advances for other groups. For instance, legal challenges that were initially narrowly tailored to allow Chinese and Mexican students to attend Whites-only schools in the American West established legal precedents and movement tactics that benefited the movement to dismantle Jim Crow schooling in the South, and that movement, in turn, drove efforts to overturn systems of separate and unequal schooling across the United States.

Fourth, we emphasize that there is nothing inevitable about educational inclusion and the concomitant broadening of citizenship categories. Many moments of inclusion in educational history came as the result of extended, relentless efforts by the marginalized to secure greater access. Given the deep stain of anti-Black racism in American life, it is not surprising that White Americans often zealously resist Black Americans' fights for educational equity and that advances in Black educational access and rights—resulting from the relentless efforts of Black families and community leaders—are often met with fierce and hugely effective countermobilizations. Although this chapter highlights education's potential to drive profound social change, the history and contemporary acts of White resistance to school integration and racial equity underscore the important role of education in maintaining categorical inequality.

Throughout this chapter, we focus on the evolving struggles over who is permitted to learn in the same building, and we contrast cases of gender coeducation with cases of racial integration.[2] We rely heavily on this contrast because it highlights how categorical boundaries can be so thoroughly redrawn and so fervently reinforced at the same time. As a society, we have come to accept coeducation by gender to such a degree that it is rarely questioned and its implementation is nearly universal.[3] At the same time, we continue to struggle to mount successful racial integration efforts even in contexts where it has widespread social support.

We also leverage this contrast to describe the role of schools in creating and reinforcing category boundaries as well as to demonstrate how schools magnify the salience of existing societal categories. In chapter 2, we primarily adopted the lens of citizenship to make sense of the struggles over educational inclusion, arguing that debates about who is entitled to educational access amount to debates about the extent to which the category of "citizen" can accommodate people of multiple genders, races, and abilities. But of course, these struggles are also about the construction of categories themselves, their definition, and the ways in which we allow these categories to shape contemporary political and social life. In this chapter, we examine the interplay between educational citizenship and gender and race, examining how the out-groups within gender and racial hierarchies challenge their educational citizenship rights.[4]

Schools do not single-handedly create the category of the citizen. Laws, political theory, and global culture working together have created this category. But schools implement this category and give it meaning. Likewise, schools do not single-handedly create racial and gender categories, which shape children's lives long before they enroll in formal schooling. Indeed, schools often attempt to undermine these categorical inequalities, driven by a universalistic and egalitarian ethos.[5] Nonetheless, educational systems reinforce racial and gender inequalities by legitimating and redrawing boundaries between racialized and gendered categories, shaping their content, and influencing the way these categories shape people's lives.

The overlap between school attendance boundaries and racial and ethnic categories in American schools is driven by a high degree of residential racial segregation, a tradition of defining enrollments primarily via neighborhood residence, and the widespread preference of White parents to send their children to predominantly White schools.[6] School segregation thus creates a set of educational categories (in this case, the school a student attends) that overlap considerably with race.[7] Similarly, educational categories that operate within schools (for example, special education, gifted and advanced placement coursework, and extracurricular activities) reinforce and co-construct racial categories.[8] By the end of secondary education, racial categories and privilege can be maintained without explicitly referencing race.[9] At this point, schools can take actions that are prima facie race-neutral but that have disparate racial consequences.[10]

Educational categories have profound implications for students' understandings of what race means.[11] Their educational experiences and category memberships shape how students racially identify.[12] Educational systems also legitimate racial boundaries and promote understandings of what race means through textbooks' racial content or lack thereof.[13] Of particular importance are the school-relevant racial meanings that shape students' understandings of what is possible—and what is probable—for their lives. For example, stereotypes about racial differences in academic abilities can create racial differences in test scores by boosting the scores of Asian students and lowering the scores of Black students.[14]

In no small part because of fierce resistance to racial desegregation efforts, race aligns closely with many of the categories in education (public school district and school boundaries, honors track, English-language learner, problem student, high school dropout, and elite university student, to name a few). By contrast, because of the norms of coeducation that emerged from the common school movement and the current assumption that boys and girls should attend public schools together, gender cuts across many educational fault lines and most youth spend the bulk of their educational career in mixed-gender schools and classrooms.

To be sure, schools play an important role in reinforcing gender categories by helping students understand what it means to be a girl or a boy and a woman or a man. School structures reinforce the gender binary when they sort students into girls and boys as they line up in gender-segregated lines to walk to the cafeteria or are seated "boy-girl-boy-girl" in the classroom. Recent debates about accommodating trans youth have only served to highlight how deeply embedded the gender binary is in everything from school architecture (for example, boys' and girls' bathrooms) to extracurricular activities. Further, schools present students with dominant gender norms throughout the curriculum.[15] Even high school biology textbooks convey inaccurate folk notions of sex and gender.[16] Education also plays an important role in providing both formal and informal socialization into gender roles. These roles—and thus the gender socialization that occurs within schools—vary by class, race, and geography.[17] Education, by structuring peer interactions as well as communicating expectations and providing opportunities, frames students' understanding of gender and gender-appropriate behavior. In this respect, education is not particularly different from other institutions that maintain gender categories by internally reinforcing society's gendered expectations. Indeed, it would be odd to expect our teachers, schools, and textbooks to be somehow immune to the biases that are more broadly present in society.

The contrast between race and gender is also instructive. America's failure to accomplish true racial integration in its schools contributes to the maintenance of a sharply unequal racial hierarchy in American civic, economic, and social life. By allowing White families to avoid racially integrated schools and consigning students of color to separate and unequal educational opportunities, American public schools allow racial cleavages to continue to undermine the citizenship category's implicit promise of political equality. By contrast, placing boys and girls into close social proximity throughout their developmental years and ensuring that they are exposed to similar curricula and educational experiences has enabled American schools to build a relatively gender-inclusive vision of citizenship.

Coeducation: Schooling as a Lever for Women's Inclusion

Most of the history that we recount in this chapter is a story of struggle for educational inclusion. "Power cedes nothing without a demand," as Frederick Douglass put it, "and it never will."[18] But we start with a story of extending schooling to new groups that was much less contested than many subsequent inclusion efforts.

In 1790, young women's literacy rates in the United States were approximately half those of young men. By 1840, U.S. youth had reached rough gender parity in literacy. And by 1870, fifty years before the Nineteenth Amendment to the U.S. Constitution extended the right to vote to women, young women had higher literacy rates than men. What happened during this period to so dramatically boost girls' access to educational opportunity?

As detailed in chapter 2, Americans were engaged in a broad effort to build schools throughout the nineteenth century. But the history of the common school movement provides only a partial answer to the riddle of educational inclusion in a society that sharply conscribed women's social roles and severely limited their power. If educational inclusion is a lever for inclusion in the category of "citizen," how did (White) women gain access to schools long before they gained political power? And given women's second-class status in nineteenth-century America, how did it come to pass that girls received the bulk of their schooling under the tutelage of female teachers while sitting shoulder to shoulder with boys?

David Tyack and Elisabeth Hansot argue that coeducation came about quietly in American schools.[19] As early as the colonial period, widows and single women throughout the Northeast operated "dame schools" out of their homes to provide basic literacy instruction as well as instruction in domestic arts to a handful of local boys and girls. Running schools as an extension of the domestic sphere was an inexpensive way to provide care for children. But it also provided a model for schooling that proved influential as communities began constructing more formal primary schools in the early republican period. Initially, many towns built formal schools only for boys and hired male schoolmasters to lead them. But these schools typically had relatively short school hours during the fall and winter months. When the school was out of session, many communities repurposed their schoolhouses in a model that echoed the earlier dame schools: they hired women to provide both basic instruction to small children and more advanced instruction to older girls.

As Horace Mann noted in 1853, these schools "smuggl[ed] in the girls, perhaps for an hour a day, after the boys had recited their lessons and gone home." From there, Tyack and Hansot argue, admitting girls to the winter session probably felt to town elders like a small additional step to take. But doing so is likely to have served as a wedge for expanded educational inclusion. With the dame school in recent memory and a local labor force of literate women to draw upon, it was only one more small step for budget-strapped small communities to replace the male schoolmaster with a woman. By the middle of the nineteenth century, coeducational one-room schoolhouses and women teachers were de rigueur in small communities across the United States. The process of coeducation was more contentious in urban schools—particularly at the secondary level, where education was seen as a more direct portal to the workforce—and it remained a topic of vigorous debate in the educational research literature through the nineteenth century. By the late nineteenth century, however, the field's most influential professional organizations had concluded that coeducation facilitated "a more harmonious development of both sexes," and mixed schooling had become the norm nationwide.

The rapid adoption of coeducation in many communities is notable because it happened with little federal coordination and relatively few limits. Few official school policies, court decisions, or laws dealt directly with gender during this time. In contrast, formal policies and legal decisions about age, race, academic proficiency, and school curricula were frequently documented.[20] The diffuse rural nature of many communities also hastened the adoption of coeducational schools because it was more affordable to fund a single school within walking distance than two.[21] The limited accounts from this period suggest that girls in coeducational schools had access to nearly the same resources as boys. What is more clearly documented is that many girls readily embraced their newfound educational opportunities, often outperforming boys in grades, grade promotion rates, and, eventually, enrollment.

Throughout this period, many educators rejected the claim that coeducation would lead to greater social inclusion, which was proffered not only by opponents who feared that coeducation would "subvert the laws of creation" but also by suffragists, who saw coeducation as a step toward full social inclusion for women.[22] These educators saw the school as a reflection of the family's social order and a means for reinforcing family structures promoted by the church. Investing in women directly maintained this order and was seen as part of investing in the next generation through the formative work of the future mothers they would become.[23] For them, it was only natural to place male principals in charge of schools in which female teachers provided care and instruction in classrooms filled with boys and girls, continuing the work begun by the family in the model of the church.[24] Rather than subverting the existing gender hierarchy, educators assumed that a gendered division of labor in the school would reproduce a society in which women cared for children while ceding power and decision-making responsibilities to men.

It turns out that this assumption was wrong: coeducation led to a reconsideration of gender roles, opening the way to women's suffrage and driving the expansion of citizenship roles for women. Although educational opportunities remain gendered in contemporary schools, coeducation marked the school as a social setting in which boys and girls could interact as relative equals. Further, it created an occupational niche for women that, in time, opened the way for broader involvement in the labor market. As coeducation has become normative in schools around the world, gender gaps in educational opportunity have narrowed. Coeducation thus appears to have been an important force in the construction of more equitable gender regimes around the world.[25]

Coeducation substantially increased educational opportunities for women and increased gender equality across the globe, but the path to greater educational equality has not been linear, and important differences remain. Women have eagerly pursued education as opportunities have been made available to them, and they have outperformed their male classmates on many indicators of participation, engagement, and achievement. In 1917 women represented just over half of students at both the University of California at Berkeley and Indiana University, and national statistics from the 1919–1920 school year indicate that 47 percent of students enrolled in higher education nationwide were women. Although women's share of higher education enrollment fell to 30 percent in 1949–1950, since 1979 there have been more female students in higher education than male students, and women's advantage in this domain has grown over time. The current gender disparity in postsecondary enrollment is particularly pronounced among historically minoritized groups. Yet substantial gender segregation persists between different fields within higher education: male students are concentrated in STEM and other higher-paying fields, and female students are concentrated in the humanities, social sciences, and applied fields, such as education. Although gender gaps in earnings have narrowed since the mid-twentieth century, women—and particularly women of color—persistently earn less than their White male counterparts with equal levels of education.

Education has remained a female-dominated field that still subordinates women in important ways. Teachers, like those in many feminized occupations, are paid poorly, and for many years female teachers were paid less than their male counterparts, who were often given preference for administrative positions. The unionization of the teaching force has reduced some of these gender inequities among educators, but many persist. Educators are continuing to lose financial ground relative to other professions that require bachelor's degrees, so that teachers are increasingly priced out of the high cost-of-living cities in which they teach. Thus, while in many ways education has proven to be a powerful vehicle for greater social inclusion for women, the institution continues to perpetuate barriers to gender equality as well.

Schools and the Enforcement of Racial Boundaries in Jim Crow America

The story of racial desegregation in U.S. public education contrasts sharply with the story of coeducation. Coeducation brought girls and women into American schools with comparatively little controversy. By contrast, American schools have been and remain highly segregated by race, and questions around racial desegregation and resource allocation across groups remain highly contested topics in American political and educational life. Whereas the acceptance of women into coeducational schools was relatively peaceful, students and families of color have had to make repeated and coordinated efforts to gain each small measure of additional educational inclusion. These boundary-redrawing efforts have also been frequently opposed, reversed, or undermined by the continued efforts of those in power to preserve White supremacy.

As we discussed in chapter 2, the common school movement offered, at best, partial inclusion in the category of American citizenship to many people of color. Mann and his colleagues fought to provide educational access to White students independent of class, creed, or gender, but few common school advocates argued for educational access for Black students and many actively articulated a preference for racial segregation. American educators launched a handful of experiments in racially inclusive schooling, but segregated schooling was common throughout the period in which the nation constructed its mass educational system. Furthermore, where Black parents advocated for their children to be included in White schools, educators enforced racial segregation with the explicit support of the U.S. Supreme Court.

Opposition to formal attempts to promote integrated schools ultimately provided the legal standing to slam the door on integrated schools for generations. In 1847, parents of a Black five-year-old, Sarah Roberts, enrolled her in the all-White school closest to her home in Boston, Massachusetts, but she was ejected. The African American lawyer Robert Morris and the abolitionist Charles Sumner (later a Massachusetts senator) sued the City of Boston on her behalf, arguing that school segregation was a violation of equality under the law and an injury to both Black and White children.[26] However, when the case was heard by the Massachusetts Supreme Court in 1850, Judge Lemuel Shaw ruled in favor of the Boston Primary School Committee and preserved its right to determine children's school assignments and enforce segregation, saying, "The committee . . . have come to the conclusion, that the good of both classes of school will be best promoted, by maintaining the separate primary schools for colored and for White children, and we can perceive no ground to doubt, that this is the honest result of their experience and judgement."[27] With this judgment, Shaw also provided legal precedent for the case that enshrined the principle of "separate but equal" in schools and public spaces across civil society for decades.[28]

On June 7, 1892, Homer Plessy, a mixed-race son of Haitian immigrants from Louisiana who attended a Reconstruction-era integrated school, purchased a first-class train ticket and boarded a "Whites only" car bound for New Orleans. Plessy was arrested under the Louisiana Separate Car Act. Although Plessy's lawyers argued that the Thirteenth and Fourteenth Amendments entitled him to equal treatment under the law, Judge Howard Ferguson, ruling that Louisiana had the right to regulate state rail companies operating within state borders, convicted Plessy. Plessy appealed the decision to the Supreme Court of Louisiana, where the judge found precedent for segregated cars from the 1849 Massachusetts decision, which argued: "To assert separateness is not to declare inferiority. . . . It is simply to say that following the order of Divine Providence, human authority ought not to compel these widely separated races to intermix."[29] In 1896, *Plessy v. Ferguson* was heard by the U.S. Supreme Court, where Plessy's lawyers as well as several legal briefs argued that Plessy should have been guaranteed the same rights as all U.S. citizens. However, the Court decided against Plessy, 7–1, and rejected his arguments based on the Fourteenth Amendment, finding no evidence that the Louisiana law violated it. Their rationale was described in Justice Henry Billings Brown's summary: "We consider the underlying fallacy of the plaintiff's argument to consist in the assumption that the enforced separation of the two races stamps the colored race with a badge of inferiority. If this be so, it is not by reason of anything found in the act, but solely because the colored race chooses to put that construction upon it."[30]

The 1896 *Plessy v. Ferguson* decision instituted a government-sanctioned racial separation across a broad array of social sectors, including housing, work, public spaces, and, of course, schools. *Plessy*'s legal framework of "separate but equal" allowed for sixty years of formal segregationist policies in seventeen states and gave federal, state, and local governments a powerful tool to enact the legal subordination of Black Americans and other individuals of color across the country.[31] Although the wording of the framework implies that the separate institutions created through this formalized segregation process would somehow be "equal," simply the process of dividing and isolating Black Americans underscored their disenfranchisement from equal citizenship rights. Under the *Plessy* decision, Black students would be relegated to separate educational spaces with fewer resources and worse facilities for decades. *Plessy* thus reformalized the racial categories that had long existed in American education, now bolstered by a new justification whose insidious logic would deprive many Americans of their full rights under the guise of so-called equality.

Let's pause here to notice a striking contrast: at the end of the nineteenth century—the very moment when American schools achieved gender integration through coeducation—the nation built a legal apparatus that allowed racial segregation in education and many other social domains. We can speculate about why the institutional and legal contexts around gender and racial categorical inequalities diverged, but for our purposes, what's important is how differently these nineteenth-century decisions positioned the institution of the school with respect to these two forms of categorical inequality. As any White girl who tried to show up to a nineteenth-century common school in pants and short hair could no doubt have attested, gender categories certainly thrived in coeducational schools. But by placing boys and girls in the same classrooms and exposing them to similar curricula and learning opportunities, coeducation recognized gender similarities in capacities to learn and relegated the work of maintaining boundaries between boys and girls to within-school cultural and organizational practices. By contrast, racial school segregation gave educational access a central and explicit role in the maintenance and enforcement of racial categories and boundaries. While the conservation of resources and effort was offered as a reason to allow coeducation in many rural areas, this was not a sufficient argument to counter the White supremacist mandate of separate, inferior, or no educational opportunities for non-White students.[32] To segregate schools, educational leaders needed to codify a racial hierarchy, make determinations about which students attended which schools, and expend additional resources to maintain separate facilities, employ additional teachers, and enforce separation. Despite the legal mandate to provide "separate but equal" educational resources, this pattern of racial segregation persisted precisely because it allowed Whites—as members of the more powerful racial category—to hoard educational resources for their own children's schools and deny resources to the schools that educated racially minoritized students.

Contesting *Plessy*: The Fight for Racial Desegregation

Legal struggles to overturn *Plessy* began almost immediately. In 1899 the U.S. Supreme Court heard a case brought by Black residents of Richmond County, Georgia—home to the City of Augusta—who argued that they should not have to pay property taxes because they had no access to secondary education after the county closed Ware High School, the county's Black-only high school. Despite *Plessy*'s invocation of "separate but equal," the Court disagreed, effectively allowing that "equal" could encompass a high school for White children and no high school for Black children.

In the decades to come, however, a series of lawsuits brought by Latine[33] and Asian communities forced the courts to confront the complexities of racial boundary work engendered by schooling, laying a legal foundation for broad attacks on *Plessy*'s logic and Jim Crow segregation. In 1924 the parents of a nine-year-old Chinese American girl, Martha Lum, sought to enroll her in a consolidated all-White high school in Bolivar County, Mississippi, because the county did not have a school for Chinese students. The U.S. Supreme Court rejected her claim, ruling that since Lum was not White, she should attend a segregated school for "colored" students. In his written opinion for the case, Chief Justice William Howard Taft argued:

> Most of the cases cited arose, it is true, over the establishment of separate schools as between white pupils and black pupils; but we cannot think that the question is any different, or that any different result can be reached, assuming the cases above cited to be rightly decided, where the issue is as between white pupils and the pupils of the yellow races. The decision is within the discretion of the state in regulating its public schools, and does not conflict with the Fourteenth Amendment.[34]

In other words, the Court ruled in 1927 that boundaries drawn around school access between White students and Black students also applied to Chinese and other Asian students, who similarly lacked the full standing of their White peers.

A few years later, however, the legal activism of Mexican American parents in California began to turn the tide on de jure school segregation. In January 1931, the agricultural community of Lemon Grove, California, east of San Diego, sought funds to build a separate school facility for Mexican children in an area where schools had previously been integrated. Parents who were furious about the substandard quality of the building and the equipment the school had been furnished with formed a neighborhood group to boycott the school and pursue legal action. El Comité de los Vecinos de Lemon Grove (the Committee of the Neighbors of Lemon Grove) hired attorneys to file a suit on behalf of the eighty-five children assigned to the new school. Using a rhetoric of Americanization, school board members argued that building a new school was justified to support the learning needs of non-English-speaking children. The students took the stand to demonstrate their fluency in English, and the judge ultimately decided in their favor, ordering their immediate return to their original school. The grassroots work of these parents, with the assistance of the Mexican consul, advanced the American citizenship claims of these Lemon Grove students and represented the first successful U.S. court ruling in favor of school desegregation.[35]

The Lemon Grove decision paved the way for a second California desegregation case, in Orange County. As in Lemon Grove, Mexican American students had long attended integrated schools in the town of Westminster. But by the 1940s, Westminster had begun to segregate Mexican American students. Gonzalo Mendez, a relatively prosperous Mexican American tenant farmer who had himself attended integrated Westminster schools, objected. Working with the League of United Latin American Citizens (LULAC), the Mendez family joined four other families to file suit in 1945.

The defense invoked racial stereotypes, arguing that Mexican American students had inferior ability and hygiene and insisting that separate schools were necessary to support students with limited English ability. But after nearly a year of weighing the evidence, Judge Paul McCormick ruled in favor of the Mendez family. McCormick's decision, which was grounded in the Fourteenth Amendment's equal protection clause as well as a rejection of the claims of Mexican American students' academic inferiority, caught the attention of the NAACP's Thurgood Marshall, who filed an amicus curiae brief. Rather than pursue the case to the U.S. Supreme Court, the Orange

County school districts desegregated. *Mendez v. Westminster* would pave the way for California's Anderson Bill, which repealed all California school codes mandating segregation and was signed by then-governor Earl Warren, who would later preside over *Brown v. Board of Education*.[36]

As Marshall and the National Association for the Advancement of Colored People (NAACP) perceived, the efforts to desegregate schools for Mexican American students in California provided an opening for other communities of color to increase their participation in American public education. The NAACP, which had been organizing legal efforts to challenge *Plessy* for decades, followed the *Mendez* template when it recruited families who were willing to fight Topeka's racial segregation policy. The named plaintiff, Oliver L. Brown's daughter Linda, was a third-grader who had to walk six blocks to her bus stop to attend a segregated Black school a mile away, though a White school was only seven blocks from her house. The Brown family was happy with the quality of the education that Linda received at her all-Black school but joined in the efforts to fight segregation because they believed in the right of children to attend any school.

Following the NAACP plan, Brown and twelve other parents attempted to enroll their children in the closest neighborhood schools in the fall of 1951. When each student was refused enrollment and referred to a segregated school farther away, the group of parents filed a class action lawsuit against the Topeka School Board. The district court that heard *Brown v. Board of Education* sided with the school board, citing *Plessy* and arguing that the state law concurred with the "separate but equal" principle that allowed for separate school facilities. The district court found that segregation in public schools had a detrimental effect on Black children, but denied them relief on the grounds that White and Black schools in Topeka were substantially equal with respect to buildings, transportation, curricula, and teachers' educational qualifications.

Brown joined four other NAACP-sponsored cases from around the country in the appeal to the U.S. Supreme Court, with the first being heard in the spring of 1953. As the *Brown* case worked its way through the courts, many Americans came to see it as a test case for American ideals in the Cold War context. In an amicus curiae brief submitted to the court, Secretary of State Dean Acheson argued that school segregation "jeopardizes the effective maintenance of our moral leadership of the free and democratic nations of the world."[37] At the heart of this petition, as well as the public statements made by many others, was the clear understanding that maintaining a segregated school system amounted to maintaining a tiered system of citizenship. While the provision of schooling asserted African Americans' educability—and thus humanity and citizenship—school segregation maintained categorical distinctions among citizens along racial lines.

In 1954, the Supreme Court voted unanimously in the Brown family's favor. The *Brown* decision hinged on the notion that even if segregated Black and White schools were of equal quality, that segregation was still detrimental for Black children and unconstitutional. Writing for the majority, Justice Warren argued that

> segregation of white and colored children in public schools has a detrimental effect upon the colored children. The impact is greater when it has the sanction of the law; for the policy of separating the races is usually interpreted as denoting the inferiority of the Negro group. A sense of inferiority affects the motivation of a child to learn. Segregation with the sanction of law, therefore, has a tendency to retard the educational and mental development of Negro children and to deprive them of some of the benefits they would receive in a racially integrated school system.[38]

As is clear from this argument, Justice Warren understood that category distinctions and formal separation based on these distinctions were harmful in and of themselves and that they reinforced the boundaries around citizenship rights.

One crucial lesson that we take from the long battle leading up to the *Brown* decision is that in cases involving categorical inequalities, border cases matter. School segregation, we argue, was all about maintaining unequal racial categories within the broader category of American citizenship. When girls started attending school with boys, it became increasingly difficult to withhold the full rights and privileges associated with citizenship from women. Many American White supremacists were loath to see racial equality follow a similar trajectory. But maintaining segregated schools required diligent maintenance of racial boundaries. As the twentieth century progressed, advocates for school desegregation—and racial equity more broadly—began to test those boundaries by contesting school segregation in border cases. While a lawsuit aiming to enroll a Black student in an all-White school would probably have gotten nowhere in the Jim Crow South, lawsuits aiming to enroll English-speaking Mexican American youth in all-White schools in California succeeded. And by succeeding, they punctured both the logic and the legal apparatus surrounding school segregation, enabling other legal challenges.

Continuing Contestation: Resistance to Desegregation

The long fight for racial integration in schools carries a second lesson as well: those who benefit from categorical inequality fight persistently to maintain these boundaries and their advantages.

As the legal scholar Derrick Bell Jr. notes, it took the threat of international scrutiny and concerns about economic development to motivate American White elites to support school desegregation. Bell describes this as an example of a broader phenomenon he refers to as "interest convergence": "The interest of blacks in achieving racial equality will be accommodated only when it converges with the interests of whites."[39] He argues that several political incentives motivated Whites to acquiesce to the *Brown* decision. In particular, there were mounting concerns about the U.S. image abroad. Professed ideals of freedom and equality in the escalating confrontation with a Cold War enemy conflicted with the perpetuation of unequal conditions among citizens at home. In addition, some argued that the rhetoric of equality espoused when Black soldiers fought in World War II should persist once veterans returned home and translate into broader movement toward equal opportunities for Black veterans and their communities. Others, motivated by purely economic self-interest, argued that segregation was hindering Southern development and should be dismantled to facilitate growth and trade in the region.

Brown's federal legal mandate failed to spur many segregated states and school districts into action. By delegating the task of ensuring that desegregation was proceeding "with all deliberate speed," the Supreme Court's 1955 decision gave states and districts across the United States legal cover to quietly delay and obstruct desegregation efforts. But in many places, state and district leaders took a more explicitly oppositional stance. Within the first two years after *Brown*, six Southern states declared the ruling null and void, and others passed laws allowing (and in some cases requiring) governors to shut down integrated schools. In many cases, these laws authorized governors to redistribute school funds on a per pupil basis to segregated schools (public or private) that enrolled students from the shuttered schools—thus creating a system of private school vouchers designed to maintain school segregation. Reflecting on this seemingly self-destructive politics, Ed Peeples, a White sociologist and Virginia racial justice activist, remarked: "There's always been a theme of opinion in Virginia by many of the elites that we didn't need education. We ought to just get rid of public education: it's insidious and it teaches egalitarianism and we're not equal."[40]

To understand the depth of Southern White resistance to desegregation, consider the famous scene that played out at Little Rock's Central High School. Under pressure from the NAACP, Little Rock hatched a haltingly cautious plan for school desegregation that involved integrating Central High while maintaining segregation based on residential patterns in the district's remaining high schools. On the first day of the 1957 school year, Arkansas governor Orval Faubus dispatched the Arkansas National Guard to support local segregationists and block the nine Black students who planned to integrate Central High School.[41]

Little Rock's school district and mayor condemned the governor's deployment of soldiers and appealed to President Dwight Eisenhower for help. Eisenhower sent in the 101st Airborne Division of the U.S. Army to protect the nine students and enforce integration, and he federalized the Arkansas National Guard so that Governor Faubus could no longer intervene. On September 24, the 101st Airborne accompanied Elizabeth Eckford and the rest of the Little Rock Nine into Central High School past the angry, taunting, White crowds. Eight of the Little Rock Nine finished the school year at Central, facing verbal and sometimes physical harassment from some of their White classmates.

The next year, Governor Faubus shuttered Little Rock's high schools for the entire school year. White students scrambled to get into segregated schools in surrounding districts and local private schools. Black students fared worse: approximately 15 percent of high school–aged Black children in Little Rock left the state to attend school elsewhere, nearly 25 percent attended another Arkansas high school, and more than half of them missed school entirely during the 1958–1959 school year.

Little Rock was far from the only locality to close schools rather than face integration. Prince Edward County, Virginia, closed its schools for five full years: from 1959 to 1964. Other districts simply dragged their feet to avoid integration, often entering into protracted court battles that forced students of color and their families to organize and assemble evidence if they were to realize *Brown*'s promise of equal educational access. In response to efforts to stall integration, a 1969 case, *Alexander v. Holmes County Board of Education*, changed the *Brown* requirement that compliance be achieved "with all deliberate speed" to "desegregate now."

Similar battles raged across the country throughout the 1960s and 1970s as Black families used the courts to protest racially gerrymandered school assignment zones and other practices that achieved racial segregation without explicitly prohibiting integration. In 1961, the courts declared the school attendance policies in New Rochelle, New York, to be in violation of *Brown*, ruling: "It is of no moment whether the segregation is labeled by the defendant as 'de jure' or 'de facto,' as long as the Board, by its conduct, is responsible for its maintenance." Similar rulings in Denver, Los Angeles, Detroit, Pontiac, Kansas City, Las Vegas, and Massachusetts[42] made school desegregation a national project.[43] In response to these court rulings, districts in the North and the South alike found themselves implementing court-ordered school desegregation plans. Often, these plans hinged on breaking up neighborhood schools by reassigning and transporting students across the district to allow for more mixing between White students and students of color. White parents in both the South and the North fiercely contested these plans. Although *Swann v. Charlotte-Mecklenburg* (1971) determined that busing was an appropriate remedy for segregation, protests and countercases established limits to this policy.[44] The inclusion of busing in the desegregation plan provided White parents with a framing that allowed them to name busing as the reason for their resistance to the plan without having to state their fears and racist motivations. Well-publicized anti-busing protests in Boston, New York, Chicago, Los Angeles, and elsewhere captured national attention, and fears over the political resistance of White families led cities to revise or withdraw their busing plans.[45]

White parents were not alone in their resistance to school desegregation. In 1971, when the San Francisco Unified School District devised plans to reassign students attending segregated schools to comply with *Brown*'s desegregation mandate, Chinese American parents organized to resist the plan, arguing that Asian-only schools helped to preserve their cultural heritage and provided primary language instruction.[46] In *Guey Heung Lee v. Johnson* (1971), the courts rejected their case, ruling that "Brown v. Board was not written for Blacks alone" and noted that students from other backgrounds also stood to benefit from the cultural and historical lessons previously reserved for Chinese-heritage schools. The courts ultimately called upon the students of San Francisco to help ease the racial tensions of desegregation: "The school children of San Francisco can be counted upon to lead the way to unity. In this and in their capacity to accept change without anger, they deserve no less than the whole-hearted support of all their elders."[47] Thus, just as schools had historically been used as sites for reinforcing group boundaries, the *Lee* decision argued that schools could also be the sites of reconciliation, and that this reconciliation work was not only needed between White and Black students and their families but needed with other groups as well.

Still Separate, Still Unequal: Racial Inequality in Contemporary Schools

To this point, our discussion of racial inequality has focused on White supremacist efforts to enforce categorical distinctions around who was allowed to attend particular schools. As laws forced schools to eliminate these boundaries, families devised new legal and political strategies for preserving privileged schooling experiences for their children, such as changing school funding allocations or pursuing district secession. Many of these avenues for preserving segregated schools and unequal opportunities within schools continue to be used today. Although the *Brown*, *Lee*, and other court decisions banished the state-mandated segregation of the Jim Crow South, less formal processes still drive racial segregation and inequalities in school quality across schools.

Local school finance practices allow some affluent communities to raise supplementary educational funds through local property taxes and other community-led efforts; this practice often reinforces between-school resource inequalities that disadvantage students of color. In the early 1970s, parents from the low-income Edgewood Independent School District sued San Antonio Independent School District, along with five neighboring districts, arguing that funding schools via local property taxes created cross-district school finance inequalities that violated the equal protection clause of the Fourteenth Amendment. The courts accepted the plaintiff's contention that school finance inequalities drove pronounced inequalities in student access to books, teachers, and counselors. In its 1973 *San Antonio Independent School District v. Rodriguez* decision, however, the U.S. Supreme Court refused to declare the school finance system unconstitutional, ruling that the Constitution did not protect a right to education and that, as a result, school finance inequalities did not violate poor students' right to equal protection under the law.[48] This decision substantially limited the federal judiciary's power to oversee inequalities in access to educational resources.

The Supreme Court's 1974 *Milliken v. Bradley* decision further reinforced inequalities across school district lines by blocking an effort to desegregate schools in the Detroit metropolitan area by reassigning students between city and suburban school districts.[49] As a result, district boundaries play a crucial role in the maintenance of school segregation and educational inequality. Parent groups in contemporary school district secession movements will organize, for example, to draw a new district boundary around a subsection of their current district, forming a new, typically more affluent and racially homogenous district. District secession gained popularity in the 1990s and continues to this day, with proposals submitted in at least nineteen different states.[50] Particularly because district secession efforts are commonly undertaken by affluent, White parent groups, these efforts often drive school resegregation and racial inequality in school resources.[51]

Families also use school choice to reinforce school segregation. Research indicates that racial composition plays an outsized role in shaping school preferences, suggesting that when families talk about "school quality," they are really talking about the characteristics of the children enrolled in the school rather than how much their children stand to learn by enrolling. School quality categories thus appear to be euphemisms.[52] When advantaged families say that they want to enroll their children in "good schools," they seem to really be saying that they want to enroll their children in schools that enroll mostly affluent, White, and otherwise socially advantaged children. The "good school" euphemism allows advantaged families to engage in practices that have racist, segregationist consequences without acknowledging that they are doing so and without violating social taboos around racism and exclusion. In this respect the "good school" euphemism is similar to what the sociologists Amanda Lewis and John Diamond describe as happening when privileged parents send their children to integrated schools in a way that hoards opportunities at the school for their own children: students from privileged backgrounds may not be in any classes with students from disadvantaged backgrounds.[53]

While affluent and privileged families have pursued a variety of strategies to evade the redistribution of resources that accompanies the equalizing of educational opportunity, students and families from marginalized groups have continued their efforts to obtain greater educational access. As before, these efforts have collided with legal and financial barriers that have stalled progress toward educational equality. If anything, the progress won by earlier legal efforts has been dismantled, calcifying inequalities and preserving unequal citizenship.

Students and families have contested the lack of equality in schools by arguing that poor school quality undermines students' rights. The impact of decisions like *Milliken* that prevent desegregation efforts across districts, combined with White flight, discriminatory housing policies, and declining economic conditions, has left some districts, like Detroit, with little funding to address substantial academic and administrative challenges. As a result, learning is difficult for students compelled to attend schools that are short-staffed, overcrowded, and forced to deal with toxic mold, insufficient heating and air conditioning, and materials shortages, including a lack of paper, pencils, and books.[54] A group of Detroit students sued the governor, arguing that they were being denied their constitutional right to liberty and nondiscrimination with the denial of their access to basic literacy. In deciding the case, Judge Stephen Murphy III noted that the schools' conditions were "nothing short of devastating" and that "when a child who could be taught to read goes untaught, the child suffers a lasting injury—and so does society" but nevertheless concluded that access to literacy is not a fundamental right that schools are obligated to provide.[55]

Law professor Lani Guinier described the transition from an exclusionary and segregated educational system to the current disintegration of attempts to rectify these inequities: "Legally compelled segregation became socially acceptable separation; separation became stigma; stigma became association with Blacks who still occupied and defined separate, albeit public, education. Integration was reduced to diversity, a benefit to be enjoyed by a critical mass, but not by the masses."[56]

Thus, despite the equal protections guaranteed by the Fourteenth Amendment and the long fights to obtain access to schools waged by students of color, speakers of languages other than English, disabled students, and undocumented students and their families and communities, challenges continue to be raised over who has a right to educational opportunities, whether those opportunities are equal, and what types of opportunities are (and are not) included in these guarantees. In many ways, the evolution of American education from a domain exclusively for the benefit of White, mostly male, higher-income children to the vast system of public schools in every city in the country is a testament to how successful the fights to broaden the boundaries around educational access have been. However, the struggles to see this educational expansion come to fruition have achieved only partial success. The *Brown* mandates and subsequent legislation calling for free and equal education for all children living in America continue to be dismantled and renegotiated. Desegregation has stalled and in many ways been reversed. To the degree that schools are integrated, they still regularly preserve the relative advantages of White and affluent children to the detriment of students of color and their lower-income peers. Inequities in school quality and access to appropriate instructional environments and resources are rampant. Despite the court decisions and mandates obligating districts to provide equal opportunities and "meaningful" education to all students, schools still provide differentiated opportunities and make categorical distinctions that deem some children more worthy of opportunities, basic rights, and resources than others.

Wrapping Up

In this chapter, we have discussed how schools construct, define, reinforce, and occasionally contest some of the most foundational categories in contemporary social life: citizenship, gender, and race. Throughout, we have emphasized the mutability of each of these categories, as well as each category's relationship to educational practice. The categories in each of these systems, the boundaries among them, and their meanings are all matters of continuous social negotiation and contestation. Likewise, how education relates to each of these categories varies considerably over time and place.

This categorical mutability is good news for students, families, educators, and leaders interested in working for social justice. The categories that define our communal lives have deep, long-lasting, and very real implications for people's lives. But because these categories are social constructs, each of us has the power to fundamentally change them. As this chapter's review of American educational history efforts makes clear, schools are strategic sites for doing this work of social reconstruction. Just as previous generations of educators used schools to create new American identities, tomorrow's schools can be sites of new, more inclusive ideas about global citizenship and collective identity. Similarly, just as coeducation paved the way for women's greater political and economic power, it is possible to develop new educational models that make space in the public sphere for the expression of trans, nonbinary, and gender-nonconforming identities. Further, we can use schools to address deep racial inequalities, confront racist systems, and build a more racially equitable society.

None of these moves toward a more equitable society are inevitable. Indeed, in each case discussed in this chapter, schools have been sites of considerable contestation and dispute. Just as White elites fiercely resisted school desegregation, the beneficiaries of unequal educational categories will inevitably resist changes that threaten their advantages. But although America still fails to fully include many children in its expansive vision of educational citizenship, education has considerable potential as a central place for breaking boundaries and drawing people into the American project. The institution of education, which in many ways is nothing more than a morass of loosely linked schools, districts, and state agencies with fairly limited federal influence, has undergone a remarkable transformation. Where we once educated only an elite few, we now attempt to make learners and democratic participants out of nearly every child living within our borders. Although the outcome is far from a forgone conclusion, this ongoing transformation speaks to the powerful role that education plays in our individual lives and in our national project.

PART II
SORTING WITHIN SCHOOL

Della Curry thought her job as a cafeteria worker at a school in the suburbs of Denver revolved around feeding hungry kids. But in a school system that provided free meals only to students whose families demonstrated financial need, Curry had another key duty: policing the boundary between students who were eligible for free lunch and their peers who were not.

Like many educators, Curry found this task—which amounted to constructing and enforcing an educational category that created inequality among the students—heartbreaking. One day in 2015, tired of being told to deny meals to kids who lacked lunch money, she rebelled. "I had a first-grader in front of me, crying, because she doesn't have enough money for lunch. Yes, I gave her lunch," Curry explained. Curry's small act of protest got her fired. But it also helped her find a platform. After losing her job, Curry went to the press, and her story helped to spark a national conversation about the practice of "lunch shaming."

The notion of categorical inequality helps to explain how school cafeteria workers find themselves withholding food from students. Since the National School Lunch Program is intended to provide nutrition to students who might otherwise go hungry, the legislation that authorizes it requires schools to collect household income information from students and their families. Students who report a household income of less than 1.3 times the federal poverty level qualify for free lunches, and students whose household income is less than 1.85 times the poverty level pay no more than 40 cents for their lunch. Thus, in 2017 a student from a family of four with a household income of approximately $33,000 qualified for free lunch, and a student from a family of four with a household income of less than $45,000 qualified for reduced-price lunch.[1] So as they dole out pizza squares and shelf-stable peaches, American school cafeteria staff help to enact a policy that sorts kids into three unequal categories—free-lunch kids, reduced-price-lunch kids, and the kids who pay full price or bring lunch from home.

In theory, assigning students to the free lunch and reduced-price lunch categories sounds simple enough. Every fall, schools ask students and their families to complete a household income worksheet and then use this information to assign students to the free-lunch or reduced-price-lunch category. In practice, however, nothing is as simple as it should be. Our research indicates that many students from very low-income families do not enroll in the program, and that some students enrolled in the program come from families who report a relatively high household income to the IRS.[2]

What accounts for this gap between the National School Lunch Program's cut-and-dry eligibility language and the way the program operates in schools? Few parents are accountants; for the majority who aren't, coming up with an accurate and inclusive accounting of their family income is a challenge. Further, some parents may be too proud to report their income accurately, while others may distrust authorities and be reluctant to report their income at all. In the face of these hurdles, educators—including district and school leaders, teachers, school social workers, and cafeteria workers—make a series of decisions about how their schools will enact educational categories. Leaders decide whether or not to take part in federal programs that are designed to decrease the burdens associated with applying for free lunches, including increasingly popular (but unfortunately underfunded) programs that allow schools to provide free meals for all students. Educators and social workers at the front lines decide which families to encourage to apply for free lunch and what sorts of help to give families with their applications. Meanwhile, cafeteria workers like Della Curry make moment-to-moment decisions about when to enforce the categories that emerge from this process and when to look the other way.

In part II, we look at the many different categories that educators, students, families, and others enact *within schools*. The school lunch categories that Della Curry hated enforcing are just one example. Others include the age-based grades that kids travel through as they grow, the academic tracks that define students' academic experiences in middle and high school, and the smaller groups of peers that students sit next to and learn with during the course of their school days. Throughout, we emphasize that educational categories are social constructs. Rather than being set in stone, these categories emerge out of the choices and actions of educators, policymakers, school leaders, families, and students themselves. Schools, like other bureaucratic organizations, rely on explicitly articulated rules as well as a set of more implicit norms and shared understandings to negotiate their day-to-day operation. A theory of categorical inequality focuses attention on these processes of category co-construction and maintenance. Realizing that all of us contribute to the co-construction and perpetuation of educational categories helps us understand that each of us has the power to alter educational categories and their consequences.

We should take that power seriously, because the educational categories that we co-construct have durable consequences for students' lives. It broke Della Curry's heart to deny food to a hungry child because she understood those consequences. American school lunches may be notoriously greasy and flavorless—"a cross between dirty gym clothes and frying oil" in one student's memorable description—but for kids from homes where the pantry shelves are empty, they can be a lifeline.[3]

But Curry's concern reached beyond nutrition. Her use of the term "lunch shaming" helps us understand that processes that mark students as poor enough to receive free lunch create class-based categories that operate throughout the school day and beyond. While many of their more affluent peers tuck into their lunch boxes for bologna sandwiches and chips, free- or reduced-price-lunch recipients often line up at the beginning of the lunch period to reach around sneeze guards and claim their hot lunches. In other words, the National School Lunch Program segregates students by income (and often by race and ethnicity as well) at one of the few moments in a school day when students can socialize without direct instructional supervision. Having been marked as poor kids, many students report carrying the "free lunch" label with them as they move through their school day. As one student put it, "If you received lunch free, it symbolized poor, unwealthy"; according to another, "the 'cool' kids ate from the [paid] snack bar and the others ate from the [free] line."[4]

The psychologist Kenneth Payne provides a moving account of his own school experience: "I learned I was poor on the new lunch lady's first day at work." Before that day, Payne received his free lunch from a veteran lunchroom employee who had memorized students' school lunch status and "passed us through the line, money or not, as smoothly as our plastic trays glided over the rail." In her lunch line, free lunch was not a salient marker of poverty. When the new lunchroom employee stopped young Payne and asked for lunch money, he "realized what my free lunch meant." This interaction changed nothing about Payne's family situation, but it fundamentally reshaped the way he saw himself. "The moment when I realized what my free lunch meant is still with me," Payne writes, "and I can feel the heat in my face as I recount it."[5]

MAKING COURSES, CLASSROOMS, AND OTHER EDUCATIONAL CATEGORIES 4

In chapter 2, we introduced the "grammar of schooling"—the institutional forms or organizational arrangements that are so deeply engrained in our conception of schooling that we find it almost impossible to imagine schools without them. We gave three examples of those forms: the distinction between teacher and student, the collection of many students into classrooms, and the status progression of grades and school level. Notably, these examples involve the construction of social categories and the sorting of students into them.

To understand how definitional these educational sorting processes are, it pays to circle back to Katherine Anne Porter's character, Stephen, in her story "The Downward Path into Wisdom." When Stephen starts school, he steps into the role of a student. In chapter 2, we considered how that role shaped Stephen's understanding of himself and his relationship to the world. But Stephen isn't just any kind of student. Stephen is a kindergartener, and as such, he goes each day to a classroom filled with other kindergarteners and does what kindergarteners do: sit in squares, count to ten, learn the ABCs, and memorize the Pledge of Allegiance.

It probably never occurs to Stephen, his parents, or even his teachers to wonder why his school sorts all the youngest kids together into the same classrooms. Age-grading is such a fundamental part of the grammar of schooling that it sometimes seems to us as though there is no other way to organize a formal educational enterprise. But of course there are other ways. In the nineteenth century, Stephen might have been enrolled in a monitorial school or a one-room schoolhouse. In the late twentieth century, if Stephen's mother had decided to go back to school to get professional training, she most likely would have gone to school with adults of many ages who were all interested in pursuing the same sort of career. If Stephen had aged into school during a global pandemic, he might have spent the whole year learning alone at home, squirming as he gazed at a computer screen. As it happens in the story, being enrolled in a school that sorts students based on their age and being placed with twenty other five-year-olds in the same classroom is likely to have lasting consequences for Stephen's development.

In the years to come, Stephen's school will probably assign him to dozens of different educational categories. Porter doesn't tell us much about Stephen's family background, but perhaps he receives free lunch. Stephen seems to be a typically developing child from an English-speaking home who has an easy time meeting his school's behavioral expectations and keeping up in class. But if that is not the case, his teachers might refer him for special educational services, or for supplementary instruction to learn English, or for an individualized education plan to accommodate disabilities. As Stephen and his classmates sing their ABCs and start reading, his teachers will sort him and his classmates into fancifully named reading groups. If he is a quick study, Stephen might be a "bluebird" and spend his class reading time reading chapter books and writing short essays. If he struggles to string letters into words and words into sentences, he might be a "redbird" who reads and rereads *See Dick Run*. If Stephen's teachers identify him as precocious, they may sign him up for extra tests and categorize him as "gifted."

In this chapter, we consider the logic of these educational categories and their consequences for children's educational experiences. Our discussion focuses on two sets of category-producing educational practices: age-grading and academic tracking. At first glance, these two categories are so different as to be virtually incomparable. Age-grading is taken for granted in the grammar of schooling, particularly in the elementary school years. Since urban monitorial schools fell out of favor and population growth and rural school consolidation rendered the one-room schoolhouse obsolete, grouping students based on their age has been an essential organizational building block of American primary schooling. Today everything from teacher training to the testing and accountability systems that drive American educational policy to school building architecture make the idea of grouping students into mixed-aged settings for instruction all but unthinkable.

By contrast, educators, activists, families, and policymakers have been arguing over academic tracking for decades. Depending on who you ask, tracking—grouping students based on educators' judgments of their academic need and potential into different and relatively skills-homogeneous learning environments—is either a technical solution to the challenge of providing effective educational opportunities to students with diverse needs and abilities[1] or a practice with roots in scientific racism that inevitably produces and reproduces inequality.[2] Age-grading is by now so deeply engrained in the grammar of schooling that schools implement the practice almost unthinkingly. By contrast, schools endlessly debate, revise, and rethink their tracking practices.

Grades and Tracks as Educational Categories

Before we dig in on these and other important differences between age-grading and academic tracking, we want to point out three key similarities between them that provide important clues about what makes a category a category.

First, both age-grading and tracking are practices that schools use to sort students for instruction. At the risk of stating the obvious, no classroom can be large enough to educate all children at once. Schools in the United States leaned incredibly heavily on instructional technology during the first year of the Covid-19 pandemic, but technology does not solve the problem of scale, since students clearly need individualized instruction and a learning community. Thus, any mass educational system simply must sort students for instruction in some way. Though they utilize very different criteria to sort students, both age-grading and academic tracking are strategies to deal with this fundamental problem facing all mass education systems.

Second, in grouping students for instruction, both age-grading and academic tracking explicitly assign labels to students. Students know these labels and carry them wherever they go, both inside and outside of the schoolhouse. As Stephen learns his place in the school, he undoubtedly learns that he is a kindergartener, and he learns that being a kindergartener is different from being a first grader. When his mother introduces him to new adults, she tells them that he is a kindergartener. And when Stephen meets new kids outside of school, he asks what grade they are in. All students, particularly as they move out of elementary school and into middle and high school, know what academic track they occupy in the school. They learn to peruse their course schedules and those of their peers, looking for the "honors" labels on courses for the academically advanced and college-bound or the "remedial" (or, in more polite schools, "developmental" or "support") labels that mark courses for the academically struggling.

Third, both age-grading and tracking assign students to categories that influence their educational experiences. Kindergarteners spend much of their day surrounded by peers who may be diverse on many dimensions—race, gender, background, school readiness, religion—but are approximately the same age. They are taught by kindergarten teachers and receive different educational experiences than do first graders, let alone second, third, fourth, or twelfth graders. Scholars and educators have noted that kindergarten curricula have become increasingly academic over time.[3] Kindergarten continues to have roots, however, in a set of ideas about childhood and youth development that prioritize learning and socialization through play rather than direct instruction.[4] Similarly, track placements influence the characteristics of students' classroom peers; the sorts of teachers to whom they are exposed; and the level, pace, and style of instruction they receive. By design, academic tracking creates skills-homogeneous classrooms. However, since many measures of academic skills correlate with student race and socioeconomic status, they also segregate students by race and class across classrooms.[5] Schools often reward experienced and well-regarded teachers with high-track classes.[6] In addition to covering more advanced material in high-track classes than in low-track classes, teachers often utilize a more interactive and participatory instructional style in high-track classes, while teachers of low-track classes more often lecture and drill students on basic skills.[7]

Category Assignment and Identity Formation

Age-grading and academic tracking have one more key thing in common: by grouping students for instruction, labeling them, and shaping their educational experiences, both practices influence identities. By converting constructed categories into powerful social units, identity formation serves as a key mechanism in the construction of categorical inequalities.[8] One well-known set of studies conducted by the social psychologist Muzafer Sherif powerfully demonstrated how easily people translate categorical assignments into powerful group identities. In the late 1940s and early 1950s, Sherif and his colleagues shipped a bunch of White, middle-class eleven- and twelve-year-old boys off to summer camp. Once at camp, the social psychologists put the boys in a single cabin, allowing them to form friendships. After a short while, they split the boys into two groups, purposely assigning friends to different groups, and then set the groups into competition. Before long, these groups had become two exclusive societies, the Rattlers and the Eagles, and their rivalry was bitter. Old friendships forgotten, Sherif's subjects readily pledged loyalty to their new group and developed stereotypes and demeaning nicknames for the other group.[9]

Other research underscores that we are quick to assign and act upon status differences among groups, even if we know that group assignments are random. In the late 1990s, Sheryl Ball and her colleagues split undergrads in an introductory economics course into two groups of equal size, then held an in-class ceremony in which the members of one group were called out by name and given a gold star and a round of applause. Next, the researchers set up auctions in which students were to sell things to members of the other group. Members in the gold-star group consistently got higher prices at auction than members of the other group, even though the experimenters had explicitly created the groups randomly by drawing names out of a hat in front of the class.[10]

School-based research suggests that identity formation is a two-sided process. That is, educational categories come to influence identity both by changing how students see themselves and by changing how others see them. The literature on tracking is particularly informative here. When students are placed into high-track classes, their confidence in their academic ability rises; when they are placed in low-track classes, their confidence falls.[11] Similarly, students are more likely to view their peers in low-track classes as "stupid" or "troublemakers" and less likely to see their peers in high-track classes this way.[12] Many teachers believe that track placements reflect students' innate and fixed intelligence rather than academic readiness, which is more malleable.[13] As a result, they typically expect more of students in high-track classes than they do of students in low-track classes.[14] All of these perceptions—student self-perception, peer perceptions, and teacher perceptions—combine to make track assignments a powerful source of identity in a school. Perhaps not surprisingly, since age-grading is taken for granted in schools, we have less evidence on how grade assignments influence student identity formation. But to anyone who has ever seen what happens to friendships between four- and five-year-olds when one goes off to kindergarten, or watched a child ask another at the playground about what grade they're in before playing with them, it's clear that this category also shapes the way students think about themselves and others.

Educational categories become more powerful when students incorporate them into their identities. Young Kenneth Payne's understanding of himself, his family situation, and his place in the world shifted when the new cafeteria employee's questions revealed his free-lunch status. But why was this interaction such a defining moment for Payne? First, it gave Payne an identity—from that moment on, Payne was a "free-lunch kid." Second, that identity had a clear meaning in that school context. To be a free-lunch kid was to be poor, and to be poor was to be lower in status, power, and esteem.

What Payne's story illustrates is that the category of "free-lunch kid" takes its meaning from the boundaries it creates and the people it separates. To make sense of his interaction with the new cafeteria worker, young Payne needed to look around himself and observe which of his classmates paid for lunch and which ones received their lunch for free. He might have noticed that free-lunch kids tended to wear hand-me-down clothes, or that they were all from the same neighborhood, while the kids who brought lunch or paid for them wore new clothes and lived on the other side of the tracks. These observations might have led Payne to start noticing patterns in how his classmates interacted with one another, or how teachers interacted with his classmates, or even how shopkeepers interacted with his classmates' parents. The power of the "free-lunch kid" category lies in this web of associations.

We often think of educational categories as independently meaningful: a student does or does not receive a free lunch, or a student takes algebra rather than pre-algebra. In truth, however, the distinctions created by categories are inherently relational, in that they are defined by their relationship to other categories. Again, academic tracking is an informative example. Academic tracks matter, first, because they influence the distribution of educational opportunities. Students in high-track classes are given access to higher-level material, while those in low-track classes are given lower-level material. But those differences are probably not sufficient to explain the relationship between tracking and educational inequality. After all, age-grading also exposes students to differentially difficult material. If tracking placed students in classes that met their educational needs equally and appropriately, students in high- and low-track classes might learn the same amount and tracks might not contribute to educational inequality. But because school leaders often treat high-track teaching assignments as rewards for their most experienced and favored teachers, and because those teachers often dedicate disproportionate time and attention to the students in their high-track classes, track assignments often correspond with resource inequalities. Further, because White students from affluent families are often overrepresented in high-track classes, track assignments also correspond with status inequalities in the school.[15] Tracking's effects on students' beliefs about their abilities, their behavior, their educational expectations, and the expectations of those around them accumulate at the intersection of these categorical distinctions.

Different Kinds of Educational Categories Produce Different Kinds of Inequality

Because educational categories gain their power in no small part from the way they shape identities and place students in a web of associations that reach from education and into other institutions in our unequal society, the effects of educational categories can be highly variable. Educational categories work as a function of the criteria upon which they are based, their relative size, the extent to which they overlap with other categories, and the nature and degree of inequality between the other categories with which educational categories overlap. How would school lunch have influenced Payne's identity differently if the school had given students free lunch as a reward for successfully completing the morning's schoolwork? How differently would the story have played out if the old cafeteria worker, who never asked Payne for lunch money, had stayed in the job throughout Payne's school career? How much of Payne's experience was rooted in the particular socioeconomic mix in his school? Receiving a free lunch, for example, might have felt different in a school where all students got their lunch for free than in a school, like Payne's, where only some students got free lunch. Likewise, getting free lunch might have meant something different in a school located in a community where the distribution of family incomes and resources was very compacted, such that the free-lunch kids were not noticeably poorer than the paid-lunch kids. And it might have meant something far different in a community with a great deal of income inequality, where the free-lunch kids lived in shacks and the paid-lunch kids lived in mansions. How different would Payne's story have been if he had attended a racially diverse school in which Black and Hispanic students received a disproportionate share of the free lunches and White kids disproportionately paid for their lunches?

To contemplate these questions, it is helpful to return to our comparison of age-grading and academic tracking. All things considered, age-grading feels like a relatively egalitarian exercise in educational category construction. Admittedly, the practice of sorting kids based on their age into grades introduces inequalities in children's exposure to educational resources. Kindergarteners are enrolled—for free—in public elementary schools, where they enjoy access to elementary school educational resources and learning opportunities. Their four-year-old neighbors, meanwhile, are left at home or in preschool as their families pay for educational opportunities that are typically less academically rigorous than those made available in the elementary school. But kindergarteners are generally given less challenging instruction than first graders. Furthermore, thanks to accountability pressures, kindergarteners, first graders, and second graders often learn from less experienced and lower performing teachers than their older peers, whose test scores are taken into account in school rankings.[16] But in the long term we expect these inequalities to disappear as kids get older and progress through the grades. After all, how else can we make sense of the phenomenon of kindergarten "redshirting"—parents (particularly relatively advantaged parents) opting to postpone their children's kindergarten entry for a year, so that they are exposed to less rigorous content than their on-time kindergarten-attending peers?[17]

By contrast, a broad consensus in the research literature holds that academic tracking substantially exacerbates educational inequality. For example, Laura Argys, Daniel Rees, and Dominic Brewer estimated the odds of student track placement for students enrolled in U.S. high schools in the early 1990s based on a variety of student and school characteristics (including student gender, race/ethnicity, socioeconomic status, and prior achievement, as well as school size and demographics).[18] Their analyses use classroom teacher survey data to categorize tracks, comparing students in classrooms in which teachers described student skills as "above average," "average," or "below average" with students in classrooms that teachers described as "heterogeneous." Their analysis indicates that tracking has modest positive effects on mean levels of student achievement, such that a typical student placed in a heterogeneous class scored approximately one percentage point lower on a tenth-grade measure of mathematical achievement than the sample mean. However, the gains associated with between-class tracking are not distributed evenly. Students placed into high-track classes scored significantly higher than they might have if they had been placed into untracked classes, while students placed into low-track classes scored significantly worse. Furthermore, these analyses indicate that track placement effects do not vary substantially with student ability. Several other studies using a wide array of data sources and methods reach similar conclusions.[19]

Our own research focuses on schools that place students who score above a test score threshold into advanced classes and students who score below the threshold into grade-level classes. We compare students just on the two sides of the threshold used for course placement to generate arguably causal estimates of the effects of advanced course placement. These analyses demonstrate that students placed into high-track classes learn more than they would have in lower-track classes, and that these positive effects persist for years after their initial track placement.[20] In sum, these analyses indicate that tracking benefits students who are placed into high-track classes and hurts students who are placed into low-track classes. Based on this evidence, we believe that it is safe to conclude that tracking exacerbates educational inequality, and that the unequal effects of track placement persist even as students transition from school to adulthood.

Structural Characteristics of Categories

If age-grading and academic tracking both produce educational categories that determine educational opportunities, how are we to make sense of the apparent difference in their consequences for durable inequality? Answering this question provides an opportunity to think through the dimensions of education's categorical inequalities. We argue that any practice that produces educational categories inevitably produces inequality of some form, but that the inequality-producing consequences of educational categories vary with the *assignment mechanisms* and criteria that sorters use to populate categories, the opportunities for *mobility* among the categories, the *number and size* of the categories produced by a practice in its context, and the *scope* and salience of the categories produced. Comparing age-grading and tracking on these dimensions helps to explain why these two educational category–producing practices have such different effects and provides an opportunity to flesh out these important dimensions of educational categories.

ASSIGNMENT MECHANISMS

Let's begin by comparing the assignment mechanisms that these two category-producing practices use. Age-grading sorts students into learning environments primarily based on their birth date or calendar age, while tracking sorts students into learning environments based on various definitions of their academic readiness or need. The differences between these two category assignment mechanisms have clear implications for the kinds and degree of inequality that the resulting categories produce.

Age is easy to measure. Every student has a birth date, and most parents have no trouble accurately reporting that birth date to the school. Most schools or school systems set a threshold for student assignment based on birth date. For instance, a typical rule states that a child who has turned five by August 31 can enroll in kindergarten, but younger kids with a fifth birthday on or after September 1 must wait a year to enroll.

Furthermore, a student's age is largely uncorrelated with many other socially important student characteristics. Unless a school is undergoing an extremely rapid demographic transformation, the students in its kindergarten classes will look similar to students in their first-grade classes on gender, ethnicity, family background, and other characteristics. Therefore, to the degree that grade assignments hinge purely on student age, we do not have to worry about race, class, or gender biases getting mixed up in age-based grade categories.[21]

Measuring student academic performance is a notoriously tricky undertaking. Indeed, fierce debates rage among educators, students, parents, policymakers, and researchers about what "academic performance" even means. Historical tracking systems attempted to measure and sort students based on their supposedly innate capacity for academic work. More contemporary systems attempt to measure and sort according to students' achievement, or their mastery of the skills and academic materials to which they have been exposed. Others have proposed sorting by mindset, attitude, work ethic, or potential to benefit from a given educational opportunity. Many contemporary public schools administer several standardized assessments to their students over the course of an academic year, repeatedly measuring their mastery of foundational skills, particularly in the core academic areas of math and language arts. But few educators believe that these assessments provide a full view of the student characteristics that should inform track assignments. Many school tracking systems thus draw upon a combination of assessment scores, student grades, teacher recommendations, and student preferences to make track assignments. In practice, track assignments are often political decisions that rely heavily on educators' judgment as well as input from a wide array of stakeholders.

As a result of these measurement challenges, tracking assignment practices are already far more complicated than mechanically sorting older children into one grade and younger children into another. But these measurement challenges are just the tip of the iceberg. Perhaps even more complicated is the normative value attached to track assignments but not to age-grade assignments. We talk about "respecting elders," and we arguably accord more prestige to the teachers who teach students in the upper grades than teachers who teach young children. But the status gradient associated with age is typically less steep than the status gradient associated with academic performance.

We celebrate kids' birthdays, but we think of birthday parties as celebrations of the child rather than as rewards for attaining a higher age. By contrast, we give our children rewards for high grades and, though we may be reluctant to admit it, many of us are likely to feel that our children have demonstrated some aspect of their worth when they ace a standardized test. To put the point differently: it has never occurred to anybody to rank law schools based on the age of their students. But ranking law schools based on their incoming students' test scores is so common as to seem the most natural thing in the world.

Furthermore, links between the criteria relevant to assignment mechanisms and categories like race, gender, and poverty play an important role in whether they are viewed as controversial. These categories operate largely independently of age, so that students of all races, genders, and different levels of resources tend to pass through age categories similarly. By contrast, regardless of how educators conceptualize and measure the characteristic that they use to sort students into academic tracks, the students they place in high-level tracks are likely to differ on a wide range of characteristics from the students they place in low-level tracks. On average, poor students and students of color rate lower than their affluent and White peers on a wide variety of metrics of academic success.[22] As a result, skills-based track placements are likely to reflect and reinforce broader social inequalities. The overlap between track and race may be a particularly potent source of durable inequality, as the work of the sociologist Karolyn Tyson has aptly demonstrated.[23] Tyson studies Black students' attitudes around race and schooling, comparing students in racially mixed high schools where Black students disproportionately take low-track classes with students in predominantly Black schools where Black students are well represented at all track levels. Tyson and her colleagues find that Black students—and their teachers—are much more likely to conflate race and academic achievement in the mixed-race high schools.[24] In these schools, tracking enhances the meaning of race, putting pressures on high-achieving Black students to avoid high-track classes and other academic distinctions and convincing low-achieving Black students that their status in the school is inevitable.

OPPORTUNITIES FOR MOBILITY

A second important way in which age-grading and academic tracking differ is in the opportunities for mobility across the categories they create. Over time, students have nearly perfect odds of moving between school grades. No student remains a kindergartener forever, and although some students repeat grades as they progress through school, the norm is for students to move between these educational categories on an annual basis. By contrast, mobility across academic tracks is rare: very few students move from low-track classes to high-track classes. In an analysis of course tracking among twenty-four thousand students in twenty-three California middle schools, we found that some 40 percent of students fell from high-track math courses to low-track math courses and 30 percent fell from high-track language arts courses to low-track language arts courses between eighth and ninth grade. But fewer than 1 percent of students made the reverse move—from low-track courses to high-track courses.[25]

There is, of course, a reason why few students move up in academic tracking systems: skills acquisition in many academic subjects is cumulative. It is extremely challenging for a student who has not mastered algebra to tackle geometry. When we talk with middle school math teachers about their school tracking systems, they are often flummoxed at the idea of track mobility. Asked to imagine how a high-performing middle-track student might fare if promoted to an honors course, one teacher told us: "I think he would miss out on a lot, because I'm finishing up on chapter 4 in the standard class while I'm finishing up on chapter 7 in the honors class. So you're missing five and six and seven. That's a huge amount to miss! What can you gain?" We have encountered a few schools that very carefully provide scaffolds—such as summer programs, condensed course sequences, and double-dose classes—to allow students to learn material that they haven't yet encountered and to promote track mobility. But since such scaffolds are rare in most contemporary middle and high schools, upward track mobility is rare as well.

Perfect mobility across grades helps to explain why age-grading is such an uncontroversial category-creating practice. Because parents understand that their children almost inevitably graduate to the next educational level, they feel no need to complain about the fact that their children are taught less advanced material than they would be in the next grade up. Grade assignments may produce inequalities in the short term, but since students routinely move between grades, these inequalities tend to fade away over time.

By contrast, the near-absence of upward mobility among academic tracks helps to explain both why tracking is such a controversial practice and why it produces durable inequalities. The stakes associated with track placement are high indeed when honors algebra in the eighth grade is the gateway to AP calculus in twelfth grade, especially given the role AP calculus plays in getting into a selective college. Furthermore, a degree from a selective college is a gateway to a top-tier law school or medical school, which is a gateway to professional success. The infrequency of upward track mobility thus confers substantial power on the educators who make track assignments and gives students who land in high-track classes early in their educational career a substantial advantage.

Furthermore, low levels of track mobility make questions about how to conceptualize and measure the student characteristics that educators use to assign students to tracks particularly pressing. Mobility provides opportunities to correct mistakes that occur when students are assigned to tracks based on criteria that imprecisely measure their capacity to benefit from the instruction the track provides. The absence of mobility—coupled with imperfect and potentially biased assignment mechanisms—ensures that misplaced students continue to suffer the consequences of misplacement throughout their academic career and beyond. Category mobility is thus a particularly salient issue for evaluating educational categories that are established relatively early in students' educational careers. And it is doubly salient in early assignment to categories—like academic tracks—that are based on measures of academic achievement or other student characteristics that are influenced by students' home environments. Since a young child's reading skills are a function of both home and school influences, systems that track students based on their reading skills in the early elementary grades are likely to create categories that correlate highly with student socioeconomic status and home resources. This is an important explanation for the finding that intergenerational mobility is lower in educational systems that track very young students than in systems that wait until students are older to sort them into academic tracks.[26]

NUMBER AND RELATIVE SIZE OF CATEGORIES

Age-grading and academic tracking systems also differ in terms of their structure—including the number and relative size of the categories that they create.

School age-grading systems typically create more categories than school academic tracking systems. Most elementary schools separate students into six or seven grades, kindergarten through fifth or sixth. By contrast, the typical secondary school tracking system sorts students into three tracks, a common configuration being developmental (or remedial), college preparatory, and honors (or advanced).

The number of categories operating in an educational setting is likely to influence how students experience these categories. The more categories a school creates, the more students will probably have in common with their peers within the category. By creating a large number of categories, schools can more effectively target instruction or other educational services to students. But the extent to which this sort of microtargeting generates or ameliorates durable inequalities may vary considerably across settings. Individualizing instruction in the elementary school setting appears to reduce educational inequality by enabling teachers to provide effective early intervention to struggling readers.[27] At the same time, the highly differentiated structure of the American higher education system may also contribute to the construction of durable inequalities. At the bottom of this system, exploitative for-profit universities saddle students who have few other options with considerable debt.[28] At the top of the system, highly selective colleges and universities channel students from advantaged family backgrounds into elite professions.[29]

Putting these two insights about the number of categories together, we might hypothesize that the more categories there are in a given setting, the smaller the degree of inequality between any two neighboring categories on a status hierarchy but the greater the degree of inequality between the highest and lowest categories. This hypothesis suggests that a school that attempts a sort of micrograding by, for example, creating one kindergarten class for kids who start the year close to their fifth birthday and a second kindergarten class for kids who start the year close to their sixth birthday and then sending students through school in these relatively small cohorts, will give the younger kindergarteners and the older kindergarteners fairly similar experiences. We can imagine, however, that such highly developmentally targeted instruction instead will maximize the differences between the educational experiences provided to kindergarteners and sixth-graders. Similarly, tracking might result in particularly pronounced between-group inequality in a high school where students are tracked on either a high track or a low track, while a more fine-grained tracking system might create more subtle between-group inequality. Overall, however, we might expect the school with fine-grained academic tracks to maximize the differences in achievement and life opportunities available to students in the highest tracks compared to their peers in the lowest tracks.

Age-grading and academic tracking also differ in the relative size of the categories that they produce. That is, most contemporary schools have approximately the same number of students in each of the grades, but some tracks can be much larger than others. Many students default into a college prep track, which sits at the middle of the tracking hierarchy and is often the school's largest track. In this typical track configuration, the developmental track is reserved for students with demonstrated academic challenges (including students with a history of course failure or diagnosed learning differences) while the advanced course is reserved for a small number of students with a history of high test scores or other extraordinary academic achievements. But this configuration varies considerably from school to school. The potential for inequality varies with the relative size of categories in a purely mathematical sense, but it is not clear that the relative size of categories is related to the magnitude of inequality in practice.[30]

CATEGORY SCOPE

Finally, educational categories can differ in the extent to which they shape students' days, identities, peer exposure, and other aspects of their educational experiences. We refer to this dimension as category scope.

Grade assignments are high-scope, particularly in the elementary school years. Elementary school students typically spend their entire school day surrounded by their grade-level peers. Further, while some elementary school students spend part of their day receiving targeted instruction from teachers who specialize in working with English-language learners or special education students, for most students their grade assignment determines which teachers they are exposed to in core academic settings.

In theory, academic tracks could be lower-scope categories than academic grades, particularly if schools make it possible for students who enroll in high-track classes in one subject to enroll in lower-track classes in another subject. In practice, however, such cross-track course enrollment is rare in American middle and high schools. Our analyses of track placements in twenty-three California middle schools suggest that students' eighth-grade math course placements are so highly correlated with their eighth-grade English course placements that if we knew only a student's math course we could predict their English course enrollment with nearly 70 percent accuracy.[31] Similar analyses reveal equally high correlations in track placements across academic subjects in a nationally representative sample of youth.[32]

Since we suspect that the scope of the categories produced by grade assignments and track placements are very similar, we do not expect scope to explain differences in the effects of these two category creation processes.[33]

Nonetheless, the higher the scope of an educational category, the more it can contribute to the production of educational inequality. High-scope categories like grades and academic tracks shape many aspects of students' educational and social experiences at school. Further, they are likely to have particularly pronounced consequences for students' identity formation. Lower-scope categories, however, are likely to have smaller consequences for inequality. To understand why, consider two schools that take different approaches to school lunch. In the first—let's call it Shady Canyon Elementary—students who receive free lunch line up and receive their lunch while their classmates who do not participate in the program sit in the lunchroom and get started on the lunches they brought from home. In the second—let's call it Sunny Ridge Elementary—all students pass through the lunch line, swipe a card, and receive a school lunch. Behind the scenes, free-lunch recipient lunch expenses are billed to the lunch program, while other families receive a bill for their children's lunches. In both schools, school lunch categories are likely lower-scope than either grades or tracks. But the salience and scope of school lunch categories are likely to be considerably higher at Shady Canyon than at Sunny Ridge. As a result, both students and educators at Shady Canyon are likely to be much more conscious of lunch status, since standing in the free-lunch line marks some students as poor, and the stigma associated with free lunch might be more likely to shape students' identity, offsetting the program's nutritional benefits and generating durable categorical inequalities.

Thinking Culturally: The Value We Attach to Categories

Above and beyond all these structural characteristics, it is important to remember that the normative social value that we assign to educational categories also influences their power to create durable inequalities. As a society, we invest both receipt of free lunch and placement in a high-track class with powerful social meaning—free-lunch students are "poor," and honors-track kids are "smart." While the latter is widely recognized in society as highly desirable, the former is not. This normative value matters. Because we see free lunch as a reflection of student socioeconomic status, students consider the free lunches that some students receive to be "poor people's food." This judgment even shapes the way food tastes—we have seen middle-class children clamor for tater tots at home but reject them as "disgusting" when they are served at school. Furthermore, the normative value attached to school free lunches may explain the stigma attached to receiving free lunch in some schools.

If anything, the cultural value associated with academic tracks is even more powerful. American schools often value student intelligence above all else, making "smart" a synonym for "good." Teachers and students alike often view track placements as a proxy for student "smarts." When students believe that their track placement is a reflection of their worth, and when teachers subtly—or not so subtly—reinforce that message (as happened when Stan Sitwell launched the color-coded ID card program at his high school), it is not at all surprising that students placed into low tracks question their own intelligence and ability to do academic work and eventually disengage from school.[34] Perhaps romanticized ideas about children and our reluctance to label them as "bad" or "unworthy" explain why explicit tracking occurs much less frequently in the elementary grades than in the middle and high school grades (although evidence suggests that teachers' use of ability groups in the early elementary grades can influence their assessment of students' behavior and students' subsequent learning, widening inequality after kindergarten entry).[35]

Wrapping Up

Most writing and thinking about education focuses on the teaching and learning that happens in schools. But if we want to understand how and why schools work, we need to look closely at a third activity that is central to contemporary schooling: categorization.

Sometimes schools build, enact, reproduce, and enforce social categories in the service of teaching and learning. If asked why their schools sort students into age-grades or academic tracks, most educators would argue that these categorization processes help teachers teach by creating groups of learners who are ready for similar challenges and have similar educational needs. Other categories that schools create may be only peripherally related to teaching and learning. Because most of us agree that combating child hunger is a valuable end in and of itself, it may seem relatively unimportant whether or not free meals affect student achievement.[36]

Regardless of why schools categorize students, these categories have long-lasting and often unintended consequences. By creating categories and sorting youth into them, schools develop templates that influence the contours of inequality throughout contemporary societies. School categories matter for the students categorized by their schools. They influence the way students see themselves and the way others see them. Furthermore, school categories matter for society at large, since they establish and legitimate the criteria by which the adult world allocates status, power, riches, and other spoils of inequality.

However, the nature of the categories that schools construct is by no means predetermined. As we have discussed in this chapter, schools enact many different kinds of categories. Furthermore, even when schools enact the same categories, they do so in very different ways. These differences matter. Categories based on criteria that are distributed relatively evenly across society, like age, tend to create diverse groups of students, while categories based on criteria that are very unequally distributed tend to create homogeneous and unequal groups. Furthermore, the practices through which schools enact categories can have implications for their consequences. When schools hide the categories they use, their consequences may not go away, even though drawing attention to their categories can give them more power. Finally, the structure of school categories matter. Categorization processes can create differences in opportunities for students between categories, and schools can build categories that permanently follow kids throughout their educational careers and beyond. Schools can put students into bigger groups or smaller groups, and they can build categories that affect either a large part of students' educational experience or only a small part.

Because these differences in school categorization processes matter, the people who contribute to the construction and maintenance of educational categories have the power to fundamentally alter the structure of inequality in our schools and ultimately across our society. Actors throughout our educational system—from the most powerful lawmakers to the youngest student—participate in the co-construction of educational categories. As such, each has some power to help rethink and reconstruct educational categories. It may be impossible to imagine educational systems that do not categorize and that therefore do not contribute to the construction of social inequality. But it is at least possible to work for more just and equitable educational categories with the hope of creating a more just and equitable society.

In the next chapter, we take a closer look at that possibility by investigating the struggles that take place in schools as educators work continuously and iteratively to build and rebuild educational categories.

CONTESTING SCHOOL STRUCTURES 5

The construction and maintenance of the categories that schools use is a messy project. Educational policy debates tend to treat schools as bureaucratized institutions that are ruled by standardized and rationalized institutional logics. Although this discourse inevitably proceeds from the assumption that our schools are in crisis, it also confidently takes for granted that all it will take is some good commonsense management to make high-quality schools that work for everybody. Listening to these debates, you can almost be fooled into thinking that we all agree about the goals that schools pursue.

We don't. Fierce and ongoing debates about educational goals are threaded through the history of American education. In the early republican period, leading thinkers put forward competing visions of education's place in the young nation that continue to define educational discussions today. In the early twentieth century, leading African American thinkers such as W.E.B. Du Bois, Booker T. Washington, and Charles Hamilton Houston navigated similar tensions as they debated education's place in the movement for Black liberation.[1] These historical debates still echo through education. Should schools aim to teach every student the same set of basic skills? Or should they use a broadly differentiated curriculum and aim to cultivate each student's unique individual capacities? Do we ultimately want our schools to build democratic citizens? Or to facilitate social mobility? Or to just socialize people to work together in an orderly fashion?[2]

We also face a great deal of uncertainty about which educational strategies best advance educational goals. Some teachers swear by group work, others want students to attack problems independently and develop their own strategies, and still others believe that "drill and kill" is the only way to lay the cognitive foundations on which mastery is built. Despite advances in the learning sciences and curriculum studies, educators are unlikely to come to an informed consensus on these questions anytime soon. Because both teachers and their students vary, even the most thoroughly validated pedagogical strategies will work better in some classrooms than in others.

Since we cannot agree about the goals that schools should be pursuing or the means to best pursue their goals, schools are sites of continuous contestation and debate.[3] These debates often take their most public form when policymakers attempt to design, enact, and enforce explicit rules that define educational categories and shape the criteria and processes that govern student assignments to categories. These high-level policy debates—about public school attendance boundaries, high-stakes tests for grade advancement, or affirmative action in college admissions—get all the attention. But often the debates that really define educational categories and the inequalities they create happen in more obscure corners of the educational system—in the committees and professional learning communities where educators and educational leaders implement educational policy and make everyday educational decisions.

Education is not a fully rationalized and rule-driven institution, and time and again high-level public policies have failed to achieve intended changes in educational practices as they have come into contact with schools' diverse and rapidly changing circumstances and the educational stakeholders' wide range of views and understandings about schooling. It's a long road from conceptualization to instantiation for educational categories, and along that road policymakers, school leaders, educators, families, and students make countless decisions, improvisations, and compromises that influence the shape and magnitude of the inequalities that these categories produce. In this chapter, we map that road, describing the dilemmas that educators face when they enact educational categories and the ways they routinely contest and reimagine the educational status quo. Although we draw examples from multiple areas, we focus on eighth-grade mathematics course placements as a case study that provides a vibrant representation of the micropolitics of educational categories and their implications.

Throughout the discussion, we focus particular attention on the ways in which teachers—the street-level bureaucrats of the educational system—contest the educational categorical inequalities that they encounter in their schools and how they work together to try to co-construct new, more equitable educational categories. Like the nurses, police officers, social workers, and other street-level bureaucrats profiled by Michael Lipsky, teachers stand at the interface between social policies and the public.[4] As such, teachers' decisions about how to distribute scarce educational resources influence the shape of educational categories and their consequences for enduring inequalities.[5]

To be clear, teacher agency is sharply constrained. Teachers, like other street-level bureaucrats, often find themselves squeezed between policy requirements and their own limited time, attention, and resources. Furthermore, they must continuously attend to the multiple stakeholders with whom they interact—including school leaders, fellow teachers, students, and their families—as well as the often-conflicting expectations and interests of these stakeholders. Nonetheless, by drawing attention to the important decision points on the way to educational categorical inequality and the ways in which teachers and other educational actors approach these decision points, we aim to highlight the agency that local educational actors have in the construction of educational categorical inequality.

In this chapter, building on our discussion in chapter 4, we describe four distinct steps in the construction of categories in schools:

1 First, educators and their constituents elsewhere in society reach a rough consensus regarding the criteria on which categories are to be based.
2 Second, they develop and implement a strategy to measure and distinguish between students according to these conceptual criteria. Stakeholders' decisions in these first two steps have important implications for categorical assignment mechanisms.
3 Third, stakeholders make important decisions about the structure of educational categories, including the number of categories used in a given setting and their relative size.

4 Finally, stakeholders enact the organizational routines that sort students into categories and give those categories meaning.

The ways in which stakeholders enact categories have important implications for the scope of those categories and the opportunities for mobility among categories. Organizational—and ultimately institutional—change in education often occurs through a process of accretion. At each step in the category creation process, educational actors articulate ideas and enact practices. Because these ideas and practices accumulate as schools continuously build and rebuild educational categories, the categorical inequalities that schools create are both highly path-dependent and potentially malleable.

Our Case: The Middle School Math Wars

Our discussion in this chapter focuses on instructional category construction in the context of middle school mathematics course assignments. As we argued in chapter 4, middle school mathematics course placement is an early and important categorical distinction in the U.S. educational system, and the point in many students' school careers at which they first encounter formal cross-course instructional tracking. Many U.S. middle schools use a two- or three-tiered tracking system in eighth-grade mathematics. In this system, most students take a grade-level mathematics course that is often labeled "pre-algebra," while a smaller proportion of high-achieving eighth-graders take algebra. In some schools, an even smaller highly accelerated group of students take algebra in seventh grade and geometry in eighth grade.

We became interested in middle school math in part because it is a key sorting point in contemporary education. Since middle school math provides a gateway to the hierarchical structure of high school mathematics courses, students who take algebra earlier than their peers are much more likely to gain access to calculus and other advanced mathematics courses during their high school years. Accordingly, this initial sorting process has consequences for students' later opportunities to learn, their postsecondary outcomes, and their transition to the labor market.[6]

We also happened to be living in a time and place—California in the early twenty-first century—in which the rules and norms that governed middle school math course assignments were very much in flux. Beginning in the late 1980s, the California Department of Education (CDE) led a national effort to expand students' access to eighth-grade algebra. At the start at least, the CDE's stated goal was improving educational equity. The CDE believed that putting everybody into courses that schools had once reserved for relatively advanced students would be a first step toward detracking schools and eliminating long-standing racial and socioeconomic inequalities in students' opportunities to learn.[7] The ultimate result, the department hoped, would be the elimination of this highly consequential categorical distinction in California schools.

The algebra-for-all effort moved to the center of California's educational policy portfolio during the 1990s, even as its policy rationale became more diffuse. The 1998 *Mathematics Framework for California Schools* identified algebra as the only appropriate mathematics course for California eighth-graders, opening the door for the algebra-for-all effort to become a part of the state's school accountability policies. At the same time, this document marked a subtle shift in how the state talked about its algebra-for-all effort: the focus changed from educational equity to academic rigor and student college readiness. Consistent with this shift in tone, the CDE's 1998 *Framework* took pains to argue that "what students are taught has a greater effect on achievement than does how they are grouped," while allowing schools to preserve differentiated instructional groupings across middle school mathematics classes.[8]

California's first comprehensive school accountability legislation, the 1999 Public Schools Accountability Act, incorporated students' middle school mathematics course enrollments in the public evaluation of California schools. Fully implemented in 2004, this law made the proportion of eighth-graders enrolled in algebra or more advanced mathematics courses a part of the summary scale used to measure school quality statewide. The California State Board of Education raised the accountability stakes associated with eighth-grade algebra even higher in 2008, when it declared that algebra was the "sole course of record" for eighth-graders. This move required eighth-graders to demonstrate proficiency on the state's end-of-course algebra standards exam to satisfy federal and state accountability expectations.[9] This requirement put schools that tracked a large proportion of eighth-graders into less advanced courses at risk of state takeover or reconstitution as a charter school.[10] However, California's eighth-grade algebra-for-all mandate was never fully implemented. Immediately after the state board's vote, a group of California school administrators and school boards mounted a legal challenge, claiming that the state had failed to provide educators with sufficient time and resources to prepare all students to enroll in algebra. Concurring, the court repeatedly postponed implementation of the algebra-for-all mandate.[11]

In the fall of 2010, California joined forty other states in adopting the Common Core State Standards (CCSS), which recommended a course of study for all eighth-graders that combined pre-algebraic and algebraic concepts but was "designed to permit states to continue existing policies concerning algebra in the 8th grade."[12] Some of the state's vocal algebra-for-all advocates decried the CCSS as a step back in academic rigor.[13] Further, the CDE discontinued the use of eighth-grade algebra enrollments in the calculation of API scores beginning in the 2012–2013 school year. However, the state's 2013 *Mathematics Framework* included a detailed appendix that attempted to guide schools toward mathematics course placement, acceleration, and sequencing policies that would maximize the proportion of students taking advanced mathematics courses.[14]

The middle school math wars continue to rage in California, and the salience of categorical distinctions between mathematics courses continues to fluctuate. In 2021 the state issued a new draft *Framework* that declared the state's algebra-for-all effort a failure and particularly decried its negative consequences for poor students and students of color. The current *Framework*—to the chagrin of many of the educators and activists who argued for acceleration, but with the support of others who believe that inequitable tracking inevitably accompanies acceleration—calls for enrolling students in skills-heterogeneous mathematics courses through middle school and beyond and argues that the path to educational equity and excellence is to provide opportunities for students to learn material deeply rather than accelerating content coverage.[15]

Carefully observing how educators respond to changing expectations and policy pressures surrounding educational category construction provides us with a unique window on category construction processes. Between 2010 and 2015, when California's algebra-for-all push was reaching its zenith and the state was beginning to reconsider its emphasis on content acceleration, we talked to dozens of math teachers at California public schools as well as school administrators and instructional coaches responsible for middle school math course placement and instructional policy. We use the data from our conversations, as well as data collected by other scholars during this turbulent period, to understand how educators thought about middle school math course assignments; the sorts of rules and procedures that they implemented to construct math course categories in their schools; and the tensions and pressures that they felt along the way.

We are consistently impressed by how thoughtfully and seriously educators approach this work. They see course assignments as both an ethical and a practical problem, and many of them told us about sleepless nights, tense conversations with families and students, and tearful meetings as they and their colleagues struggled to design and implement instructional categories that reflected their ideals. Educators struggle to design category construction processes that are morally defensible and pedagogically effective. Throughout the following discussion of these placement processes and the dilemmas that educators face, we draw particular attention to the constant contestation in schools and district offices as educational leaders and teachers negotiate with one another and with families and students in an attempt to square their practice with policy, research, pedagogical instincts, local cultures, and perceived student needs.

To organize our discussion, we divide the process into the four rough steps described earlier. Not every category construction process will follow these steps in order, but they represent key decision points on the path to the creation and maintenance of virtually any educational category.

Step 1: Selecting Criteria for Category Construction

In light of ongoing debates about the goals of education and the best ways to pursue those goals, contemporary schools use diverse criteria to sort students into many different kinds of educational categories.

As the sociologist Christopher Jencks memorably noted, "Americans never argue about whether educational opportunity should be equal," but, he notes, "we have dramatically different views about *whom* educational institutions should treat equally and whom they can legitimately treat unequally."[16] Jencks illustrates this by describing the dilemmas facing an elementary school teacher committed to providing equal educational opportunity to all the students in her classroom. Such a teacher might start by trying to allocate her time and energy evenly across all her students, an approach that Jencks describes as "democratic egalitarianism." But she might decide that this approach spreads her efforts so thin that no student is well served. Instead, Jencks suggests, this equality-minded teacher might pursue the path of "compensatory egalitarianism," focusing her efforts on struggling students in an attempt to level the playing field and compensate for the disadvantages that account for their struggles. Alternatively, she could invoke a principle of "moral egalitarianism," using her time and energy as a reward for student effort and perceived worth.

Jencks's argument is that each of these approaches represents a principled and valid interpretation of the ideal of equal opportunity. "The enduring popularity of equal educational opportunity," Jencks concludes, "probably derives from the fact that we can all define it in different ways without realizing how profound our differences are."[17]

The educational categories that contemporary schools enact reflect each of these ideas about equal opportunity, and then some. Although it is impossible to distribute identical educational experiences to all students in so large and varied an educational environment as U.S. schools, practices like lottery-based admissions to high-demand schools or age-grading within schools approach the ideal of democratic egalitarianism, since they allocate resources in a way that attempts to be independent of important student background characteristics. The National School Lunch Program, on the other hand, explicitly pursues compensatory egalitarian goals. Based on the assumption that poor children need supplementary resources, the program categorizes students into free, reduced, or full-priced lunch categories based on their financial need and allocates supplementary resources to the most economically disadvantaged. The same can be said for special education, specialized English-language learner programs, and other programs that aim to provide focused resources to students in need of specific educational supports. By contrast, a wide range of programs use educational resources to reward students' efforts and prior achievement, consistent with moral egalitarianism. High schools confer diplomas when students have satisfactorily completed a specified course of study; selective universities admit undergraduates based on a notion of merit; elite PhD programs select students based on judgments about their odds of advancing scholarly inquiry.

Teacher thinking about tracking in middle school mathematics reflects the ethical dilemmas that Jencks highlights as well as more practical debates about how to provide effective educational opportunities. Most contemporary middle schools sort students into separate classrooms for mathematics instruction based on their prior achievement. Many advocates for this sorting system argue that it facilitates efficient instruction of diverse students with diverse needs. When we talked to middle school mathematics teachers about skills-based tracking, many noted that grouping students into classes based on their prior achievement allowed them to meet students where they were. Many recounted working with students in low-track eighth-grade classrooms who struggled with basic arithmetic; others noted that students varied in their motivation to study mathematics and in their classroom behavior. Tracking, in these teachers' telling, was a technical solution to the challenges associated with sorting students with different abilities and needs.

Other advocates frame the argument for tracking in middle school mathematics in more normative terms. One teacher told us that she liked "that the advanced kids are separated, because then those kids are not in a class where it is constantly a behavior thing happening. . . . I think they've earned that. They've earned the right to be in an advanced class." Another teacher echoed this sentiment, using a slightly less moral tone: "When I have my honors cluster in here, I definitely identify with those kids. And many of those kids have a lower tolerance for students who are going to disrupt instruction and they get very frustrated."

But many teachers feel deeply ambivalent about the practice of sorting students for instruction. One middle school teacher told us:

"I don't believe in the honors system. I believe that all kids should be deserving of a high-quality curriculum." This veteran teacher refused to teach the honors classes that his school offered because he believed that tracking was both unjust and ineffective. By denying some students the opportunity to engage with challenging academic content and engaging instruction, he argued, tracking undermined the goal of equal opportunity in schools. Further, this teacher was not convinced that skills-based tracking was necessary to create effective learning environments for accelerated students. "People still think that if they have the H by their class name they're learning something better. That's not always the case." Another teacher we spoke to agreed, arguing that classrooms that purposely mix highly skilled students and less highly skilled students—skills-heterogeneous classrooms, in educational parlance—provide particularly rich learning environments. In fact, this teacher liked to sort students into working groups within his classes. "At each table, there is one high-scoring student, one low-scoring, and two students who scored in between. . . . The student who is high-scoring seems to benefit from being asked to explain to the medium-level students and to help them along. The low-scoring student definitely benefits from hearing how to do the math from peers instead of just the teacher."

As these discussions reveal, educators think hard about sorting for instruction. Indeed, in our discussions, it became clear to us that educators and educational leaders continuously engage in difficult conversations about these issues. Educators formulate both normative commitments concerning the educational opportunities that students deserve as well as professional judgments about how to effectively deliver those educational opportunities. Sometimes those normative commitments and professional judgments conflict. Furthermore, educators know that they represent just a part of this ongoing discursive process. Every teacher we talked to recounted navigating discussions about course assignments with students, families, and school leaders. Others gestured toward state and local policies that limited the range of possibilities for collective decision-making. Nonetheless, educators understand that their deliberations regarding course assignments play an important role in setting the terms for category creation.

Step 2: Operationalizing and Measuring the Criteria

The second step in the construction of categories is measuring the criteria that will be used to sort students into categories. Even when the criteria upon which category assignments will be based are conceptually clear—such as the notion of economic need that governs the allocation of free lunch—this measurement process is difficult and imperfect. Under federal policy, schools are to measure economic need formulaically based on just two factors: family income and household size. But as simple as these two factors initially appear to be, neither is simple to measure. When a form asks a parent to report annual household income from all sources, should the parent report income from the last year or expected income from the next? Does income from social safety net programs count? What about income from noncash goods or services received in the context of a bartered exchange? And which family members should count as householders? If Uncle Bill lives in the house for three months while going through a rough patch, does he count as a household member? In the case of the National School Lunch Program, it's taken years of legislative horse-trading and fine-toothed regulatory parsing to come up with answers to these questions, which are then hidden in the fine print on the application that families are asked to complete in order to enroll their children in subsidized meals.

Furthermore, household income and family size are only imperfect proxies for economic need. Other factors—including family wealth (or debt), the local cost of living, social capital, and income volatility—also matter. A mom and two kids with a household income of $30,000 living in a New York City rental probably has much more acute economic need than a two-parent, one-child family with the same household income living debt-free in an inherited house in Omaha, Nebraska. We suspect that educators often quietly look for hints from students to formulate a more holistic assessment of student need and then take such assessments into account as they decide which students to encourage to apply for free lunch.

Of course, these measurement issues are even more complicated when the criteria governing selection are amorphous or subject to ongoing debate. To take a common example for the three of us, consider the dilemmas facing educators tasked with determining which students to admit to PhD programs. Although the criteria that govern these decisions clearly vary across institutions, fields, and even faculty reviewers, we suspect that most of our colleagues would agree with the economist who told Julie Posselt, "You're basically looking for people who are going to be first-rate researchers and leaders in the field," or the classicist who said, "We want to have somebody who is going to finish the program and thrive—thrive here and go on to be a successful faculty member somewhere."[18] But selecting such candidates requires an ability to predict how a student will do in the future based on relatively limited information. We suspect that most of our colleagues would also agree with the classics professor who called graduate admissions "a crapshoot" because "we don't know who's going to blossom and who isn't. We have not found reliable predictors."[19]

The same dilemmas apply to middle school mathematics teachers, department chairs, and administrators contemplating course assignment processes. Educators have a firm conviction that the learning opportunities they extend to children matter, and they believe that they have a strong professional obligation to match children to educational opportunities that meet their needs. But they are perpetually dissatisfied with the processes they use to match students to classes or academic tracks.

In our interviews, educators described their use of many different strategies to assess students' academic readiness. Virtually all contemporary American middle schools administer a battery of tests designed to measure student aptitude as well as their mastery of the mathematical topics that are foundational to middle school mathematics. Schools also keep extensive records of students' prior course-taking experiences and detailed grade reports. In addition, educators frequently consult with their fellow educators and take seriously their colleagues' assessments of student behavior, motivation, approaches to learning, and abilities. They also often receive both solicited and unsolicited input from students and their families about their academic desires, plans, and expectations. In many cases, therefore, the primary challenge for educators is not an absence of data. Indeed, educators often feel like they are drowning in relevant data. More often than not, the primary challenge for educators looking to measure student readiness and make academic track assignments is deciding which of these measures to use and how.

Standardized assessments are typically the measures that most heavily influence track assignments in contemporary schools. A recent study by the Council of Great City Schools indicates that the average middle school student in sixty-six large urban school districts spent approximately twenty-five hours annually taking ten or more mandatory tests during the eighth-grade year.[20] These include the standards-based tests that states require schools to administer for accountability purposes, the lower-stakes tests that schools administer repeatedly during the school year to track student progress, and the many teacher-made tests that determine a student's grade in the course. Although schools use these tests for many purposes, from school accountability to teacher evaluation, district leaders report that approximately half of the tests they administer are used to match students to instructional opportunities.

As a matter of policy, some school systems require that educators use only test scores to make track assignments. In 2010, for example, the public schools of Wake County, North Carolina, implemented a policy that automatically placed students into middle school mathematics classes based on an aggregate of their mathematics test scores in prior years. Although the placement policy was not strictly enforced, its implementation substantially reduced racial and socioeconomic inequality in access to high-track classes in the county's schools.[21]

Nonetheless, schools have a difficult time implementing and defending class placement systems that use only test scores. Test scores have an alluring patina of objectivity and impartiality, but many educators worry that they systematically understate poor and minority students' abilities.[22] Another concern is that tests provide limited information about these children's work habits and approaches to learning. Accordingly, grades are the measure that educators describe as the second most influential factor, after test scores, in academic track assignment processes. It is far from clear that grades are less subject to bias than test scores; teachers, who are disproportionately White and middle-class, are just as subject to implicit racial and class bias as the rest of us.[23] However, teachers often consider student effort as well as achievement when they grade students' work. One eighth-grade math teacher told us, "Half of my class grades are based on homework, and I grade homework entirely based on whether they took the time to answer all the questions and show their work."

As a result, many teachers believe that grades can provide information for class assignment that would be unavailable elsewhere. Similarly, many teachers favor systems that solicit recommendations from their fellow teachers for student track placement, arguing that working closely with a student provides a more nuanced view of that student's skills and dispositions than a test score can.

Teachers are far less supportive, however, of providing opportunities for student and family input into track placements. In higher-poverty schools, teachers worry that families may not understand the consequences of track placement, while in more affluent schools teachers accuse families of undermining their authority and pushing for inappropriate high-track assignments. As one administrator in a relatively affluent school told us: "Every parent here thinks their child is on his way to MIT, and they'll fight like crazy if we don't place them in the highest possible track. We sometimes have to do what we can to keep parents out of the conversation." This teacher's district experimented with a test-based middle school math placement process that was very much like the process that Wake County implemented in 2010. One spring, the district required all seventh-grade students to sit for a challenging mathematics test that was designed and graded by a group of eighth- and ninth-grade math teachers. The district then gave all students who scored above a predetermined threshold the option to enroll in high-track eighth-grade algebra while requiring the rest to take grade-level mathematics. The policy was explicitly designed to protect course placement decisions from family influence. As a teacher told a group of parents at a meeting describing the system: "You can beg, bribe, talk, or cajole your student's teacher. It does not matter. The placement decision is made by the placement test, not the teacher."

However, educators find it hard to exclude socially advantaged parents from consequential educational category assignment processes. When the affluent district where "every parent . . . thinks their child is on his way to MIT" implemented its test-only math course placement policy, the proportion of students enrolled in the eighth-grade algebra classes dropped by half, angering many parents. After being flooded with angry phone calls and facing down room after room full of angry middle school parents, the district reversed course and replaced the test-based system with a system in which teachers were tasked with making course placements only after considering test scores, grades, and their own judgment of student potential to succeed. Such political confrontations are relatively common: in their 2015 book *Despite the Best Intentions*, Lewis and Diamond describe how affluent parents' angry reactions led another suburban district to abandon an effort to purposefully mix high-achieving and low-achieving students in high school math classes.

In the face of all the measurement error and uncertainty around course assignment—not to mention families' considerable scrutiny of course assignments—schools constantly tweak their assignment mechanisms. Viewed from a distance, school strategies for designing classroom assignment processes therefore look like an endless process of trial and error. The history sketched earlier of the California Department of Education's recommendations about middle school math course assignment mechanisms is emblematic of this process of trial and error. Over the last several decades, the state's guidance about eighth-grade math placement strategies shifted from algebra-for-some to algebra-for-all, then back to algebra-for-some before settling on an approach that recommended doing away with eighth-grade algebra courses altogether. Given that shifting guidance, it is perhaps not surprising that school-level educators also continuously revisit their course placement strategies. Our analyses indicate that approximately 10 percent of California schools set a threshold based on seventh-grade test scores, placing students above that threshold into advanced math courses and students below it into grade-level or standard courses.[24] We also find, however, that fewer than one in four California schools keep purely test-based placement systems in place for more than a year at a time.

Teachers and school leaders can rattle off the shortcomings of previous track assignment processes: "A parent said that their kid was in honors last year, so they should be this year. But you know what? They were not performing well in seventh grade. So the administrator said, it's going to be to their disadvantage if they're placed in eighth-grade honors because they couldn't handle the class last year. And he was right. So now we make recommendations without the parent feedback."

But even though teachers are often eager to discuss the importance of measurement for track placement and their frustration with available measures, they struggle to articulate any better approaches to measuring student readiness for tracked course placements.

Furthermore, even in category assignment processes that are highly formalized and draw upon multiple sources of rich data, educators' decisions can be highly idiosyncratic. Schools are paradigmatic examples of what sociologists call "loosely coupled" organizations.[25] Faced with a broad set of highly contested and hard-to-measure organizational goals, as well as considerable uncertainty about how to best meet those goals, educators are often given discretion to make decisions about how to construct educational categories and deliver instruction. As a result, schools could not be more different from factories and other "tightly coupled" organizations that operate on a command-and-control logic. Educators carefully defend that discretion and often work to undermine the attempts of policymakers and educational leaders to more closely monitor and control their behavior.[26] Teachers use their discretion as they place students into educational categories. Sometimes they use the available evidence to provide post hoc justifications for decisions that they have already made based on observation and intuition.[27] At other times they use their discretion to provide advantages to students from high-status families.[28] And sometimes the decisions they make appear to be nearly random.

Step 3: Designing Categories and Sorting Students into Them

The third step in the creation of educational categories is determining how many categories to create and how many students to place in them. Ground-level practitioners often have limited direct input into this step of the category creation process. Federal policy, for example, defines the three categories that operate in the free and reduced-price lunch program, and so the economic situation of students in the school determines how many students are eligible and how many are not. Even in this case, however, educators may have a role to play: they are the ones who inform families about the program and have the power to decide how vigorously to encourage families to complete applications.

Policymakers also attempt to influence the number, size, and dimensions of the educational categories that schools create to facilitate instruction. Organizational theory suggests, however, that since these categories sit at the center of the school's organizational mission of teaching and learning, organizational actors will work hard to effectively maintain their power over these operations in a process that theorists describe as "buffering the technical core."[29] We see this happening in California middle schools during the eighth-grade algebra-for-all era. Beginning in the late 1990s, California schools faced growing accountability pressures to increase eighth-grade algebra enrollments. As we noted earlier, however, California middle schools received ambiguous signals about what algebra-for-all meant for instructional differentiation, particularly during the transitional period that we studied. On the one hand, the algebra-for-all effort took inspiration from the school detracking effort as well as from the many teacher professional development and curricular resources developed by the state and educational professional organizations to encourage instructors to equalize students' opportunities to learn by enrolling all students in skills-heterogeneous eighth-grade algebra courses.[30] On the other hand, by the time the state introduced accountability incentives for eighth-grade algebra, the CDE had explicitly clarified that schools could maintain skills-differentiated instruction even as they universalized eighth-grade algebra enrollments.

Accordingly, there were at least three different ways in which California middle schools could respond to the state's algebra-for-all effort. First, given the loose coupling of the state's educational system and the policy's weak incentives, they could ignore the algebra-for-all push and continue to enroll relatively few students in eighth-grade algebra. Second, consistent with the algebra-for-all movement's early calls for heterogeneous instruction, they could detrack, replacing a middle school math course placement system that sorted students between eighth-grade pre-algebra and eighth-grade algebra courses with a system that placed all students in eighth-grade algebra. Or third, faced with pressures to maintain instructional differentiation, they could "track up": enrolling more students in eighth-grade algebra while maintaining differentiation in middle school mathematics by creating a new, doubly accelerated, eighth-grade geometry track.

Our analyses indicate that all three of these approaches were taken by different California schools.[31]

In this case—and indeed in many cases related to educational categories—distinct conversations within schools and districts contribute to organizational variation in category creation practices, even in the face of common policy and structural pressures. A decade later, the California Department of Education has reversed its algebra-for-all effort and is now encouraging schools to wait until ninth grade to enroll students in algebra courses. Some of the state's large school districts are following this guidance, arguing that accelerated algebra assignments violate local visions of equitable schooling and are inconsistent with the instructional scaffolding laid out in the relatively recently implemented Common Core State Standards.

Emily Handsman, Caitlin Farrell, and Cynthia Coburn provide a behind-the-scenes look at one district's decision to end math acceleration and enroll all eighth-graders in detracked grade-level math courses.[32] In this district's case, the new CCSS and the CDE's guidance disrupted existing educational practice, opening the door to new conversations about educational goals and pedagogical strategy. Their account demonstrates that this conversation unfolded in a wide variety of settings across the district, including district department meetings, school-level math educator planning meetings, teacher professional development sessions, conversations with external partners (such as researchers and curriculum providers), and open houses designed to solicit family input. They describe a process through which important decisions about district policy "accrete" as key ideas come to frame the discussion, defining some strategies as viable alternatives and pushing others out of consideration.

In other cases, educators working at the school level can make and remake policy by simply ignoring higher-level directives. For example, one district that we worked with adopted an eighth-grade algebra-for-all policy that made the high-track algebra course the default course for all students. In this policy's first year, the district instructed school-level educators to carefully place students into skills-heterogeneous mathematics classrooms. The curriculum specialist recalled, "We had the idea that everybody needs to get the same thing and you need to teach them all in the same way, so we wanted high flyers and struggling students to be spread across all classrooms." Although teachers largely complied with the policy in the first year, many struggled to effectively teach academically challenging algebra content in classrooms that included many students who had not yet mastered division alongside students who were already comfortably solving for *x*. "It was a complete failure," one teacher reported.

Teachers complained to district officials, noting that more than 70 percent of students failed algebra under the new policy. Nevertheless, the district retained the placement policy into a second year. This time, however, teachers and school leaders took matters into their own hands and quietly created three levels of eighth-grade algebra classes, sorting students among those three levels based on their seventh-grade test scores. In doing so, these teachers created three equally sized eighth-grade mathematics tracks—reducing categorical boundaries on paper while reinforcing them in practice—in a policy environment that was designed to eliminate middle school math tracking.

Step 4: Enacting the Categories

Once schools construct educational categories and sort students into them, they must enact these categories. This fourth step in the process of constructing educational categories is often the step at which teachers can most directly influence categories and their implications for durable inequality.

To understand the power that teachers have over the implementation of educational categorical inequalities, consider two teachers who teach eighth-grade math in adjoining middle school classrooms. Both teachers have been assigned honors-level and standard-level math courses to teach. The first of these teachers, whom we will call Mr. Zaxby, believes that students in his standard-level course should be exposed to the same material as students in his honors course. Mr. Zaxby, a veteran teacher who describes himself as "somewhat conflicted" about the practice of academic tracking in middle school math, uses the same textbook in his standard and honors courses and moves through the material at the same pace. Doing so, he says, helps to keep open the possibility of moving across tracks for students who excel in the standard class. Mr. Zaxby differentiates his instruction across the two classes, but he does so in a fairly subtle way. For example, he says, "I'll typically give my standard-level kids a problem and then ask them to show me every single step of how they solve the equation. So that's just for my regular math class. My advanced kids have to come up with their own word problem and solve it. So it's a little bit deeper, a little bit harder." This strategy is designed to provide more instructional scaffolding and direct instruction for the students in the standard-level class and an opportunity for students in the honors-level class to develop deeper familiarity with the content being covered.

By contrast, the teacher in the classroom next door, a relatively novice teacher we will call Ms. Eberson, sees her standard-level and honors-level classes as very different learning environments. "Sometimes we need to go over the same material a few times in my standard-level class, and the honors-level kids are able to shoot ahead." Unfortunately, one result, Ms. Eberson says, is that "last year we didn't get through the textbook in the standard-level class." She attributes her standard-level class's inability to cover all of the topics in the intended course curriculum to the class's academic disengagement and its tendency toward disruption. Commenting on her struggles to maintain order in the standard-level class, Ms. Eberson remarks: "If I could teach five honors-level classes, that would be so great."

These two teachers are enacting the same educational categories, but in very different ways. Although Ms. Eberson's approach is relatively typical for the teachers we interviewed, we encountered other teachers who took an approach like Mr. Zaxby's. We suspect that teachers' different ways of enacting categories play an important role in determining the size and nature of the inequalities that they produce. For example, it seems reasonable to expect that Mr. Zaxby's approach to tracked instruction, if executed well, will yield more track mobility and fewer durable inequalities than Ms. Eberson's approach. Unfortunately, the large and growing literature on teacher effects to date provides little guidance on this sort of question.

On Agency and Constraints in Educational Categorization

Throughout this chapter, we have intentionally emphasized the malleability of educational categories and drawn particular attention to the ways in which educators work to transform the categories their schools enact. Categorical inequality theory indicates that the categories that generate durable inequalities are socially constructed. By transforming the practices that construct categories, social actors have the power to transform social inequalities. We see educators as crucial social actors in educational contexts, and we hope that our analyses help them cultivate the agency to push toward more equitable practices.

Based on our conversations with teachers and school leaders, we are convinced that educators have both the will and the power to change the educational categories that they create. The teachers and school leaders we talked with had a wide range of ideas about how to group students for instruction in middle school mathematics, or opinions on why such grouping should be avoided. They were thinking carefully about placement categories and policies and their implications for their students.

When educators give voice to their thoughts, they help to shape conversations about educational practice that have key implications for categorical inequality. Since many key educational decisions are made in an iterative, discursive fashion, it can be hard to see this educator influence; educator feedback often takes potential categorical strategies off the table before they even become serious contenders for implementation. Similarly, educators often work quietly in their own classrooms to shape the implementation of educational categories (or, on occasion, to ensure that policy-defined categories are not implemented in practice).

That said, we want to be careful not to exaggerate the degree of power that individual educators have over educational categories. We would point out that educator power is often collective. Earlier, we described one California district's response to the end of the algebra-for-all era by placing all eighth graders in detracked grade-level courses. These educators helped to push the district in this new direction by interpreting the instructional sequence in the new Common Core State Standards as pedagogically inconsistent with eighth-grade acceleration and by consistently articulating equity-based concerns about sorting students into higher- and lower-achieving math courses. But as we have noted, educators often disagree deeply about educational categories. What if these educators had not come to a consensus around these two ideas? We suspect that substantial disagreement among educators about the CCSS's pedagogical implications or the equity of acceleration would have provided an opportunity for affluent families—many of whom favored acceleration—to more forcefully intervene in the discussion.

Relatedly, questions of institutional legitimacy also constrain educator agency. Mr. Zaxby and Ms. Eberson may have the power to organize their eighth-grade math classrooms and instructional strategies in two different ways. But their practice must align with the rules and norms that define their educational field. This is why, even though Mr. Zaxby would like to do away with the honors label altogether, he continues to teach honors eighth-grade mathematics courses. Families, administrators, and other actors in his setting take honors coursework for granted as a legitimate part of a middle school experience, so despite his qualms, Mr. Zaxby has no choice but to teach honors classes and to justify his instructional practices in these classes, even as he tries to decrease this categorical distinction's salience.

Finally, structural factors also play an important role in defining the shape of the categories that schools construct. In California's eighth-grade algebra-for-all effort, one factor that discouraged schools from enrolling all students in a skill-heterogeneous eighth-grade algebra class was the number of teachers on staff who felt trained and prepared to teach algebra content to eighth-graders. Although schools were eventually able to train teachers to teach the course, the lack of trained teachers was one reason why some schools acted much more slowly than the state would have liked to enroll more students in eighth-grade algebra. The shape of educational categories are also influenced by the exigencies of course scheduling systems. For example, one teacher told us about their school's trouble with placing English-language learners in appropriate classes. This school offered a mathematics support class that provided both supplementary mathematics instruction and socioemotional support for students who were struggling in standard-level mathematics. But although 40 percent of the students at this school were English-language learners and many of them struggled in mathematics, none of these students were enrolled in the supplementary mathematics course. The reason? There was just not enough time in their schedules to receive supplementary instruction in math and English. Faced with this scheduling dilemma, the school had decided that "they should be reading first."

Understanding the Effects of Different Tracking Systems

In the popular conception, a highly "tracked" school is one in which curricula are highly differentiated, students are grouped into very skills-homogeneous classrooms, access to high-track classes is confined to a relatively small proportion of high-achieving students, and track scope is high while track mobility is low. In this conception, it seems reasonable to categorize schools as "tracked" or "untracked" and to expect little movement among these categories within a school over time. Our analyses suggest, however, that school tracking systems vary in ways that this simple "tracked" versus "untracked" dichotomy simply does not capture. Indeed, in our study of middle school math classroom assignment practices in twenty-three schools across three academic years, we found that these dimensions of school-based educational categorization systems were relatively independent of one another. For example, some schools placed all eighth-graders into the same grade-level math class but sorted high-achieving students into different classrooms from low-achieving students.

We can use these data to test the independent relationships between these different aspects of school tracking systems and the distribution of student achievement. These analyses indicate that school practices that place students into skills-homogeneous math classrooms often hurt their achievement growth in mathematics, and that this negative effect is particularly pronounced for low-achieving students. This finding suggests that students may benefit from placement in relatively skills-heterogeneous classrooms for secondary mathematics instruction. Based on this finding, we believe that teachers who have developed strategies to help diverse students learn from one another in skills-heterogeneous classrooms may be pointing the way to more equitable educational opportunities in middle school mathematics.

Our analyses also suggest, however, that efforts to place all students in relatively advanced courses for mathematics instruction may be misplaced. Consistent with several recent policy analyses, including our own, these findings suggest that efforts to detrack instruction by enrolling more students in accelerated courses can have unintended negative effects.[33] From a practitioner's perspective, therefore, our findings point to a tension between the benefits of skills-heterogeneous learning environments and the shortcomings of instruction that is insensitive to student skills. One promising strategy for resolving this tension that could be incorporated into curricular reform efforts is simultaneously providing disadvantaged students with access to higher-achieving peers and sufficient skill-building opportunities.[34]

Wrapping Up

If this chapter has a single lesson, it's that the creation and maintenance of educational categories is a messy, contentious business. Educators, students, families, school leaders, community members, employers, politicians, and many, many others have an interest in how schools work and ideas about how to make them work better. Because the opinions and interests surrounding education are so diverse, it feels almost ridiculous to ask "what works" in education. But in fact, even assuming a simple set of educational goals, we know very little about what works in schools, not to mention where, why, and how it works.

Amid these many competing voices and considerable uncertainty, schools muddle through, continuously improvising educational strategies. You might expect educators to feel discouraged and disempowered in the midst of all this disagreement and ambiguity, and of course sometimes they do. But most of the time educators embrace their professional responsibility to work through the messy philosophical, political, and strategic questions as they struggle to build educational categories that feel just, equitable, and responsible. In this chapter, we have provided an overview of four key decisions that educators must regularly make as they construct educational categories: (1) decisions about the criteria upon which categories are constructed; (2) decisions about how to operationalize and measure these criteria; (3) decisions about the number, size, and composition of educational categories; and (4) decisions about how these categories will be enacted in the day-to-day life of their school.

As our research indicates that educational categories can vary in a number of ways and that this variation matters for students, we are glad that educators approach the construction and maintenance of educational categories with such care and attention.

PART III
SORTING INTO THE WORLD

In 1699, the centenarian Huang Zhang and his great-grandson sat together for the Peking prefectural examinations.[1] The examiners marked Zhang's test attempt with considerable ceremony, and his great-grandson marched with him into the examination room carrying a lantern and a banner marking the occasion.

The Chinese civil service examinations, which were in use in some form (with brief exceptions) from 650 to 1905, held an outsized place in Late Imperial China, where the common view was that "to obtain a high examination degree is to ascend to heaven."[2] The exams were designed to match test takers to civil service careers. But at more than one hundred years old, Zhang probably was not concerned about job opportunities. Rather, we can only guess that Zhang put himself through "China's examination hell" because he understood that his society regarded educational success as a mark of moral worth.[3]

Passing the civil service exams was said to require the "sprightliness of a stallion, physical strength of a donkey, fortitude of a beetle and perseverance of a camel."[4] But in a society in which "centuries of conditioning made commoners accept their inferior status *vis-à-vis* the educated elite," the exams provided the only path available for Zhang to achieve the level of social status and regard to which he aspired.[5] Indeed, the pomp and circumstance paid to the centenarian's perseverance can be understood as an attempt by officials to confer some of the status rewards associated with passing the test to those who persevered despite failure, and to circumvent questions about the legitimacy of a system in which the overwhelming majority of those who took the exams failed.

The Chinese civil service exams were deeply elitist in that studying for the test required resources that were not widely available and the small cadre of examinees who passed wielded considerable power. Furthermore, the exams reinforced a patriarchal social system by allowing only men to take the examinations. But as a system to allocate positions of power and status based not simply on social origin, the exams were also fundamentally egalitarian.[6] In this way, the Chinese civil service exams, much like contemporary educational systems, served two critical social functions.[7] First, they acted as a gatekeeper and pipeline for powerful elite positions. This role can be understood as largely technical: by supposedly measuring test takers' abilities, the exams ensured that social power flowed to those deemed the most deserving. This role can also be understood as purely symbolic: by creating a ritual and associating it with social value, the exams created a mechanism for separating elites from commoners. Either way, the exam system also served a second function: co-opting opposition to the emperor by providing an established path to social power for would-be revolutionaries and other ambitious men. This is what Emperor Taizong of the Tang dynasty—who ruled from 626 to 649—meant when he described the civil service exam system as a trap that ensnared those who might have become heroes of the opposition.[8]

Given the low odds of success, it is perhaps puzzling why people persisted in taking the exams generation after generation. Clearly the tests and the mastery of Confucian philosophy that it assessed held a privileged position in Chinese culture. As the oft-repeated aphorism had it, "All ten thousand vocations are lowly, book reading alone is noble."[9] Cultural explanations alone, however, fail to account for the fact that the exams overshadowed the content they were testing: knowledge of the teachings of Confucius. In a statement echoing contemporary concerns regarding high-stakes testing, Emperor Qianlong noted in an imperial edict of 1740 (quoting the Confucian scholar Zhu Xi) that "if Confucius were alive today, he would have to take part in the civil service examinations, but examinations would have deterred Confucius from striving to be a sage."[10]

In part, the centrality of the examination system was maintained by its monopoly on upward mobility and the societal rewards that came to those who earned this educational credential. This monopoly, coupled with its exclusivity, made the examination system's legitimacy self-fulfilling. Because so many failed the exams, passing was a mark of distinction. And because passing the exams ensured entrée to the elite, prior generations' accomplishments reinforced the test's status.

It's easy to spot the parallels between the Chinese examination system and the education system in the contemporary United States.[11] Just as Chinese scholars needed to prove their mettle on the exams to enter the elite, contemporary American youth must be able to demonstrate their academic ability if they are to access many of our society's most sought-after positions. Further, the contemporary American educational system wraps itself in the mantle of "merit," associating educational success with moral worth in much the same way as the Chinese examination system did. In both Imperial China and the contemporary United States, societal inequality is justified on the grounds of this merit, and the legitimacy of the merit-generating system is protected by ensuring that merit aligns with existing structures of advantage while also being understood as being broadly accessible.[12]

In part III, we explore these parallels as we consider both the processes through which education confers social value on the educated and the implications of organizing society around this sort of educational meritocracy. In chapter 6, we consider how educational categories translate into lasting inequalities in the adult world. The association between educational success and merit is a key component in this process. In the contemporary world, educational experiences deeply shape our sense of self and worth. Furthermore, these identifications are fundamentally positional—the status enjoyed by those with more merit comes at the expense of others. The profound power of educational categories grows out of their ability to demarcate people who are more meritorious from those who are less meritorious. But to maintain that power, we argue, educational categories must be broadly understood as fair, while at the same time ensuring that the meritocratic elites they produce conform with broad social expectations. Striking this balance—maintaining an educational contest that is open to all while consistently producing a recognizable elite—is the fundamental challenge of educational legitimacy.

In chapter 7, we describe the many ways in which social actors challenge educational categories. Some forms of contestation seek to maintain the legitimacy of the educational system, while others are agnostic or even seek to undermine the system's legitimacy. Students who cheat, for example, contest their placement in an educational hierarchy when they subvert the rules that govern education's distribution of merit in an attempt to access higher-status educational categories and their rewards. We argue that cheating does not explicitly challenge education's role in creating merit but actually depends on the legitimacy of educational merit. Other forms of contestation, however, reject the legitimacy of educational merit and seek to establish alternative systems of merit creation.

We conclude by underscoring that the creation of merit is a primarily political project that inevitably results in the production of inequality. Many critiques of contemporary meritocracy attempt to concern themselves with the processes through which education produces merit. We argue that these critiques fall short. Since merit is positional, meritocratic logics are necessarily ableist and deeply dehumanizing.

MAKING MERIT 6

The Chinese civil service examinations in use during Late Imperial China may have been conceived in utilitarian terms as a relatively fair and efficient way to sort ambitious young men into some of the most powerful and high-status positions in dynastic society. But as the image of Huang Zhang being paraded into the exam room at over one hundred years of age illustrates, the exams' power transcended their practical purposes. Success on the civil service exams conferred enormous honor on Chinese test takers in part because it provided access to prestigious jobs. But just as importantly, success on the civil service exams provided a very public signal that the successful test taker *deserved* access to one of those prestigious jobs.

Educational categories play a similar role in the contemporary American meritocracy. Of course, our educational system differs from the Chinese civil service exam system in many important ways. Our schools aim to provide all young people with instruction in socially valued skills and aptitudes, while the Chinese system only focused on assessing those skills. Further unlike the Chinese civil service exam, which sorted people into a highly structured system governed by a series of tests, our educational system produces a wild diversity of cumulative educational categories (including high school graduates, business AAs, mathematics BAs, MFAs, JDs, and sociology PhDs, just to name a few). But like the Chinese civil service system, our educational system works as a mechanism to differentiate members of society. Some of this differentiation is qualitative—as is the distinction between different majors in higher education—and some is more quantitative, reflecting the amount of education the student obtains.

Furthermore, just as Imperial Chinese society viewed distinctions based on civil service exam performance as a marker of human moral worth, our society treats educational achievement as a mark of value. We think of educational credentials as categories that summarize people's educational careers, thus bringing educational inequalities into the workforce and broader society. As such, they serve as gatekeepers for many high-status social positions. Doctors, lawyers, and teachers in contemporary society are all expected to have completed a base level of education that prepared them to practice their profession. But perhaps even more importantly, educational credentials confer *merit* on their recipients. The MD next to your doctor's name tells you—and for that matter, tells your doctor—that they *deserve* to call themselves a doctor, to do the work that doctors do, and to enjoy the wealth and social status that comes with being a doctor.

In part I, we discussed the "social magic" of the knighthood ceremony and argued that going to school transforms a child into a citizen in much the same way that being dubbed by the monarch's sword transforms a commoner into a knight. Educational credentials—the document with our name rendered in calligraphy above an impressive signature that we frame and hang on our office wall or stash away in a storage box—perform a similar sort of social magic. When we process in a commencement ceremony, accept that credential, and throw our mortarboards into the sky in celebration, we are celebrating the way these educational categories fundamentally shape both the way we think of ourselves and the way others think of us. We are celebrating merit and our entrance into a new social category.

The social magic of merit allows educational categories to produce profound and lasting inequalities in contemporary society. Because our society associates educational success with merit, it grants resources, status, and power to the educationally successful, effectively allowing educational categories to shape people's entire lives. In this chapter, we investigate how this social magic works. We first examine how educational categories construct merit and confer it upon students and graduates. Central to this process is how educational systems teach students about their identities and their place in the world. Sometimes educational systems intentionally impose identities on students, and other times they do so unintentionally. Either way, the identities that students derive from their educational experiences often stick with them throughout their lives. Building on a rich tradition of sociological thinking about credentials and their social consequences, we argue that many of these educational identities are positional, rather than absolute, goods. In particular, educational systems operate as a sort of tournament in which those who are successful in earlier rounds win permission to compete at higher and higher levels.

Several aspects of our educational system help convince us that the results of this tournament reflect our worth as a person. First, public rhetoric emphasizes the myth of equal opportunity. Second, educational administrators constantly adapt their sorting criteria to ensure that they reflect prevailing ideas about social worth. Third, educators reference the tournament structure to motivate students by constantly reminding them of the educational competitions ahead. Fourth, although the educational system creates opportunities for educational mobility—and celebrates mobility when it occurs—it takes care to produce an elite who meet the social expectations of the elite. To do so, putatively "merit-based" educational gatekeeping processes are structured to guarantee positions for children of the elite among the educationally successful.

Our mission in this chapter is to understand how educational categories create lasting inequalities. To do so, we need to understand the values and inner workings of our educational meritocracy. But we want to be clear that we believe that the social order created by this educational meritocracy is both deeply unjust and unsustainable. By constructing an educational tournament that sorts people based on their supposed "merit," we have built a society that values people based on a narrow set of human attributes, devalues countless other people whose gifts and passions lie in domains that go unmeasured or unappreciated in educational contexts, and directs the more educationally successful into an endless and ultimately unfulfilling quest for opportunities to demonstrate their merit.

Educational Categories Endow Identities

Categories structure our educational experiences and friendship networks, ultimately shaping who we understand ourselves to be. These categories have lasting consequences for our lives in part because they publicly impress identities that purportedly reflect deep underlying truths about who we are. These identities persist long after our educational career ends, following us into our social and romantic lives, influencing our self-concept and our health, and shaping our opportunities to work and exercise social power.

The process of imposing identities on students is particularly clear in the rituals of elite boarding schools, many of which see character building and identity construction as central to their mission. In their classic study of American boarding schools, Peter Cookson and Caroline Hodges Persell describe "the loss of self" that these schools require of students, noting that one headmaster they spoke with shared that "habit formation is the basis of freedom."[1] By this the headmaster meant that the boarding school's rituals lead students to form new habits that become second nature and shape their daily lives, thus becoming ingrained in their understanding of who they are. As difficult as this process may be for the students, the educators at elite boarding schools see their school's rituals as a crucial part of preparing students to become members of the social elite.

Shamus Khan recounts this process in his ethnography of life at St. Paul's School in Concord, New Hampshire, where each school year starts with a "taking one's place" ceremony in the school's storied chapel.[2] At the start of the ceremony, returning faculty seat themselves in the chapel, arranged according to seniority. After faculty come returning seniors, who seat themselves just in front of the faculty on the chapel's tiered seats, followed by juniors in the lower rows and sophomores lower still. Once the returning members of the community are seated, a hush falls. Then, one by one, new faculty members process through the chapel and claim their seats at the bottom of the faculty hierarchy, followed by new students who claim their seats in the freshman rows at the bottom.

As Khan notes, the "taking one's place" ritual and the hierarchical seating arrangement in St. Paul's chapel echoes aristocratic seating arrangements in European cathedrals. But because St. Paul's rituals are conducted in a school, they reinforce the unique nature of educational categorical inequality. "In an aristocracy," Khan writes, "members do not 'climb'—indeed the very point of an aristocracy is that relationships are fixed. . . . For the new elite, the seats of the hierarchy are fixed and there is an order of things, but students learn how to work within these positions to ascend."[3]

In Khan's telling, therefore, the ritual of "taking one's place" socializes students into an organization and legitimates their movement up a hierarchy. As students age through the school, they move from the bottom of the chapel's seating plan to the top. The chapel seating ritual—like countless other rituals that reinforce the status that students attain as they progress from freshmen to seniors—helps to teach students that graduating from St. Paul's is an accomplishment, by virtue of which they have earned a place in the elite. "I worked hard to get here," an unexceptional St. Paul's student tells Khan as they walk through the chapel, "and I feel good when I get to chapel in the morning and see how far I've come."[4] Consistent with Cookson and Persell's claim that life in elite prep schools is difficult by design because "privilege must appear to be earned," Khan demonstrates how the internal hierarchies at St. Paul's legitimate students' privilege and convince students that they deserve power and prestige upon their graduation.[5] Further, consistent with Cookson and Persell's finding that Black students and middle-income students at elite boarding schools report lower levels of self-efficacy and belonging, Khan contrasts how casually legacies and affluent students approach the school with other students' striving and reverence. For example, when Kahn asks a Black eleventh grader about why Black students at St. Paul's take more classes than their White peers even though their grades seem to suffer, he is told: "If you saw where I'm from, you'd know. You wouldn't have to ask. . . . This is my chance. I'm making the most of it."[6]

St. Paul's socialization of students into elite identities is similar to the ways in which other schools socialize students into identities that are more suited to positions in the working and middle classes.[7] Jeannie Oakes, for example, memorably points out parallels between the punitive and ordered environment typical in lower-track high school classrooms and the alienation that graduates from these classes are likely to experience in working-class jobs.[8] By contrast, Oakes observes that high-track classes give greater freedom to their students, effectively socializing them for entry into the professions.

More recently, Joanne Golann has described the strict dress and behavioral codes prevalent in predominantly minority "no-excuses" charter schools.[9] While these schools ostensibly aim to send all their graduates to college, their culture emphasizes diligence and compliance. Students in these schools, Golann makes clear, learn to turn in homework that is "neat, complete, on-time, and best effort," to follow rules, and to signal respect for teachers. However, Golann notes, these schools provide students with little room for cultivating their own interests and managing their own time and relationships—skills that are essential for success in higher education and beyond. Rather than socializing students for the professional classes, these "no-excuses" charter schools appear to be socializing them for highly regulated low-wage work environments. Similarly, Victor Rios describes the harsh carceral landscape of a public school for high school students flagged for disciplinary infractions: teachers and security guards line students up, submit them to security screenings to move from one part of the school to another, force them to wear bright orange shirts modeled on prison uniforms as a form of punishment, and create classroom environments that reward compliance over intellectual engagement. In criminalizing youth, Rios argues, these schools create a pipeline to prison.[10]

Importantly, in each of these cases schools do not simply teach different skills to students based on their social backgrounds. Rather, school cultures and rituals more deeply imprint student identities by conveying important information to students about how they should expect to be treated as adults. While St. Paul's shepherds its students toward a sense of themselves as entitled leaders, no-excuses charter schools teach students to think of themselves as rule followers and disciplinary schools teach students to understand themselves as potentially dangerous criminals.

To appreciate the power of these identities, consider the color-coded ID card system that we described at the beginning of this book. When Stan Sitwell implemented this system in his California high school, he very publicly branded students with identities, based on their academic success, that they carried with them throughout the school day. The kids who scored very high (in the top category) on all tests got the platinum ID cards and were honored as academic superstars; the kids who scored fairly well (in the top two categories) on all tests got gold ID cards and identities as academic successes; and the rest of the kids got white ID cards and were given stigmatized academic identities. Importantly, however, the ID card program had an additional clause: no student who experienced a drop in their test score category between school years could get a gold or platinum card. This meant that students who scored in the highest category in all subjects in their sophomore year (and thus received the highest-status platinum card) but then scored below the threshold in one subject in their junior year experienced a precipitous decline in card status. Rather than dropping from platinum to the still relatively high-status gold card, they would drop from platinum all the way to the low-status white card.

Our analyses indicate that when a student "fell from grace" by dropping from the highest-status platinum ID card to the lowest-status white ID card—sometimes based on small year-to-year test score variations—this fall fundamentally changed their student experience. We found that they were subsequently more likely to be suspended from school and that their grades and test scores also fell appreciably. Given that honors students told a white-card honors class student that "honors classes aren't for white-card students," and white-card students reported feeling dumb, the experience of going from a visibly marked position of privilege to the less desirable category of white-card student seems likely to have challenged students' understandings of themselves as academic high flyers.

At this point, we should note that schools inculcate a wide range of identities and that students may adopt many different identities as they move through a school day. When Stephen, the kindergartener in Katherine Anne Porter's short story, becomes a high schooler, he may think of himself as a band geek in the morning, a popular kid at lunchtime, a history buff in the afternoon, and a school bus rider before and after school. More generally, he may identify as a sophomore and as a Riverside High School "Pirate." If Riverside High School has a color-coded ID card system like the one Stan Sitwell implemented, Stephen might have thought of himself as a gold-card student at each of these moments of his school day. And of course, these explicitly educational identities are just a fraction of the social identities that might matter to Stephen, who may also identify as a man, as a teenager, as a Texan, as queer, as asthmatic, and so on.

Stephen's educational experiences probably contribute to the construction and definition of each of these identities, though the school's role is likely to differ from one identity to another. Stephen's identities as a Riverside High School Pirate and as a gold-card student are both inexorably tied to his school experiences. If Stephen were to attend a different school, he might not adopt these identities (though he might adopt analogous identities in different school contexts). By contrast, Stephen's identities as a man and as a Texan are perhaps less directly linked to education. As we think about how education constructs merit in contemporary societies, it makes sense to pay particularly close attention to categories that schools create most directly. As we discuss in more detail later, education has claimed a place in our society as a legitimate arbiter of merit.

Importantly, we can think of each educational identity as categorical in the sense that it is defined in relation to other identities. Stephen identifies as a history buff because his teachers, grades, course assignments, and peer interactions have told him that he's better at history than other students. Note that this process relies on both Stephen's self-understanding and the way others understand him. A student who loves history but consistently receives low grades is not likely to identify as a history buff. Nor is a student who receives high grades in history but does not particularly care about the class. All identities are similarly two-sided: Stephen may identify as a Texan because he feels a sense of affinity with his classmates, teachers, neighbors, and relatives who have roots in Texas, or that identity may be based on a sense of difference from classmates, teachers, and neighbors whose roots lie elsewhere. In this sense, identities at school can be both self-created and externally imposed.

The Positional Rather than Absolute Nature of Educational Success

To understand how educational categories create merit, it is helpful to take a quick detour to understand the difference between what economists and sociologists call "absolute" and "positional" goods. Briefly, absolute goods are things that are valuable to people irrespective of whether other people also have them. For example, the nutritional benefits that a child obtains from eating a leaf of kale do not depend on who else is eating kale. By contrast, the value of a positional good is defined precisely by what others do and do not have. For example, the value of a diamond comes from the fact that not everyone has one. Most goods are situated somewhere on a continuum as partly positional and partly absolute: while the nutritional value of a meal at a three-star restaurant might be relatively absolute, its positional value leads diners to brag about their three-star meal. Similarly, some housing markets are governed by a positional logic where buyers are extremely conscious of the status of a neighborhood relative to other neighborhoods, or the size of a house relative to other houses in the neighborhood, but when we think of housing as a basic human right, housing functions more as an absolute good.

Our educational system can be thought of as creating goods that fall along this continuum: some of its goods are relatively absolute (such as basic health knowledge) and others are close to purely positional (for example, elite prizes). Although the skills taught in schools may create largely absolute goods, the categories and categorical identities created around this knowledge function largely as positional goods.

Categorical identities are positional because they exist and are defined in relationship to other categories: what it means to be in any particular category is defined by the boundary between that category and the categories around it. The meanings and benefits of category membership are thus not fixed but rather positional, and they change as the categories around them change. When people create categories and maintain the boundaries between them, they make categorical identities meaningful by distinguishing them from other categories and identities. Importantly, the creation of categories and the maintenance of their boundaries vis-à-vis other categories enable the members of one category to exploit and hoard resources and status at the expense of the members of other categories.

Indeed, some of the categories created by education are created explicitly to hoard resources at the expense of others. Take, for example, the categories that Stan Sitwell created around high school achievement by requiring students to wear color-coded ID cards. The categories created by the ID card system mattered almost exclusively because of their positional value, as the status of platinum-card students came at the expense of white-card students. The ID cards were simply slips of colored plastic, emblazoned with students' names and photographs and carried around on lanyards throughout the school day. They had nearly no intrinsic value, and they signaled very little about students' shared experiences. Nonetheless, everybody in these schools knew that it was better to be a platinum-card student than a white-card student. And Sitwell plastered posters all over the school proclaiming that "membership has its privileges" to make sure that nobody forgot the positional status of the platinum- and gold-card students. On its face, the intent of the ID card system was to inspire all students to attempt to become a platinum-card student and achieve elevated status. Although theoretically possible, this goal was ultimately unattainable for many students, and the system thus served as a daily visual reminder of the white-card students' academic inferiority.

By contrast, other categories are less clearly governed by a logic of opportunity hoarding. While the ID card system was explicitly designed to make it better to be a platinum-card student than a white-card student, it is less clear whether it is better to be a high school band geek or a high school football player. Here the answer probably depends on the educational context, who you ask, and what you mean by "better." Football players clearly enjoy a great deal of status in many high schools, but the band geeks we know have no shortage of pride. In addition, identification as a band geek may more reliably open doors to postsecondary and other opportunities that pay off in earnings and status over the life course. While the status of football players may be a strongly positional good, camaraderie with teammates and bandmates and the skills learned are less positional goods. Insofar as many of the opportunities and benefits provided by being a band geek or a football player come not entirely at the expense of students in other categories, we might argue against understanding these high school subcultural identities as purely positional categories.

To this point, we have argued that because categories are defined by their relationships with other categories, they have a strong positional orientation. We also note that making merit is one of education's key functions. Importantly, merit—like categories—is fundamentally positional, as is vividly illustrated by the color-coded ID cards. That is, it does not make sense to think about somebody having merit unless somebody else does not (or is at least less meritorious).

Once again, the color-coded ID card system provides an excellent illustration of why this is the case. Sitwell's system conferred a handful of token benefits on platinum- and gold-card students, including small discounts on tickets to high school football games and dances. But of course, the ID cards redefined the life of the school because they explicitly positioned a small group of students as the school's academic elite, another group of students as second-tier high-flyers, and the rest as academically run of the mill. Put differently, the ID card system declared that each year's standardized test scores would be the criterion for building a new and highly visible hierarchy of merit in the school. And having done so, it proclaimed—loud and clear—which of these students were the best in the school based on this criterion and situated all other students in positions relative to this academic elite. Sitwell may have meant only to reward and encourage academic high-flyers. But because the ID card system publicly declared the merit of platinum- and gold-card students, it also marked white-card students as lacking in academic merit and relegated them to a lower social status within the school.

Merit-based categories thus layer the positional nature of categories on top of merit, which is itself inherently positional. Given that the creation of merit-based categories is a central task of contemporary educational systems, it is perhaps no wonder that our educational systems are so strongly oriented toward the creation of hyperpositional goods. As exemplified by the color-coded ID card categories, these merit-based educational categories exist explicitly to create merit for some at the expense of others, and we can think of them as designed specifically to hoard merit. We conjecture that, with few exceptions, merit-based educational categories are designed not only to hoard merit but also to hoard as many opportunities as coherently possible, from course assignments to the perceptions of peers, teachers, and society to success in the labor market and recognition in elite society.

We see our focus on positional educational categories as a corrective to a dominant strain of contemporary thinking about education's social role that focuses on the skills students learn in school and views these as absolute goods. These skills are particularly central to the account provided by human capital theory. In this telling, students learn skills in school that boost their productivity in the workforce and thereby increase the value of their labor. This line of reasoning leads human capital theorists to see the wage premium associated with educational attainment as a direct reflection of the skills that students learn on their way to educational credentials. It further suggests that educational expansion is a key mechanism for narrowing economic inequalities, since providing more access and more equal access to educational opportunities will tend to narrow the skills gaps that, according to human capital theory, drive inequality.

A categorical inequality perspective, however, points to a credentialist understanding of education and inequality. Credentialism argues that educational credentials signal a graduate's position in a hierarchical system of relationships as much as anything else.[11] Although this theoretical perspective does not deny that students learn skills in school, it suggests that many of these skills may be arbitrary. Skills matter, but a categorical perspective argues that they matter mostly because they serve as the basis on which schools assign merit.

To understand this argument, think about the nontrivial relationship between a high school student's performance in high school calculus and their potential lifetime earnings. Calculus often serves as a key gatekeeper for elite college admissions and access to a wide range of high-status majors in math, science, and the social sciences. Passing through these gates is likely to help students access further opportunities. Recruiters for some of the most highly respected consulting and finance firms recruit exclusively in the Ivy Leagues, and currently it is rare for students to gain admission to an Ivy League university without successfully completing calculus in high school. But do Ivy League–trained entry-level employees at white-shoe consulting and financial services firms actually use calculus on the job? Rarely. These employers aren't hiring for calculus skills; rather, in their own words, they are hiring for "pedigree," a term that seems to represent a set of common experiences and dispositions as much as particular skills.[12]

Not convinced? Consider, then, this elite Wall Street recruiter's comments while screening Ivy League applicants for an entry-level position: "I'd have to pick Blake and Sarah. With his lacrosse and her squash, they'd really get along . . . on the trading floor."[13] In this instance, the lacrosse and squash skills—and identities as lacrosse and squash players—that applicants no doubt started honing as adolescents helped pave the way to six-figure positions straight out of college. Why? Surely not because dexterity in obscure ball sports comes in handy on the job. Rather, a categorical perspective suggests, these skills and identities matter because they position Blake and Sarah as members of the elite social category from which this firm hires.

Positional educational goods—like lacrosse and squash skills—matter because they are aligned with an understanding of elite culture. If all elementary schools taught lacrosse and squash, mastery of these games would cease to signal social background, and elite Wall Street firms would look elsewhere on their applicants' résumés for marks of pedigree. This insight has important implications for how the value of educational categories changes over time. When, in the nineteenth century, relatively few Americans held a high school degree, these degrees conferred a considerable status and economic power upon their holders. As they have become more common over time, they have come to confer less status and economic power. Today a young person arguably must attain a college degree to obtain the positional benefit once associated with a high school degree. It's important to note that the value of a high school diploma declined during a period in which secondary education became dramatically more rigorous. Studies of historical textbooks indicate, for example, that contemporary middle school students routinely work on mathematics problems that would have been considered too advanced for most high school seniors in the late nineteenth century.[14] Tracing this pattern into the future, we might expect that someday people will need graduate degrees to obtain the same positional advantages once associated with high school diplomas.

To be clear, when we draw attention to the positional nature of educational goods, we do not deny that the content of instruction and the skills that students acquire matter in absolute terms. Learning to read, for example, is currently a largely absolute good. Its value does not decline as more people learn to read—in fact, if anything, the reverse is probably true, since universal literacy makes the written word increasingly ubiquitous and increases the number of resources available to readers. However, even this largely absolute good has positional elements. In any system that uses a measure of literacy as a criterion for sorting people into hierarchically ranked educational categories, what matters is not whether or not a given student can read but whether they can read better than the other students vying for a particular categorical assignment. In a school with a color-coded ID card system in place, for example, English-language arts test scores function to form identities that produce a hierarchy of merit among students. This sort of hierarchical or positional categorization inevitably creates winners and losers.

In a society that sees education as a legitimate source of merit, educational winners claim the mantle of merit and gain access to desirable and high-status social positions, while educational losers are seen as less meritorious and lower-status. It is important to pause and emphasize this point: educational legitimacy is a key part of how our meritocracy converts educational categories into durable inequalities. Positional inequalities are political, in the sense that the rankings of positional categories are social constructs defined by existing power relations. If students in Sitwell's high school simply ignored their IDs, refusing to acknowledge a difference between platinum, gold, and white cards, then these categories would become meaningless and lose their ability to contribute to conceptions of merit and to lasting inequality. Similarly, if we all agreed that educational credentials provide no information about their holders' intelligence, skills, or other abilities, these credentials would lose social cachet and market power. Thus, the whole system of educational inequality that this book describes hinges on the legitimacy of educational positional categories and, by extension, educational institutions' legitimacy as arbiters of merit.

If that legitimacy were to erode, not only would meritocracy crumble as a social system, but presumably many educational institutions would simply cease to exist. In the absence of a broadly shared belief that educational categories reflect merit, it would likely be impossible for schools to convince governments and philanthropists to support their work, and it would become harder and harder to recruit tuition-paying students. Maintaining educational legitimacy is therefore a central task for educators and educational institutions. In the remainder of this chapter, we consider what this means for educational practice.

Structuring a "Fair" Educational Tournament

Perhaps the most essential component of educational legitimacy is the widespread belief that schools can fairly and impartially judge human talent. Our educational system fosters this belief by claiming to be a contest that lines students up on a starting line and then allows them to compete according to the same set of rules.

This claim hinges on the myth of equal educational opportunity. If we believe that educational opportunities are distributed equally across our society, we are prepared to believe that the inequalities that come out of educational systems reflect the talents and dedication that students demonstrate during their educational careers rather than the advantages and disadvantages that students bring to school because of the conditions of their birth. However, when people's faith in the myth of equal educational equality starts to fray and the educational contest starts to look rigged, the system's legitimacy is compromised, and it gets harder and harder to view the inequality produced by educational systems through the lens of "merit."

To maintain education's legitimacy, therefore, it is crucial that people at all levels of the educational system believe that every student has the ability to succeed academically. This notion is deeply embedded in early educational settings in particular; these schools almost willfully overlook differences in academic skills among young children in order to provide them with a common set of educational experiences. We know that children come to school with wildly divergent skills and abilities, and we know that these inequalities are closely linked to the socioeconomic and racial inequalities that divide our society. The average affluent student enters kindergarten with math skills that it takes the average poor student much of the kindergarten year to master, and racial inequalities in preschool skills are nearly as pronounced.[15] But rather than build educational categories based on these preschool inequalities, elementary schools sort students by age and give students in the same grade similar instruction. As a result, even though most students enter kindergarten with basic counting skills and the ability to recognize shapes, recent analyses of nationally representative data indicate that kindergarten teachers spend the majority of their mathematics instructional time on exactly these foundational skills.[16] This is not to say that schools never sort young students based on their skills and other attributes. But even when they do, they often create relatively opaque ability groups in order to maintain an appearance of equality. For example, although elementary teachers often sort young students into reading groups based on their early reading scores, they rarely label these groups in a way that draws attention to the distinctions among them.

As students age through the educational system, however, it becomes more and more acceptable to explicitly rank students hierarchically based on their educational abilities. Educational status hierarchies also tend to grow more rigid as students age, and as we saw in chapter 4 with the example of math course placements, upward mobility in particular becomes more difficult. As they age through this system, educational categories and students' position in the educational hierarchy begin to play an increasingly central role in how they understand themselves and their role in society. The transformation of our comfort with hierarchical ranking and our willingness to tie identities to the educational hierarchy is a central part of the construction of "student" as a social category. Students can be ranked, categorized, sorted, and differentially valued in ways that "children" cannot be.

Schools facilitate this transition between the assumed equality of opportunity and a socially legitimated inequality of outcomes by closely and explicitly linking status rewards to educational performance. A Northern California high school that we know provides an example of this status linkage. This school requires students to wear a standard school uniform, with one notable exception: seniors who have been accepted to college can wear apparel bearing their future college's logo. This exception to the school's uniform policy acknowledges the status associated with college in the high school by rewarding college-bound students with a measure of sartorial freedom, thus creating a culture that reminds younger students about the value of academic success as measured by college admissions. This uniform exception arguably comes at a cost, as school uniforms otherwise downplay class and taste distinctions among the students.

What's more, the uniform exemption grants redundant status rewards to college-bound seniors. The students who get to ditch the school uniform and don college sweatshirts have already reaped a substantial reward for their educational success. Having applied to and been accepted to college, these students have already been sorted into the hierarchical landscape of higher education. In a few short months, they will launch their college careers in an explicitly stratified system. These students don't need an incentive to compete in the high school's educational contests—they've already won their prize.

The uniform exception at this high school calls attention to contradictory logics embedded in contemporary American education. On the one hand, we seek to create educational environments that treat all students equally regardless of their origins, as when a school requires all students to wear matching uniforms. On the other hand, we orient much of our educational system toward the high-stakes gatekeeping decisions of the college admissions process, encouraging students to develop ambitious educational expectations and teaching them how to package themselves and curate their experiences in a way that maximizes their appeal to elite colleges and universities.

We often resolve this contradiction by emphasizing egalitarian educational goals at the start of students' educational careers and the processes of hierarchical sorting at the end. To illustrate, consider the following thought experiment: if we somehow knew at their birth what institutions of higher education children would attend, at what age would we be comfortable replacing their student uniforms with clothes representing their eventual postsecondary institution? The week before graduation? Freshman year of high school? Middle school? Kindergarten? We suspect that while some readers may share this high school's perspective that its uniform exception is unproblematic for seniors, fewer readers would be comfortable with the presence of such status labels on kindergarteners.

The college apparel exception to the uniform policy recognizes admission to an elite college as an educational goal and celebrates college-bound seniors' educational successes. But these college-bound students are not really the policy's intended audience. The policy's primary intention is to send a signal to younger students who look up to their older schoolmates. For these younger students, watching seniors come to school in college sweatshirts can motivate them to strive toward the day when they too can proudly ignore the school dress code and sport their own elite college sweatshirt. The college apparel exception of this uniform policy thus serves as a mechanism for engaging students in the educational tournament by using its rewards as an incentive for student effort. It's a ritual that creates a college-oriented culture throughout the school.

Stan Sitwell's color-coded ID card system is, of course, another example of an educator's effort to use positional rewards to motivate student effort and engagement. With a background in athletics, where the logics of talent and rankings are more salient than in the classroom, Sitwell saw the ID card program as a way to make the unspoken plainly visible: students who were the academic elite at the school were going to end up in higher-status postsecondary positions, be they colleges, jobs, or other positions. Given that this sorting was bound to happen at the end of high school, from Sitwell's perspective the ID cards simply made the implicit academic hierarchy both explicit and more salient to students' day-to-day lives. Sitwell imagined that the color-coded ID card program would organize student activity around a set of academic goals, much as high school athletic programs have varsity and junior varsity teams, elect team captains and MVPs, and participate in leagues with standings that rank the teams from best to worst based on their performance. The color-coded ID cards would allow students to understand that there were strong status consequences of their achievement once they exited secondary school. Indeed, from this perspective, the primary differences between Sitwell's ID card program and the Northern California school's dress code exception were whether they applied to non-seniors and the explicitness of their links to highly legitimized college inequalities.

In these cases and countless others, educators create rituals and incentive systems in an attempt to make the educational tournament and its stakes immediately apparent to students. They know that disengaging from the educational meritocracy has serious consequences for students. If students stop competing in the educational tournament while still in high school, they forfeit. At that point they have lost educationally. Our educational system provides the occasional second chance—nonselective community colleges, for example, provide paths to higher education for students with lackluster high school careers. But in many ways, education operates as a single-elimination tournament; particularly for poor students and students of color, one wrong educational move can have lifelong consequences.[17]

These rituals also reflect a deeper anxiety among educators about the educational system's legitimacy. If enough players forfeit, a tournament simply falls apart. While the players who stick it out to the end may still technically "win," their win may be of dubious value if the forfeits made it impossible for them to demonstrate their academic merit. Similarly, if young people disengage en masse from the educational system, education's power to mark talent and ability is degraded. Student disengagement thus threatens the link between educational categories and merit.

The Iron Law of Educational Category Legitimacy

Many students who disengage academically and opt out of the academic tournament do so because they've come to question the criteria upon which the system allocates privileged positions. "When am I ever going to use this in my real life?" is an utterly sensible question for a young person to ask their high school math teacher. But for many high school math teachers, the question can feel like a veiled threat to their pedagogical authority—at least for those who may struggle to make a cogent argument for trigonometry's relevance for young people who aren't planning to use star charts to navigate at sea. The question can rankle in no small part because it threatens to expose the extent to which high school mathematics acts as a positional rather than an absolute good. In doing so, it opens the door to questions about the legitimacy of the unequal categories that high school mathematics courses help to create.

It's worth noting that high school math students are not the only people who threaten the legitimacy of educational categories with questions like "When am I ever going to use this in my real life?" In Imperial China, critics wondered whether it made sense to allocate elite bureaucratic titles based on test takers' mastery of Confucian philosophy. Some went so far as to note the irony that Confucius himself, if faced with such an exam, might not have had the time or energy to write down the aphorisms that Chinese scholars so carefully studied as they prepared for their imperial exams. In the seventeenth century the Oboi regents, who came to power via the military, mounted a challenge to the imperial exam system, arguing that a literary test provided limited insight into test takers' facility with the martial skills that Chinese officials needed.[18] These critiques have a great deal in common with the steady stream of complaints that we hear in the contemporary world about the disconnect between academic standards and the skills that employers are seeking from their workforce. Others critiqued the exams' criteria on the grounds of social justice. In 1861 the educational reformer Feng Guifen, in pointing out that the Chinese imperial exams did little more than measure the social status of the test taker's family, essentially argued that the test was nothing more than a test of cultural capital.

As the philosopher Michael Sandel notes, Donald Trump's political ascendency was built at least in part on related questions about the legitimacy of academic criteria and the educational elite they helped to construct.[19] Trump, who once famously declared, "I love the poorly educated," positioned himself as a mouthpiece for Americans—many of them White, male, and identifying with an industrial working class—who felt disrespected by the "eggheads" and "cultural elites" upon whom our educational meritocracy confers status and power. As economic inequalities have widened, occupational opportunities for those without college degrees have dwindled and education has tightened its hold on status and power. People who have experienced limited educational success have every right to feel like the meritocracy is stripping away their dignity and life chances. Trump's rhetoric often amplified these Americans' legitimate frustrations. By championing wealth, masculinity, and "real American" cultural identity—and by openly flouting the procedural rules that enforce meritocracy in governmental employment and contracting—Trump also mounted a critique of the academic criteria upon which educational meritocracy relies.

Each of these critiques of educational criteria threatens the educational system's legitimacy as a producer of merit. As we discuss in the next chapter, cheating is occasionally justified by defining the education system primarily as a mechanism of distributing status and arguing that it is divorced from other aims such as providing skills or other absolute goods. An educational system can become the victim of its own success: after successfully advocating for the adoption of its vision of merit, education, having thus monopolized the legitimation of status, can become defined solely by its relationship to status. The reduction of education to a monopoly over status creates a moment of definitional crisis for the system.

While it is therefore crucial for educational institutions to articulate defensible category selection criteria in order to maintain their legitimacy, these criteria can go only so far. In his detailed history of admissions at Harvard, Princeton, and Yale, the sociologist Jerome Karabel articulates what he describes as the iron law of admissions: "An institution will abandon a particular *process* of selection once it no longer produces the desired result."[20] This law, we posit, holds for a wide range of socially consequential educational categories, including not only the college admissions processes that Karabel describes but also the status-laden categories that operate at other educational levels. It implies that, although educators tend to emphasize the procedural rigor of their category selection processes, describing a process that articulates a criterion and then faithfully enacts that criterion to sort students into categories, they inevitably engage in post hoc examinations of the categories that they produce, asking about the extent to which those categories reflect their own and others' expectations.

Describing admissions at Harvard, Princeton, and Yale, Karabel notes that,

> though the view that scholastic performance should determine admission was not uncommon among the faculty, the top administrators of the Big Three (and of other leading private colleges, such as Columbia and Dartmouth) recognized that relying solely on any single factor—especially one that could be measured, like academic excellence—would deny them control over the composition of the freshman class. Charged with protecting their institutional interests, the presidents of the Big Three wanted the latitude to admit the dull sons of major donors and exclude the brilliant but unpolished children of immigrants.[21]

The examinations that these elite institutions developed in the early twentieth century to determine admissions served both practical and rhetorical functions. Practically, entrance examinations allowed faculty to articulate the skills that they considered essential prerequisites for a college education and to eliminate from the admissions pool those students who lacked the necessary foundational skills. Rhetorically, they affiliated elite institutions with the notion of meritocracy, allowing them to claim that they were extending opportunities to talented youth from modest backgrounds.

Exam-driven admissions were thus particularly popular with elite university faculty. On his way from the Princeton faculty to the U.S. presidency, Woodrow Wilson served as president of Princeton, where he implemented and fiercely defended an admissions system that relied particularly heavily on admissions testing. In a speech, Wilson proclaimed:

> Not long ago a gentleman approached me in great excitement just after the entrance examination. He said we had made a great mistake

> in not taking so and so from a certain school which he named. "But," I said, "he did not pass the entrance examinations." And he went over the boy's moral excellencies again. "Pardon me," I said, "you do not understand. He did not pass the entrance examinations. Now," I said, "I want you to understand that if the angel Gabriel applied for admission to Princeton University and could not pass the entrance examinations, he would not be admitted. He would be wasting his time."[22]

Reliance on entrance examinations, however, presented a fundamental problem for Harvard, Princeton, Yale, and other Ivy League institutions. The sons of the elite often did not test well, while young men from the nation's growing urban immigrant communities—especially those from Jewish communities—often did. By 1920, Jewish men represented more than 20 percent of the students at Harvard, and Harvard's president, Lawrence Lowell, began to openly worry that Jewish students would "ruin the college."[23]

In 1922, Lowell formed the aptly named Committee on Methods of Sifting Candidates for Admission. The committee began with a project of retrospective categorization. Poring over surnames and other data, the committee labeled every student who had enrolled in Harvard between 1900 and 1922 on a system that ran from J1 ("the evidence pointed conclusively to the fact that the student was Jewish") through J3 ("the evidence suggested the possibility that the student might be Jewish") or "Other" and then linked these data to campus Honors Court records in order to show that Jewish students caused more trouble on campus than their non-Jewish peers. Having established the "problem," the committee set about to design a solution. Ultimately the university discarded purely academic admissions and implemented an informal quota system designed to ensure that Jews made up less than 25 percent of enrollments. To produce this goal, Harvard developed an intensive set of admissions interviews and added a requirement that students provide photographs with their admissions packets. These interviews made it possible for admissions officers to advocate for admitting students from the right families based on their "moral qualities" rather than exclusively on their measured academic abilities. In the years that followed, most of the rest of the Ivy League followed suit.

Harvard and the rest of the Ivy League thoroughly internalized the lessons of their early-twentieth-century experience. In the mid-1950s, Wilbur Bender, Harvard's dean of admissions from 1952 to 1960, argued that the key question for admissions was not "What are the criteria on which we select?" but rather "What kind of student body do we want at Harvard and how do we get it?" Making a distinction between "desirable students" and "top brains," Bender argued that "if we go too far out in left field, we lose our capacity to influence and contribute to American life." Rather than take the risk of becoming "too isolated from America" by admitting via academics alone, Bender developed an admissions system in which officers considered a wide range of criteria—including grades and scores, but also extracurricular activities, essays, interviews, and family connections—in order to identify "Harvard men." As any ambitious high school senior can tell you, that system remains in place today at Harvard and other elite institutions.

Today Bender's "holistic" review system helps to create educational opportunities for children of the elite. After spending a year working as an elite university admissions officer, Mitchell Stevens documented a wide array of biases that plague holistic review in college admissions.[24] Stevens argues that the cultural and material resources that high school students need to shape their lives into a compelling narrative for admissions are unevenly distributed across the student population. Affluent students, legacies, and those who come from families and communities that are intimately familiar with elite college admissions know, from a relatively early age, that they must assemble a portfolio of notable experiences and accomplishments in order to gain admission to an elite college. Doing so requires far more than success at school or high test scores. Successful elite college applicants travel, volunteer, cultivate unique talents, and lead in their schools and communities. And then, having accomplished all this, they package these experiences and accomplishments into essays and applications tailored to the eyes and interests of college admissions officers, often with help from elite school counselors or private college search consultants. In such a system, it's difficult for students who lack this insight into the admissions process or the resources to make their case.

College admissions officers and websites argue that the holistic review system is the fairest of the available options for college admissions, noting that it allows colleges to build cohorts that are diverse on a wide range of dimensions—including race, gender, and geography as well as subject matter and extracurricular interests. These justifications are crucially important for maintaining the legitimacy of the educational categories that college admissions processes create. As we argued earlier, if the public believes that educators sort students into categories based on arbitrary or unreasonable criteria, the link between these categories and merit becomes tenuous. But even as educators must credibly argue that their criteria are fair, the proof is in the pudding. To maintain legitimacy, educational category processes must produce categories that reflect the expectations of the moment. To be sustainable, a meritocracy needs to produce elites who look like elites.

Recent research on the reciprocal relationship between elite universities and high-status firms provides a striking illustration of the co-construction of these categories. As Amy Binder and her colleagues demonstrate, elite university career offices funnel students toward a small number of high-status employers.[25] These firms, in turn, develop a nearly exclusive recruiting relationship with elite universities. Recruiters describe candidates' alma maters as their "pedigree," a term that neatly encapsulates the assumption that members of the category of elite university graduates share a set of desirable capacities, values, cultural norms, and skills.[26] The status advantages in these hiring processes are reciprocal. That is, even as being hired by an elite firm helps graduates secure the advantages that elite universities convey, these graduates confer status upon the firms for which they choose to work. Lower-status firms, meanwhile, recruit largely from lower-status schools.[27] In the process, the postbaccalaureate labor market reinscribes inequalities forged in the college admissions process.

Similar processes are at work throughout the educational system. Elite colleges attain their elite status in part by recruiting students from elite high schools. Elite high schools, in turn, trumpet their ability to send students to elite colleges, understanding that these institutional links are essential to the maintenance of their elite status. Colleges and universities not only establish so-called feeder relationships with particular high schools but also seek out class valedictorians (the elite students from within schools), thereby translating categorical inequalities generated in secondary schools into postsecondary institutional categorical inequalities.[28] Secondary school tracking systems, meanwhile, emulate elementary school instructional groupings, and elementary school instructional groupings set students on an academic course and acclimate them and their families to the logic of categorization in schools. Because schooling is not a single event but a sequence of educational contexts through which students move, school contexts shape students by changing their odds of exposure to various future educational contexts. In the process, educational categories accumulate across the life course to generate lasting inequalities.[29] In this way, the categorization processes operating in adjacent organizations constrain schools' agency to manipulate the categories they produce.

Wrapping Up

The rise of the educational meritocracy has endowed educational categories with extraordinary social power. Because we collectively view educational success as a marker of merit, educational categories serve as the basis for inequalities that last across lifetimes and, indeed, across generations.[30] To maintain this power, educational organizations create categories with which individuals build important parts of their social identities.

Both categories and merit are inherently relational concepts. Categories are defined by their boundaries, which position them in a landscape relative to other categories. Likewise, it only makes sense to think about one person's merit relative to the merit of others. Given that both categories and merit are fundamentally positional, educational systems that are designed to create merit-based categories exist at the intersection of these two positional goods and are hyperpositional. Because of the hyperpositionality of education's merit-based categories, education plays a central role in creating and legitimating inequality in contemporary societies.

To ensure that the categories of merit (and inequalities) produced by schooling are broadly socially accepted, educators and schools are often fiercely protective of their legitimacy. We allow schools to sort us into an unequal society only because we collectively believe that education represents a fair contest in which we can prove our social value.

Unfortunately, however, this broad belief in the educational tournament's fairness and the resulting equation of educational success with personal merit comes at a profound cost. Not only does education sort us into an unequal society, but it tells us that we deserve our fate. It is easy to see how demoralizing this equation of educational success and personal worth is for people who struggle in school. In fact, there is good reason to think that failure in a meritocracy can be literally fatal. In his history of the Chinese imperial exams, Benjamin Elman tells the story of a test taker who died of heartbreak after being stripped of a top ranking in the civil service when the examiners realized that his exam had been improperly scored.[31] And in the contemporary American context, Anne Case and Angus Deaton note that men who do not have a bachelor's degree are three times more likely to die a "death of despair"—from suicide, drug overdose, or alcoholic liver disease—compared to men with college degrees.[32]

But even educational winners suffer in this system, which places all of us on a never-ending treadmill that compels us to perpetually compete in order to improve ourselves and demonstrate our moral worth. This meritocratic culture starts early. Today, rather than trusting schools to socialize their children, affluent families routinely invest considerable financial and time resources in their children's development, ensuring that their children have a leg up from the beginning of their formal education. And such efforts last through the life course. Rather than resting on their laurels, meritocratic elites believe that they must continually outwork others in order to reach the next level in a lifelong tournament that proves the personal worth of its winners. This is why, in a dramatic reversal of prior social orders, contemporary elites regularly report working longer hours than those in the middle class.

Understanding the positional nature of education highlights the relationship between education and other dimensions of equality. As we noted earlier in discussing algebra expansion, in some contexts advantaged families responded to efforts to enroll all eighth-graders in algebra classes by pushing their children into even more advanced geometry classes. This pattern is sometimes referred to as "effectively maintained inequality"—privileged actors using their wealth, power, and other resources to claim positional advantages in a situation in which a positional educational good (algebra instruction) is becoming more universally available.[33] As we have discussed, a large body of research highlights the role of educational institutions in reproducing inequality from other domains. The value of education may not be dependent on scarcity per se, but the logic of merit requires some exclusivity to maintain the justification for bestowing elite status on some students. Put differently, to generate inequality that is viewed as legitimate under a meritocratic system, education must nominally give all people (or at least all people who are seen as fully human) an opportunity to succeed, while at the same time ensuring that not all of them can actually succeed. Further, education must ensure that educational success mirrors existing societal understandings of privilege and elite status, while simultaneously preventing mass disengagement.

We build on these arguments in chapter 7 to underscore that because merit is made, and because, like all categories, it is made through an inherently political process, merit can also be contested.

7 CONTESTING DEFINITIONS OF MERIT

In 1843, Hong Xiuquan, frustrated after having failed the Chinese civil service exam for a fourth time, decided that both the exam system and the dynasty that it supported were corrupt and illegitimate. Hong Xiuquan, rejecting the Confucian teachings tested by the examinations and claiming to be the younger brother of Jesus, went on to lead the Taiping Heavenly Kingdom. Hong Xiuquan rejected not only the examination system's assessment of his merit but also its definition of merit more broadly and its legitimacy as a way to define merit. That said, Hong Xiuquan did not reject the idea of an examination system; in fact, the Taiping Heavenly Kingdom instituted its own examination system, which had substantially lower rates of failure than the Chinese civil service exam system.[1] The conflict between the ruling Qings and Taipings was the bloodiest civil war in recorded history: it was responsible for over twenty million deaths before the Qings eventually prevailed.[2] Although Hong Xiuquan's wholesale rejection of the civil service examination system was unusual in its scope and consequences, contesting categorical assignments and definitions of merit is relatively common.

In this chapter, we discuss the many ways in which students and others contest educational categorical assignments. We begin with a discussion of the behaviors often referred to as "cheating." Cheating has a long history, and accounts of Imperial China's civil service examination system are filled with instances of scholars sneaking in notes, hiring professional test takers, and bribing examiners. In response, examiners implemented extensive measures to prevent cheating and preserve the legitimacy of the exam.[3] In contemporary society, cheating is endemic in educational systems. Students routinely copy one another's work and sneak "cheat sheets" into testing sites; companies sell bespoke paper-writing services as anti-plagiarism software makes it increasingly difficult for students to turn in secondhand writing; and recent investigations have uncovered elaborate conspiracies involving both opportunity-hoarding parents and idealistic educators seeking to obtain their desired outcomes from educational category construction processes. Sometimes cheating is motivated by individualistic concerns, as when students game the educational system to ensure a high grade. In other cases, the motivation for cheating may be more community-oriented; in rural Jordan, for instance, East Bank tribes used a loudspeaker to announce the answers to an exam needed to apply to university outside the testing center.[4]

But regardless of motive, cheating contests educational categorization processes. At its core, cheating in school is about securing a desired educational category. Cheaters reject existing categorization processes because they might not yield the desired categorization. Yet cheaters typically accept the educational categories and do not explicitly challenge the criteria and institutional structures that sort people into them.

Although those who game the educational system display a willingness to ignore the system's rules, their actions are predicated upon the educational system's enduring legitimacy. Put differently, cheaters contest their own place in a system of unequal educational categories, but they do not contest the existence of these unequal categories or the processes through which educational systems allocate individuals to categories. Gaming the educational system works only if the educational system remains stable. Cheaters know that fundamental changes to educational category construction processes would render their gaming strategies ineffective. Likewise, they know that if everybody were to cheat, widespread cynicism could undermine the value of the very educational categories that they cheated to attain.

Other approaches more directly challenge the educational system's legitimacy, values, and processes. For example, individuals sometimes work around the educational system, creating alternative systems of credentialing and evaluation in an attempt to confer status on people who might otherwise feel undervalued by existing meritocratic criteria. Some of these alternative systems—such as the Freedom Schools of the 1960s and the Zapatista community-led schools in Chiapas, Mexico—are developed in marginalized communities as a means of affirming community knowledge and values. In other cases, such efforts are spearheaded by individuals or groups hoping to subvert traditional systems for their personal gain. Consider, for example, the entrepreneurs who build unaccredited and often fraudulent universities that grant "credentials" based on life experiences instead of coursework. We argue that both the Freedom Schools and schools that grant unaccredited credentials based on life experiences seek to redefine merit, and as such represent a fundamental threat to meritocracy's legitimacy.

Finally, we describe reformist efforts to work within existing educational and governance processes in order to propose new rules and systems that address perceived failures in educational valuation and credentialing. Like people who game the educational system by cheating, reformists are deeply committed to education's legitimacy. Unlike cheaters, however, reformists work to change the criteria, values, and processes through which education builds unequal social categories, lobbying for new educational criteria and sorting processes that more closely align with their vision of educational justice.

We conclude with a critique of the concept of merit itself. Most critiques of meritocracy focus on the way biases and intergenerational inequalities disrupt the meritocratic allocation of status.[5] Our critique, by contrast, is more wide-ranging. We argue that merit is necessarily hierarchical, and as such any educational system based on merit inevitably creates inequality. Further, to the degree that merit-based educational systems sort people into categories based (however loosely) on their abilities, we argue that these systems are inherently ableist. Contesting merit might thus involve not only contesting merit's definition and the rules for allocating individuals into merit-based categories, but also the very idea of merit as a neutral and unproblematic goal.

Gaming the Educational System for Personal Gain

Meritocracy implies competition. Schools and society police this competition via explicit rules and broader cultural agreements about fair play in educational settings. Our society embraces fierce academic competition that aligns with these rules and norms as part of a meritocratic sorting process. We expect students to study for high-stakes exams, for example, and therefore accept as legitimate the advantages that students accrue via cram sessions. However, educational systems define other student efforts to influence categorical assignments as deviant. We often call these behaviors "cheating." So while having a tutor help edit an essay or provide supplementary instruction on difficult material is typically understood as legitimate, having a tutor write the essay or take a test for a student is viewed as an illegitimate (although not unprecedented) approach to contesting one's category placement. We argue that the educational system treats cheating as a challenge to its legitimacy not only because it contests an individual's category placement but also because it implicitly challenges the rules that govern this process.

That said, even individuals who game the educational system often have a strong interest in maintaining the system's legitimacy. As we discussed in chapter 6, educational categories matter because they place people in a social hierarchy in which status is understood to reflect individual merit. This profound social power—the fact that categories matter so much for gaining access to resources, status, power, and even a sense of self-worth in contemporary societies—helps to explain why educational categories are also highly contested. If education were trivial, there would be nothing to be gained from cheating and people would not find cheating scandalous. Cheating embraces education's positional roles—its power to allocate individuals to unequal social categories and to associate these categories with merit—while repudiating its less positional goals, such as training youth in basic skills and socializing them in the behavioral norms that facilitate our collective life. Cheating thus divorces education from nonpositional goals and repositions it purely as an arbiter of status.

Before advancing this argument, we should pause to consider the line that separates socially acceptable educational activities from the activities that we describe as "gaming the system" or—even more judgmentally—as cheating. Few contemporary observers raise an eyebrow when families enroll their children in expensive test preparation courses and other forms of tutoring to boost their children's academic credentials. Countries like South Korea have developed complex "shadow education" industries to provide these supplemental educational supports to help students improve their academic performance on high-stakes exams. Likewise, few people would consider it problematic for families to sign children up for sports and other extracurricular activities, even when these extracurriculars are explicitly understood as a means to increasing their children's success in elite college admissions. It is noteworthy, however, that many of these enrichment opportunities take place after school or in the summer. It is as if by moving these activities outside of the school day, we push them out of view, allowing us to celebrate these supplementary educational opportunities as marks of good parenting and to ignore their consequences for inequality.

But when an FBI investigation uncovered a vast conspiracy in which wealthy parents falsified their children's extracurricular records, had others take their tests, and bribed college admissions officials, the public reacted with fierce condemnation and more than fifty people faced criminal charges. The 2019 "Operation Varsity Blues" parents clearly crossed the line separating loving parenting from parental cheating. But where does that line lie? What distinguishes socially acceptable uses of parental privilege in the educational category assignment process from the uses of privilege that we consider deviant? Similarly, what distinguishes the student who receives social accolades for effort and dedication to educational success and the student whom we accuse of cheating?

Broadly speaking, although our society is comfortable with a wide array of parental and student efforts to claim educational opportunities and boost performance—from choosing certain schools and neighborhoods to hiring tutors and college consultants—we object to direct interventions in the educational evaluative processes that assign categories. When the parents implicated in Operation Varsity Blues employed a professional test taker, they clearly crossed the line between involved parenting and fraud.

It's also worth noting that the line between appropriate academic behavior and cheating often depends on who is engaging in the behavior. Behavior like sharing memes for a digital media project might be celebrated as teamwork, collaboration, and group creativity in an upper-class White classroom, but punished as messing around and cheating in a poor, majority-immigrant classroom.[6] That said, many of the highest-profile cases of contemporary cheating have involved students in highly selective educational settings. Harvard, for example, investigated roughly half of the students in an introductory-level government class for cheating in 2012. Although Harvard introduced an honor code in 2015, by 2017 it was dealing with large-scale cheating in a popular computer science course. A *Harvard Crimson* poll revealed that 23 percent of respondents cheated in an academic context as undergraduates and that just over 40 percent reported having cheated in high school.[7]

It's not just Harvard. Cheating appears to be common everywhere high school students compete for selective college admissions. Stuyvesant High School, New York City's elite public exam school, recently disciplined seventy students in an elaborate cheating scheme in which students took pictures of New York's Regents Examination with their cell phones, texted them to each other, and sent each other answers. One of the ringleaders explained that he was strong in physics, and so he helped his classmates with their physics exam; in exchange, he received help in subjects he felt less confident about, such as American history and Spanish.

Some cheating—like the cheating uncovered in Operation Varsity Blues—is rational in the sense that it aims to provide the cheater with access to educational categories that could change their life trajectory. But sometimes families and students cheat even when doing so seems unlikely to have material consequences. This was the case in the Stuyvesant Regents Exam cheating scandal. Although students must pass the Regents Exam to graduate from high school, the Stuyvesant students implicated in cheating on the exam were at little risk of scoring poorly enough to experience its consequences. So why did they cheat on this relatively simple exam? Perhaps because the test scores are listed on high school transcripts and because Stuyvesant's school culture fosters competition around academic outcomes, students saw their Regents test scores as a marker of their human worth.

The Stuyvesant students said that cheating was common, and they described a hierarchy of cheating: copying homework, in their view, was relatively permissible, while they saw cheating on a test as more problematic. Yet Stuyvesant students articulated few qualms about getting help from friends on a test or sharing questions on a test that they had just taken with friends who would take it later in the day. In all, some 83 percent of the 329 students who took a student newspaper survey (which had an approximately 10 percent response rate) reported having "committed academic dishonesty," and 71 percent reported having "ever cheated on a test (Copied off someone, knew the answers beforehand, etc.)." Interestingly, only 14 percent reported having cheated on the Regents Exam, and just 9 percent said that they had cheated on another standardized test, such as the ACT, the SAT, or the exam used to determine entrance to Stuyvesant.[8] While the Stuyvesant episode is a high-profile example of cheating, it is not unique. Approximately 60 percent of high school students nationally report having cheated on a test.[9]

Stuyvesant students defended their behavior using a variety of rationales. A senior characterized cheating as a survival strategy, a way to negotiate a trade-off between failure and integrity. Other students argued that the decision not to cheat put them behind in the competition for admission to elite colleges; they described the intense pressure to perform well and characterized cheating as a time management strategy. (Consistent with this explanation, cheating appears to be most common among students in their junior year of high school, a key period for securing entrance into college.) Both defenses seem to be predicated on the assumption that high school students' primary educational task is to get into an elite college and secure their place in the social hierarchy. Since students think cheating simply assists them in this process, they regard cheating as eminently compatible with educational competition.

Students also suggested that cheating was just an accepted part of life at Stuyvesant High. According to one student: "We all are just helping each other out. Stuyvesant breeds a culture of cheating, and you're honestly stupid to not take advantage of it."[10] Teachers were sympathetic to cheating given the pressure that students were under, saying that they were unwilling to report cheating out of a fear of "ruining students' lives." These accounts justify cheating as a normal part of an educational system designed to help students "take their place" in society. In this telling, cheating does not challenge the educational system's legitimacy. Rather, it frames cheating as an activity that aligns with the educational sorting processes that create positional goods (for example, unequal social categories) while downplaying the aspects of education that create absolute goods (for example, knowledge creation).[11]

However, some Stuyvesant student justifications attributed cheating to a crisis in educational legitimacy around education's absolute goals. One Stuyvesant alum explained, for example, that it was acceptable to cheat when teachers failed to earn student respect and effectively teach the material. Another Stuyvesant student justified cheating when the workload was overwhelming, saying, "Teachers can't expect us to be reasonable when they are unreasonable." Still another student noted that "many homework assignments are tedious and meaningless. Although some classes legitimately benefit from homework, some teachers assign homework for the sake of it, even if there is nothing to be gained from it."[12] In these cases, the student said, teachers should expect students to cheat. It is noteworthy that these student critiques focused on particular teachers or classes, rather than casting doubt on the system of education more broadly. We might speculate that students at Stuyvesant avoided questioning the system more broadly because they were already winners in an educational tournament and occupied an advantaged category in the social hierarchy. These students were willing to raise local questions about education's moral authority, but they may have recognized that raising questions about education's broader legitimacy might undermine their own position in the meritocratic hierarchy.

The sort of cheating that we see in these examples from Harvard and Stuyvesant—which we might call cheating for individual gain, or selfish cheating—simultaneously undermines and maintains the legitimacy of educational categorical inequality. Students turn to this form of cheating only because educational credentials carry social value. Cheaters cheat because they want to claim that value for themselves. If education loses legitimacy, that value dissipates and cheating ceases to be worth the time and effort. Therefore, although many people who engage in cheating might be personally cynical about the educational system, they have a vested interest in maintaining broad public faith in the system's ability to legitimately sort people in an unequal society.

This suggests that cheating can only be tolerated at a small scale, or that instances of large-scale cheating must be hidden or somehow rationalized as legitimate. Practices related to admissions for legacies and the children of donors are prime examples of such rationalization. To name one high-profile example, in 1998 New Jersey real estate developer Charles Kushner gave Harvard $2.5 million. Not long after, Harvard admitted his son Jared. According to an administrator at the future presidential son-in-law's high school: "There was no way anybody in the administrative office of the school thought he would, on the merits, get into Harvard. His GPA did not warrant it, his SAT scores did not warrant it. We thought for sure, there was no way this was going to happen. Then, lo and behold, Jared was accepted. It was a little bit disappointing because there were at the time other kids we thought should really get in on the merits, and they did not."[13] At a moral level, it's hard to distinguish between the quid pro quo that seems to have gotten Jared Kushner into Harvard and the more explicit bribes that sent parents to jail in Operation Varsity Blues. Although it is not entirely clear how society makes sense of such practices, it is perhaps rationalized based on the idea that the donations benefit the university broadly, or perhaps because it follows Karabel's iron law of elite college admissions by perpetuating the advantages of the existing elite.

Beyond rationalizations, educational systems bolster their legitimacy by meting out severe punishments for cheating. These punishments—jail terms for the conspirators wrapped up in Operation Varsity Blues or expulsions for students caught cheating—serve to both dissuade individuals from cheating and assert that cheating is aberrant and rare. When, in the spring of 2021, at the height of the Covid-19 crisis, the West Point military academy began to suspect students of cheating on an online calculus exam, it quickly mounted an investigation. After expelling eight cadets and putting fifty additional cadets on a yearlong leave, the academy's superintendent explicitly positioned these expulsions in terms of legitimacy: "West Point must be the gold standard for developing Army officers. We demand nothing less than impeccable character from our graduates."[14]

Likewise, measures guarding against cheating can be viewed in terms of bolstering the legitimacy of the educational system. While the industry of cheating is lucrative, it is also constrained by the need to maintain the legitimacy of the educational system. Cheating has made Chegg and other services that provide answers to students' homework and test questions a multibillion-dollar industry, but Chegg and its competitors cannot afford for society to lose faith in the educational system because this would obviate the demand for their services.

India's medical and engineering exam cheating scandals in 2021 provide important examples of how too much cheating can destabilize the legitimacy of educational systems. In both exams, organized groups of individuals employed by test preparation centers stole test questions; posed as test takers to sit for others' exams at multiple in-person testing facilities, using digitally altered photo IDs that morphed the faces of the test taker and the person paying for cheating services; and hacked into exam center computers to solve answers remotely. Understanding just how important it was to reassure people that the legitimacy of the admissions process remained intact, the Indian government deployed the Central Bureau of Investigations (CBI) to resolve the crisis. Ultimately, a wave of arrests were carried out in conjunction with the cheating rackets, and the students involved were prohibited from retaking the tests for three years.[15] But the unfolding discovery of the extent of the cheating spawned broader public conversations that included allegations of a government cover-up; calls for the tests to be discontinued, including formal pleas to the Supreme Court and petitions to the education minister; and widely circulated social media critiques.[16] The cheating scandals also revived longer-standing concerns about the legitimacy of such admissions exams because of caste-based inequality in the likelihood of receiving a top exam score. A state-appointed committee investigating the exam argued "that NEET [the medical school entrance examination] undermined the diverse social representation in . . . medical studies, favouring mainly affluent segments of society while equally thwarting the dream of pursuing medical education by the underprivileged social groups," according to a bill introduced following the committee's investigation.[17]

From examinees bribing examiners in China and India to Stuyvesant students sharing homework, the power of educational credentials leads individuals to attempt to co-opt the educational system to attain a desired categorization. Although they refuse to accept the position in the hierarchy that education would assign them, they nonetheless depend on others' acceptance of education as legitimate in order to validate their desired categorization. In doing so, they often justify their efforts on the basis of education's outsized role in sorting students into a hierarchical society, while also downplaying the role of schools in imparting skills.

Gaming the Educational System for Collective or Altruistic Ends

Not all attempts to game the educational system are motivated by self-interest. Rather, in many contexts, cheating reflects a broader community effort to redress perceived biases in the production of educational categories. Although the line between individuals who are seeking their own advantage and those who cheat because they view the system as fundamentally unfair is perhaps blurry (after all, people who are cheating for individual gain can be viewed as rejecting the rules of the educational system that relegate them to an undesired position as unfair), in some contexts cheating is clearly a political act that makes broader community-level status claims.

Take, for example, the case of the East Bank tribes in Jordan, where cheating is widespread and arguably, at least in some contexts, normalized and expected. Members of East Bank tribes are understood as having a right to university admittance, which is widely understood as a form of political patronage, and cheating is normalized to the extent that riots have sometimes broken out when proctors did not allow cheating.[18] In one of the more blatant acts of contestation, the correct answers to the Tawjihi, an exam that must be passed in order to be eligible to apply for university admission, were read over loudspeakers outside of the testing facility. A Ministry of Education investigation "acknowledged that some people had used loudspeakers outside examination halls to help students cheat," but deflected responsibility for this by arguing that only external security forces had the authority to stop such behavior.[19] In organizing these efforts, communities were clearly attempting to boost their children's chances at gaining high-status positions. At the same time, they were signaling a broader rejection of the test as a legitimate basis for the allocation of resources in their society.

Likewise, as the journalist Rachel Aviv recounts, a "star teacher" at Parks Middle School in South Atlanta, Damay Lewis, lost his job in 2010 when investigators uncovered systematic cheating at dozens of

Atlanta Public Schools.[20] Lewis believed that Parks Middle School was making a difference in an impoverished community and changing students' lives; he saw his students' slow and steady achievement growth as a testament to their resilience and the effort invested by both students and teachers. But test scores at Parks were not improving at a fast enough pace to meet expectations under federal school accountability policy, and Lewis and his fellow teachers worried that the school would be closed.

Aviv makes it clear that teachers at Parks were deeply committed to their students. They helped students and their families pay for food and medicine. Lewis took his students' laundry home and washed it for them and opened his home to students whose parents were absent or high. Lewis was horrified by the idea of the school's closure, especially since many students had entered Parks with artificially inflated scores because their elementary schools had cheated. Further, Lewis objected to the fact that the test scores made no allowance for the incredible challenges his students faced on a day-to-day basis.

And so, motivated by a sense of duty to Parks and its students, Lewis and several of his colleagues engaged in an elaborate April ritual of changing students' scores. Noting the work that students put in and the incremental progress they were making, Lewis justified this cheating by saying: "I'm not going to let the state slap them in the face and say they're failures." A lawyer who was present during interviews conducted as part of the investigations contrasted the cheating that occurred at Parks with the cheating scandals at Harvard and Stuyvesant High School. In those cases, students were cheating to secure a more favorable outcome for themselves, while the teachers at Parks cheated because they believed that the tests were inaccurate instruments for measuring their students' worth; they saw falsifying answers as a means to keep the school open in order to be able to make a difference in their students' lives.

Damay Lewis and his colleagues saw their collective efforts to inflate student test scores as an act of civil disobedience. Knowing that he was breaking the rules when he covertly altered student test scores, Lewis justified this rule-breaking as a strategy to undermine a system that systematically underserved and undervalued his students and schools like Parks. We take these arguments seriously and believe that Lewis and many other actors saw their efforts to game the educational system as principled actions. In rejecting the educational system's rules, this sort of principled cheating critiques a particular set of rules (like the No Child Left Behind Act's school accountability policies) even as it mounts a broader critique of the fitness and legitimacy of how educational systems create and allocate merit.

To be clear, this sort of gaming the system has a very different moral valence from the lunch-counter sit-ins of the 1950s and 1960s, or the street blockages of the 2020s in which activists have openly confronted a system they believe to be unjust in order to force a more public accounting. But cheating like what occurred in Atlanta nonetheless has the potential to undermine systemic legitimacy by raising questions about the definition of merit in educational contexts and the extent to which educational categories really do reflect merit. As such, while the self-interested cheating of the Stuyvesant student or the Operation Varsity Blues parent hinged on systemic legitimacy, the efforts of the teachers in Atlanta and the community members in rural Jordan can be understood as questioning the legitimacy of educational systems.

Working Outside the Educational System

Cheating breaks educational rules to contest the categories to which students are assigned, but even when cheaters are working to undermine education's legitimacy, they typically focus their efforts on reassigning students in a way that is viewed as equitable rather than redefining merit. By contrast, other strategies work outside of the educational system by developing and participating in alternative systems that both rewrite the rules governing status allocation and distribute credentials or other markers of merit based on alternative criteria. The educational landscape is littered with organizations and initiatives that repurpose the grammar of schooling for alternative goals. Some of these organizations operate with mercenary motivations as they pass off counterfeit educational credentials on unsuspecting educational consumers. Others, such as the "dropout grants" given by Peter Thiel, explicitly challenge societal understandings of merit and seek to disrupt traditional educational structures. Religious seminaries and avant-garde artistic workshops are examples of a third group of educational outsider organizations that simply seek to serve their community's distinctive needs and are relatively indifferent to the broader social context. Finally, a fourth set seeks to provide educational opportunities that center marginalized communities and experiences while reimagining educational goals; this group includes organizations like the Mississippi Freedom Schools and the Zapatista schools. Although these initiatives are diverse, each features actors who work outside of and around the educational mainstream to create alternative definitions of merit in order to attenuate the links between educational categories, merit, and inequality.

Consider, for example, the diploma mill. According to some estimates, as many as half of the people in the United States who claim to have earned a PhD do not have a degree from an accredited university. Some people who receive degrees from unaccredited universities are the victims of educational fraud. For example, FastTrain College, a Florida-based for-profit college, fraudulently secured millions of dollars in federal Pell grants for students who were ineligible because they lacked a high school diploma or equivalent credential. FastTrain, in a former student's words, was "not interested in teaching students but rather interested in processing student loans for financial gains."[21] California-based Corinthian College, a for-profit university, recruited unhoused students to enroll in programs that didn't exist, signed them up for federal loans, and left a trail of student debt in its wake when it abruptly filed for bankruptcy.[22]

But other "students" who seek degrees from diploma mills are not clearly the victims of educational fraud. Erwin Sniedzins, for example, is a Toronto resident, the CEO of a small educational software company, and a proud alumnus of Kings Lake University. Sniedzins rejects the monopoly of the traditional educational system to legitimate human capital. As such, he saw a natural match between his educational philosophy and Kings Lake, a university that offered degrees based on certifying professional skills and experiences. After Sniedzins sent pages of documents describing his professional life—along with thousands of dollars—to Kings Lake, the university mailed him a diploma as well as a cap and gown and conferred on him a "Master of Education in Technology in Education." When reporters from the Canadian Broadcasting Corporation contacted Sniedzins as part of an investigation of diploma mills, he refused to believe that the university was illegitimate. "Sniedzins repeatedly told CBC Toronto that he never suspected a degree based on life experience that required no academic work, studying or exams could be fake as it was in line with his approach to education."[23] Similarly, a counselor with a PhD in biblical counseling from the diploma mill Alameda University who was contacted as part of the same investigation insisted that he had earned his degree and produced a twenty-five-page dissertation, of which 30 percent was plagiarized.

Both Kings Lake and Alameda University are operated by Axact, a company that makes millions of dollars per month selling fake degrees. Former Axact employees note that some customers appear to be aware of the fact that they are purchasing a fraudulent degree, but that others appear to be searching for a legitimate degree.[24] In either case, degrees conferred by Kings Lake and Alameda challenge the dominant model of educational credentials by attempting to claim the status and merit associated with educational categories while circumventing many of the rituals and expectations that maintain the social legitimacy of these categories. Just as Kings Lake appealed to Sniedzins's sense that his experience had value that traditional educational institutions failed to recognize, diploma mills trade on customers' dissatisfaction with the traditional model of educational certification by allowing consumers to determine their own educational merit and fitness for credentials.

The distinction between a diploma mill and a legitimate educational organization is maybe not as clear as we might hope, as universities often award honorary degrees to individuals who have made substantial, but non-academic, contributions. And indeed, as noted by Arthur Levine, a former president of Columbia University's Teachers College, universities sometimes give these honorary degrees as a reward to particularly generous donors.[25] As such, Erwin Sniedzins's sense that educational institutions should be willing to recognize the extracurricular achievements of individuals—for a price—is not so very out of line with existing practices in mainstream universities. To the degree that the donations typically required to be considered for an honorary degree are beyond the means of most people, one could even view diploma mills as making the logic of honorary degrees more broadly accessible.

Furthermore, the line between claiming a fake degree and receiving a legitimate degree is also fuzzy. Using nationally representative data, Paul Attewell and Thurston Domina highlighted discrepancies between how individuals represented their educational credentials and the credentials listed on their transcripts.[26] Their work reveals that 6 percent of people who claimed to hold a bachelor's degree and 35 percent of people who claimed to hold an associate's degree did not have transcript-verified credentials. Many of those claiming a degree not listed on their transcript, however, had accrued sufficient credits for a degree but were presumably missing specific classes required to satisfy institutional distributional requirements. This finding raises a series of questions: Has a person who has taken and passed all of the courses associated with a college degree with the exception of, say, a PE requirement earned a college degree? And if that person's answer to the question is different from their university registrar's answer, who should we trust? Is it fair for accredited educational organizations to have a monopoly on the legitimate allocation of credentials?

People who fudge their educational records—either by buying a degree from a diploma mill or by claiming to hold a degree that they have not actually been granted—contest the educational system's monopoly on credentialing by claiming the right to categorize themselves. Such actions make sense because education's role in shaping individuals' life chances in contemporary society has begun to overshadow less positional roles such as inculcating skills or creating citizens. This disconnect between the positional and absolute logics of education characterizes not only those who buy their degrees from diploma mills or fabricate them from their lived experience but also the Stuyvesant cheaters, the Jordanians announcing answers via a loudspeaker, the Atlanta teachers erasing and replacing student answers on a Scantron, and others who game the education system.

Others intentionally subvert educational systems, often posing a much more direct threat to legitimacy. Consider Peter Thiel's Thiel Fellowship, which awards $100,000 over two years to young people who have opted out of school. According to the Thiel Foundation, the "dropout" grant was created to empower those "who want to build new things instead of sitting in a classroom" to pursue their own ideas rather wait for a credential from an institution of higher education. "College can be good for learning about what's been done," the foundation proclaims, "but it can also discourage you from doing something new." But the Thiel Fellowship also traffics in some of the very same status marking that we associate with higher education. Thiel brings fellows together into a cohort, gives them a badge signifying merit, and provides access to a network of investors and potential collaborators. As such, the Thiel Fellowship mounts a critique of educational categories by creating a new high-status category of its own, thereby challenging those who believe in the value of education as well as the dominant role it plays in shaping young adult life.

Many community based-efforts led by marginalized communities in the United States and elsewhere have also worked outside of the traditional state-run educational system to provide educational opportunities. But in contrast to individual-oriented, advantage-maximizing efforts to redesign the educational system, these efforts are often directly centered on contesting educational hierarchies and providing the educational rights and privileges that society withholds. Take, for example, the Freedom Schools that emerged in African American communities in Mississippi during the Freedom Summer of 1964. These schools followed in a long tradition of liberatory schooling efforts that flourished in secrecy among enslaved Africans in the eighteenth and nineteenth centuries, as well as the efforts of Septima Clark and others who formed Citizen Schools to teach citizenship rights and literacy skills to African Americans in the 1950s.[27] Building on those examples, the Student Nonviolent Coordinating Committee (SNCC) created a progressive summer curriculum for secondary students that included academic, citizenship, and recreational components and aimed to counter the "sharecropper education" that students were receiving in their regular high school classrooms.[28] Courses, which were largely taught by student volunteers, centered the historical experiences of the African American community and their efforts to organize for social change and civil rights. Reflecting back on the experience, the historian Howard Zinn pinpointed the direct challenge that the Freedom Schools levied against a merit-based system by proposing instead an educational system with egalitarian goals:

> The Freedom Schools' challenge to the social structure of Mississippi was obvious from the start. Its challenge to American education as a whole is more subtle. There is, to begin with, the provocative

> suggestion that an entire school system can be created in any community outside the official order and critical of its suppositions. . . . Can we, somehow, bring teachers and students together, not through the artificial sieve of certification and examination but on the basis of their common attraction to an exciting social goal? Would it be possible to declare boldly that the aim of the schools is to find solutions for poverty, for injustice, for race and national hatred, and to turn all educational efforts into a national striving for those solutions?[29]

Similar efforts aimed at organizing alternative educational systems to drastically reorient educational goals away from merit and status competitions have arisen outside of the United States as well. The Zapatista education program arose in the 1990s in Chiapas, Mexico, when leftist rebels who were protesting globalization and efforts by the Mexican government to dispossess indigenous communities of their land organized to provide education to children in Zapatista communities.[30] These schools intentionally resisted outside influences and supported community development grounded in the principles of Zapatista self-government.[31] Each community creates course content for its Zapatista school from the bottom up through participatory democracy and communal decision-making. Classes are instructed by parents and other community members—called "education promotors"—to emphasize indigenous values, including land stewardship, food sovereignty, and instruction in indigenous languages to help preserve those languages and promote bilingualism.[32] Although they are not without implementation challenges and conflict, these schools seek to foster a communalist orientation aimed at supporting an autonomous, self-preservationist community, in direct opposition to the competitive orientation of state-funded schools.[33]

These alternative systems have very different purposes and goals, yet each is attempting to move outside of the categorical structures available within mainstream school systems. The new categorical identities forged by these efforts provide opportunities for individuals or communities to draw their own boundaries. They simultaneously challenge the legitimacy of the educational system while also ignoring and thereby minimizing the power it wields over the people who participate in it.

Redefining the Rules

Efforts to game or work around educational systems can undermine education's role in the production of social inequality without directly critiquing the educational system. But there is a third strategy for contesting educational categorical inequalities: direct critique.

Paradoxically, the strategy of direct critique and efforts to reform systems of merit allocation often reflect a profound commitment to education's legitimacy as a source of social inequality. People who game the system or cheat are willing to break the rules that govern educational category construction. Those who work outside or around the system by building or participating in alternative systems are willing to ignore the categories created by existing educational institutions in favor of newly constructed categories. By contrast, people who engage in direct critique and systemic reform efforts work to reinforce systemic legitimacy by redefining the rules by which education allocates merit.

Suggesting the criteria used to determine category membership be changed can be controversial, as evident in a recent debate over admissions to elite public high schools in cities across the United States. In New York City, the Department of Education admits rising ninth-graders to Stuyvesant High and a handful of other high-profile specialty public high schools based exclusively on their performance on a single standardized test. Stanley Teitel, a recent principal of Stuyvesant, positioned this test-based admissions system at the heart of the school's identity, saying, "One of the things [alumni] love about the school is that it remains a true meritocracy. You only get into Stuyvesant because you proved it on an exam."[34] This principle is deeply held, to the point that New York state law specifies that admission to Stuyvesant and two other selective New York City public schools must be based on combined math and reading achievement scores as measured on one (potentially highly biased) test, the Specialized High Schools Admissions Test (SHSAT).

Others, however, question the legitimacy of a system that offers fewer than 10 percent of the spots in New York City's most prestigious public high schools to Black and Latine students when two-thirds of the city's middle schoolers are Black or Latine. New York Mayor Bill de Blasio, for example, argued, "If we want this to be the fairest big city in America, we need to scrap the SHSAT and start over."[35] Similarly, the New York City chancellor of schools commented, "Why are we screening for admission? I don't get that. We're a public school system in one of the most diverse cities . . . in the world. Why are we screening kids in a public school system? That's, to me, antithetical to what I think we all want for our kids."[36] Motivated by similar critiques, Boston, Chicago, and San Francisco have revamped their public exam school admissions systems. In some of these new systems, officials sort students into tiers based on the socioeconomic conditions of the neighborhoods in which they live and allocate an equal number of exam school positions to each of these neighborhood groupings. The system then admits students based on traditional criteria—GPA and test scores in the Boston case—but structures the decision such that students are competing only with students from socioeconomically similar neighborhoods for a coveted exam school spot. In other cities, like San Francisco, the district went a step further by eliminating the competitive admissions process altogether and assigning students to all high schools through their neighborhood-weighted admissions lottery for a year, until the decision was reversed following political pressure and an election to recall three school board members.

These extraordinarily controversial decisions make it clear how highly many families value meritocracy and how closely it is linked with perceived quality. When Mayor de Blasio attempted to do away with test-based admissions in New York City schools, the billionaire Ronald Lauder spent millions of dollars on an advertising campaign to oppose the shift and the New York State Legislature ultimately refused to endorse the plan. When Fairfax County, Virginia, tried to eliminate testing for admissions to its elite Jefferson High School, families sued, claiming that the decision discriminated against Asian Americans and inflicted harm on high-achieving students.

This debate over admissions to high-status public high schools centers on questions regarding what constitutes fairness in the construction of unequal educational categories. While some might argue for the abolition of selective high schools, that argument is not at the center of this debate. Rather, the argument pits a status quo vision of educational fairness that rates students exclusively according to their performance on a measure of educational aptitude against a reformist vision that worries about biases in measures of aptitude and argues that educational category construction processes should also consider representation and diversity among elite categories. These different visions of fairness are evident in the signs held by parents both defending and protesting the lottery-based admissions system put into place for San Francisco's Lowell High School at a highly charged school board meeting. Both sides invoked equity in their signs: supporters of a test-based system held up signs reading MERIT = EQUITY, while lottery supporters held signs reading, LOTTERY HELPED EQUITY.

As the debates over elite high school admissions in New York, Boston, Chicago, San Francisco, and Fairfax County illustrate, sorting regimes emerge out of political compromises between stakeholders. These compromises are essential to the functioning of educational systems, since education's social power hinges on the broad legitimacy of the categories that it creates. Reformers—people who engage in political efforts to revise the educational processes that sort people into unequal educational categories—thus play an important role in maintaining systemic legitimacy. Many such reforms seek to implement systems aimed at ensuring that members of diverse social groups are represented in high-status educational categories.

Reforms seeking to ensure that the educational elite reflects the salient groups in society are not new. Elman's history of the Chinese imperial exam system, for example, details the system's adoption of a variety of quotas designed to reinforce the legitimacy of the examination system.[37] When, for example, the Mongolian Yuan dynasty came to power in 1271, leaders were initially inclined to eliminate the imperial exam system because these exams, which traditionally emphasized Han culture rather than Mongolian culture, had historically excluded Mongolians from civil service positions. In time, however, the Yuan dynasty came to appreciate the legitimacy that the imperial exams granted to their government. Ultimately, the Yuan kept the exams in order to maintain the impression of meritocratic assignment to the civil service. But Yuan leaders also created a quota to ensure disproportionate Mongolian representation. Although Mongolians and other non-Han Chinese were roughly 3 percent of the population, the examination system that they approved in 1313 ensured that they represented half of those who passed the exam.[38] A later quota from 1333 allocated the one hundred spots evenly between four (very unevenly sized) groups: the Mongols, the Semu, the Han, and southerners. In doing so, the Yuan dynasty was able to maintain power while also benefiting from the legitimacy of the existing system.

Approximately fifty years after overthrowing the Mongolian Yuan dynasty, the Ming dynasty also implemented quotas. The Ming quotas were not aimed at consolidating power, but at solving the "southern problem" and uniting the northern and southern regions of China.[39] In 1397—before the Ming quota was implemented—all of the fifty-two scholars who passed the test hailed from the south of China. Incredulous, the Ming emperor demanded that the chief examiner regrade the exams. In an argument that has been echoed by contemporary advocates of test-based admission systems, the chief examiner reaffirmed the fairness of the grading process and insisted that no changes were needed, proclaiming: "In our selection there has been no division between northerners and southerners. It is just that south of the great Yangtze there are many outstanding literati. Northern literati themselves just don't compare to southerners."[40] The emperor protested, "Can it be as you say that there are no outstanding literati north of the Yangtze?," before commanding the public execution and dismemberment of several exam readers.[41]

When the emperor scheduled a second examination almost immediately after the execution, sixty-one literati passed, all of whom were northerners. In time, however, as the memory of the 1397 exam reader purge faded, southerners once again began to dominate examinations. By 1420, over 80 percent of successful test takers came from the more prosperous south. The implementation of regional quotas in 1425 sought to solve this problem and ensure that the elites from both the north and the south had access to official positions. Under this quota, 40 percent of civil service spots were reserved for northerners.[42] It is also noteworthy, as Elman highlights, that although this system was effective in equalizing the number of those who passed, it did not equalize the highest scorers. As a consequence, even as the quota system evenly distributed the number of officials from different regions, it did not evenly distribute prestigious positions, which were typically allocated based on exam scores.

Ming leaders justified their quota system by noting that literary talent alone was not sufficient grounds for selecting officials, and that "practical and moral" considerations also had to be taken into account.[43] This appeal to moral character as a consideration in educational selection processes prefigured the changes to admissions policies at Harvard, Princeton, and Yale in the early twentieth century, discussed in chapter 6, when these institutions moved away from test-based systems in order to preserve the access of White Anglo-Saxon Protestants.[44]

In contrast to the Mongolian Yuan dynasty's use of quotas to maintain and legitimate Mongol privilege without disassembling the existing bureaucracy, and the Ming dynasty's implementation of regional quotas to counteract societal inequalities among elites, we also see efforts to use quotas for students from marginalized backgrounds in service of education's universalizing goal. This universalistic impulse was evident when, in 1762—roughly 250 years after the Ming dynasty instituted regional quotas—a provincial governor in the Qing dynasty sought to incorporate the P'eng minority by instituting quotas on a lower-level examination used to staff local government positions.[45] Similar policies were later proposed elsewhere in China to facilitate the inclusion of the Miao as well as the Hui (Muslims); records from this period also suggest the use of quotas that accounted for a family's historical social origin, though not surprisingly, how social origin was defined (ancestral status versus the status of the previous three generations) is somewhat ambiguous.[46] These examples also highlight the unintended power of the categories used in educational quotas: sons from military families would often take exams as commoners, and there were concerns that members of the Han majority would claim minority group membership in order to take advantage of the easier quotas. Research in the contemporary United States finds evidence of similar tactics; for example, the number of individuals who identified with minority groups changed in response to the introduction (and later the removal) of race-based affirmative action.[47]

Moving from Contesting Visions of Merit to Contesting Merit as an Organizing Principle

Schools sort students for a wide range of purposes. Some educational categories are primarily logistical—a school categorizes a child as a kindergartener not because this category reflects their merit, but because sorting children by age is simply more convenient for the purposes of instruction. But other categories are explicitly designed to reward success and convey status. These are the categories that structure the availability of opportunities and set students on paths that lead directly to stratified outcomes in our economically and socially unequal society. When a high school celebrates student achievement by naming an honor roll or asking the valedictorian to give a speech—bedecked in gold tassels and other ceremonial regalia—it associates grades with merit, communicating a hierarchy of merit to the whole community. Our educational system's tournament structure continuously reinforces and refines these merit-based distinctions as it repeatedly communicates to each of us messages about our worth and standing relative to one another.

The activities that we describe in this chapter contest the construction of educational merit. When students, families, or educators game the system, they short-circuit established rules to place themselves in categories that might not have been available to them had they followed the rules. When entrepreneurs, consumers, or other actors create unaccredited educational credentials or claim degrees that schools have not conferred upon them, they work around the educational system's monopoly on merit in an attempt to build alternative systems of social worth. And when activists or other stakeholders protest educational processes and build political power in order to change the rules governing educational categories, they import new notions of merit and value into existing educational categorization systems.

Because merit is the mechanism through which educational categories shape inequality in contemporary societies, each of these forms of contestation checks and redirects education's power to create lasting social inequalities. None of these forms of contestation, however, mount a fundamental challenge to merit.

We believe that the categorical inequality framework provides important tools for undertaking a more thorough critique of educational meritocracy and the inequality it creates. Viewing educational systems in terms of category creation helps make sense of how education can be an egalitarian institution that creates inequality. On the one hand, providing educational opportunities where they did not exist before—for instance, through the expansion of pre-K or higher education—produces more egalitarian outcomes. But on the other, profound inequalities persist and even grow in contemporary schooled societies, in which nearly all young people spend a dozen or more of their most formative years engaged in formal education. We should not attribute this persistent inequality solely to education—it seems likely that education is more egalitarian than the family, the criminal justice system, the labor market, and many other inegalitarian institutions in contemporary society. But schools clearly play a role in the maintenance of contemporary inequality.

In contemplating how education might be reimagined, it is important to recognize that any system of education that creates merit necessarily creates inequality, and that it does so by creating, defining, and reifying categories. Status, relative position, and merit are clearly deeply embedded in our contemporary educational system's DNA, where students scramble to distinguish themselves in order to gain admission to schools that in turn attempt to turn away as many students as possible in order to distinguish themselves based on their selectivity. But alternative educational systems are possible. We might imagine, for example, an educational system that is solely organized around the transactional transfer of skills (without the status signal). Such a system could reassert the absolute value of knowledge and also reconceptualize education as an absolute good that is valuable independent of how educated others are (in the same way that the nutritional value of kale does not depend on who else eats kale). We might imagine technology playing a central role in such a system. As our children like to say, "You can learn anything on the internet," and it does sometimes feel as though a future in which internet-enabled autodidacts can skip out on the educational system's elaborate status-signaling apparatus is possible.

But it's also worth noting that many innovative efforts to enable individuals to direct their own lifelong learning often end up re-creating the categories that are so central to contemporary educational inequality. Consider, for example, Google's Career Certificate program, in which learners pay a monthly fee to access learning modules focused on skills that are in high demand in the contemporary labor market. Although the program promises flexibility, independence, and individuality, it also clearly recognizes the importance of legitimacy, status, and hierarchy. Learners in the Google Career Certificate program log course time and complete assessments in order to gain access to the "Google certified" category. Google and the consortium of corporate partners that recognize Google Career Certificates attempt to position Google in a traditional educational status system by often equating these credentials with four-year degrees. As such, rather than creating an educational system built solely around skills acquisition and other absolute goods, the Google Career Certificate program inserts itself into the existing educational system and its merit-based category hierarchy.

When education creates merit, it creates and signifies value. Education not only creates a system of categories that sorts people into a hierarchy based on whether they have the skills and knowledge that are valued by society but also helps structure how knowledge is organized and which skills are understood as valuable. This is apparent in the cultural knowledge that is celebrated in curricula, the voices that are amplified or marginalized, the degree programs that are offered at different universities, and the status of different degrees. The role of educational categories in bestowing and signifying value is at the center of decisions to limit or expand access to education. Importantly, because the value imparted by education is merit-based, it has the limitations of merit. Although we all claim to believe that all humans have equal value, the logic of merit in contemporary society is relative: merit, rightly or wrongly, is defined as a zero-sum game, such that increasing the position of one individual in the meritocracy necessarily comes at the expense of others.

In highlighting how current definitions of merit are constructed and how merit is allocated, prior research underscores that the educational system does not provide all students with equal chances of success. We agree with critiques arguing that the educational system should allocate opportunities more equitably and define merit more broadly. However, we understand merit as the product of a set of political compromises; thus, as Marxists and other critical scholars have long argued, merit-based processes inevitably favor the powerful. Further, because merit is definitionally hierarchical, any system built on merit is necessarily hierarchical and definitionally unequal. We thus argue that merit-based attempts at creating an egalitarian system are, at some level, fundamentally misguided.

Understanding the discourse of merit as inherently problematic means acknowledging that building our educational system around merit forecloses the possibility of equality. And yet, references to merit and talent are ubiquitous in descriptions of universities' commitment to diversity, equity, and inclusion. Universities proclaim their mission of including talented individuals regardless of background in ways that categorically exclude those who do not have the abilities needed to be defined as meritorious or talented, such as those with profound cognitive disabilities. The University of California, for example, notes its "commitment to the full realization of its historic promise to recognize and nurture merit, talent, and achievement" and its "acute need to remove barriers to the recruitment, retention, and advancement of talented students, faculty, and staff from historically excluded populations who are currently underrepresented."[48] Although the university's rhetoric around diversity and inclusion specifically highlights individuals with disabilities as a group with an important and underrepresented perspective to offer the university, given the language of talent and merit, it is difficult to envision the university community embracing an initiative to hire professors with certain cognitive disabilities. The university, even in its attempt to be broadly inclusive, definitionally excludes individuals who are not considered talented in the ways valued in this setting, because the benefits to the university community offered by the greater inclusion of individuals with some cognitive disabilities is inconsistent with its understanding of merit.

As this example makes clear, when we celebrate merit or participate in a meritocracy, we perpetuate an ableist system. We cannot have a meritocracy without differentiating and differentially rewarding individuals based on their abilities. Put simply, any educational system that creates merit is a system that traffics in ableism.

The deep link between ableism and merit is particularly evident in the creation of categories for those deemed ineducable. Christine Sleeter describes the American anxiety in the wake of the Soviet Sputnik launch that reshaped the nations' educational infrastructure. Contrasting American high schools ("relaxed and enlivened with banter") and the Soviet educational system (in which "laggards are forced out [of school] by periodic examinations and shunted to less demanding trade schools and apprenticeships"), Americans remade their schools for the Cold War context.[49] The resulting focus on academic rigor helped equate academic success with merit in

American culture. But it also created the problem of how to think about students who struggled with this new, more academically focused curriculum. Schools often pathologized academic failure, attributing failure to inadequacies in homes and neighborhoods, particularly those of poor White students and students of color.[50] But pathologizing the failure of White, middle-class students who struggled academically was untenable, so this context also produced the concept and category of "learning disability." It is no coincidence that at the very moment when American schools came under fire for a perceived failure to produce pathbreaking scientists, they also created new categories of unmeritorious students.

In telling this history, Sleeter eloquently lays out a program for reorienting education away from categorical inequality:

> Schools need to focus much greater attention on how to teach children rather than on how to categorize those who do not learn well when offered "business-as-usual." But it is not enough to search for better ways to remediate those who have the greatest difficulty achieving standards for school success as long as society still expects schools to produce "products" with certain kinds of skills developed to certain levels of competence, and to rank-order those "products" based on their achievement of those skills. Those who come out on the bottom will still be destined for the lowest paying jobs or the reserve labor force and will still experience the pain of failure when compared to their peers. And members of advantaged social groups will still advocate treating their failing children in ways that maintain their advantaged status as much as possible. We need to shift our perspective from the failings of individuals or the inefficiencies of schools to the social context of schooling. Rather than attempting to remake children to fit social needs, we must first give greater consideration to the possibility that society's expectations for children and society's reward structure for their performance may need remaking.[51]

Broader social change is needed if Sleeter's appealing educational vision is ever to be realized. Reaching far beyond education, the notion of merit pervades contemporary American social and economic life. As Victor Tan Chen documents in his study of life in the abandoned factory towns of the Upper Midwest, this understanding of merit also pervades our current social safety net, and policy responses to unemployment from both liberals and conservatives hinge on identifying and supporting the "deserving" poor.[52] Like merit, the notion of the deserving poor is predicated on the exclusion of the undeserving poor, and these categories rest on the understanding that some people have more intrinsic value than others.

In contrast to merit-oriented systems, Chen argues for what he refers to as a grace-based system. Such a system would recognize the fundamental worth of each person rather than tying their worth to their abilities. This principle has radical implications. It would likely lead to a deepening of democracy and a more serious commitment to the idea that all people should count equally and have the right to self-determination. It might also lead to a rejection of the capitalist logic that people should be differentially rewarded for their contributions to the market.

Educational merit in the contemporary context is deeply implicated in this capitalistic logic, as the goal of a meritocracy is to distinguish people with more and less merit so as to reward them accordingly. Fundamentally, the concept of merit implies differentiation. Like citizenship and other categorical groupings defined by their boundaries and by who they exclude, the concept of merit implies that some people are more meritorious than others. Since merit implies hierarchical relationships, not everyone can have equal merit; if they did, the concept of merit would cease to be useful. The central problem with a meritocracy, then, is that it stems from an understanding of humans as hierarchically differentiated. At some fundamental level, if equality is a desired outcome, then building an educational system around the rhetoric of merit is inherently problematic, regardless of how broadly merit is defined or how equitably opportunities to attain merit are distributed.

PART IV
SORTING TOWARD A BETTER FUTURE

This book makes two fundamental observations about schools and inequality. The first is that education plays a central role in creating, maintaining, and reproducing inequalities in the contemporary world by constructing, enforcing, and perpetuating social and organizational categories. The second is that education—at least as institutionalized in contemporary society—is motivated by an egalitarian ethos.

The concept of legitimacy helps to explain how both sides of this paradox can be simultaneously true.[1] Education's egalitarian ethos enables hierarchical categorical projects because education's egalitarian commitment powers its institutional legitimacy. Put in plainer language: schools have the power to sort people into unequal categories because people generally believe that schools are committed to providing equal opportunities for all. This is why the movements for social inclusion we described in part I so often succeed when they place educational access demands at the center of their platform, why the educators we described in part II kept coming back to sticky questions of fairness as they debated and designed middle school math trajectories, and why the educationally advantaged favor the language of meritocracy to justify their privileged place in society, as we discussed in part III.

The thing about legitimacy, however, is that it hinges on appearances rather than reality.[2] As long as schools can convince the stakeholders that their practices and goals are consistent with education's egalitarian ideals, they can maintain legitimacy even in the face of stratified outcomes. And indeed, as we pointed out in part III, some aspects of education's institutional legitimacy routinely cut against these egalitarian goals. Every society carries a set of expectations regarding the composition of its elites, and in order for educational systems to maintain legitimacy, they must produce elites who match these expectations. In patriarchal societies, those expectations lead educational systems to ignore women's capacities and to elevate men to the most powerful and highest-status educational categories. Similarly, educational systems in White supremacist societies pursue legitimacy by stacking the deck against people of color. Educational organizations continuously navigate these competing legitimacy demands to maintain the appearance of fairness and convince those who lose that they had a shot and those who win that they earned it.

But even if the appearance of fairness satisfies the demands of legitimacy, we feel driven from a normative perspective to find ways to reorganize educational practices to better align with our understandings of social justice and equity. In part IV, we lay out some ideas about what a more equitable educational system might look like and how educators, educational leaders, policymakers, scholars, students, families, and others might use insights from categorical inequality theory to pursue more just educational outcomes. By analyzing how our actions contribute to the construction of educational categories and adjusting our actions accordingly, each of us has the power to reshape our social world, even if only in small, local ways. Indeed, we believe that educators and students around the world do exactly this on a daily basis. When educational stakeholders commit to careful reflection and courageous action in the pursuit of educational equity, educational organizations can continuously adapt to changing social imperatives and build categories that more closely reflect ideals of justice and equity.

BALANCING CATEGORICAL LOGICS 8

To build more equitable educational categorization processes, we need a framework to evaluate existing educational practices and imagine more equitable alternatives.

This is a tall order, in part because our society holds several divergent visions for education at the same time, often without recognizing their mutual incompatibility. Some people prioritize a vision of education as a garden in which we attend to each individual flower so that they can bloom and achieve their unique beauty. Others advance a view of education as a giant communal campfire around which children from all walks of life come together and learn to live together in peace and harmony. Still others prize a vision of education as a grand sorting machine that slots students into the roles in which they can optimally contribute to society's functioning. Questions about which of these utopian visions are appropriate for education to pursue are debated regularly in both the larger civic sphere and in local conversations about what educational categories to create and how to categorize students. But importantly, each of these visions sees education as an essential tool that allows people to live good lives and universal education as an essential component of a just and equitable society.

With gratitude to David Labaree, who memorably described educational debates in the early American republic and beyond as an effort to balance the goals of individual mobility, democratic citizenship, and social efficiency, we suggest that contemporary educational debates circle around three different categorical logics.[1] Each of these logics has a different understanding of the goal of education and proceeds from a distinct premise about what it means to live a good life. As such, each has a distinct idea about the school's primary social function. Each logic therefore leads educational organizations to approach the construction of educational categories differently, suggests different criteria for judging categories and the inequalities that they produce, and envisions a different archetype for individuals in contemporary society. In table 8.1, we lay out these three categorical logics and describe some of their key distinguishing characteristics.

The first categorical logic summarized in table 8.1 aims to facilitate each student's *self-actualization*. This logic is deeply individualistic and humanistic. It starts from an awareness of each person's value and positions the fundamental function of schools as cultivating each individual's unique capacities. The great jazz pianist Thelonious Monk was not thinking about education when he said, "The genius is the one most like himself," but the sentiment resonates deeply with this logic.[2] Educators in this model see their job as helping each student find their special genius and then giving each student the freedom and resources they need to feed that genius. This logic takes it as a matter of faith that the most fully self-actualized people are the people who contribute the most to our collective well-being, and that in an ideal world all people are the fully self-actualized protagonists of their own lives. As such, an educational system oriented around this logic would create highly differentiated and individualized categorical systems. Taken to its extreme, the self-actualization logic might lead educators to create a system in which there are as many educational categories as people in the hope of creating educational organizations in which each individual learner has access to their own personally optimal learning opportunities.

Contrast this logic with a vision of schools oriented around *solidarity*. According to this logic, education socializes students to function as active and engaged citizens in their communities. This communitarian educational logic proceeds from the premise that we are fundamentally social creatures and that engagement with a social collective brings each of us joy and strength. This logic seeks to bond students to one another and to the broader society, helping them come to share a common identity and training them in the behavioral norms and dispositions that enable collective life. When pursuing solidarity, schools orient instruction around overarching categories—such as

Table 8.1 *The Logics of Education*

Goal	*Premise*	*Function*	*Categorization Ethos*	*Conceptualization of Justice*	*Archetype*
Self-actualization	Each person has value	Schools cultivate	Categorical pluralism	Definitions rather than ends (each person has the power to define what is good)	Protagonist
Solidarity	Each person belongs	Schools bond	Categorical universalism	Democratic (formal equality)	Citizen
Efficiency	Each person is useful	Schools allocate	Technocratic matchmaking	Capitalistic (reaping what one has sown; responsibility)	Worker

Source: Authors.

national identity—rather than smaller instructional categories. In contrast to an individualistic understanding of human dignity, individuals are defined primarily in relationship to the group.

Finally, a third categorical logic focuses on *efficiency* in sorting students into the roles in which they can optimally contribute to society. This logic proceeds from the premise that each person has utility and that the school's function is to allocate students to the positions where they can be most useful. An efficiency logic understands students primarily as future workers. In our capitalist context, schools often assume that they are preparing students for paid labor, though efficiency logics can also lead schools to prepare youth for caretaking and other unpaid positions. From the efficiency logic's perspective, the most troubling forms of educational inequalities are the biases that lead schools to "waste potential" by overlooking youth aptitudes and failing to sort young people into positions where they can contribute.

A Case for Balancing Logics

Each of these categorical logics is important. We want to live in a society where children develop the rights, duties, and mutual respect of citizenship; transition from schooling into positions that enable them to contribute to society; and grow and thrive as wonderfully unique individuals. And every day, schools across the country engage in the work of socializing students for citizenship, preparing students for their roles in adult society, and identifying and cultivating students' unique capacities.

That said, we acknowledge the fundamental tension among these three categorical logics and the educational goals they pursue. In his history of the early-nineteenth-century value conflicts that helped to cast the mold for the U.S. educational system, Labaree situates the effort to strike compromises among disparate and conflicting goals as a key source of educational dysfunction. "The history of American education," Labaree writes, "has been one of ambivalent goals and muddled outcomes."[3]

Nevertheless, we argue that educational systems in contemporary society must achieve a balance among competing categorical logics because the risks of ignoring any one of these three logics are profound.

Indeed, we view education's responsibility to simultaneously uphold these three educational logics (and the premises, promises, and categorical ethos associated with each) as a source of education's power, stability, and legitimacy as a social institution.

Balancing these three divergent and mutually incompatible logics thus lies at the heart of both education's remarkable transformational promise and its often dystopian reality. Each logic implies a distinct way of thinking about how education should be organized and the sorts of educational categories that schools should create. We believe that particularly toxic forms of categorical inequality are born when we build educational institutions that do not appropriately balance these three logics.

The color-coded ID card program that we described at the beginning of the book is emblematic of this challenge. Principal Sitwell was frustrated by an educational system that judged schools according to an efficiency-oriented logic based on test scores, while buffering students from this logic and allowing them to pursue other meaningful identities (such as athletics or drama) and maintain a sense of belonging in the school. Sitwell thus created new categories to realign the social pressures at the school and create an ecosystem that resolved the contradiction between these logics. From Sitwell's position in the heart of a bureaucracy that rewarded administrators and teachers for test scores, the fact that test scores mattered was a given. The challenge was finding a way to organize school social life to satisfy this efficiency logic. Sitwell's ID card program addressed this challenge by yoking student identities and sense of belonging to the school accountability policy's testing and ranking systems.

Sitwell's color-coded ID card program was controversial, and district administrators discontinued it after two years. We argue that it was controversial in part because it prioritized efficiency at the expense of solidarity and self-actualization. Students, parents, and journalistic accounts did not contend that the program was ineffective at raising achievement; indeed, our analyses indicate that the program worked as intended in that regard. Rather, criticisms of the program focused on the divisions that it created (the costs to solidarity) and the ways in which it discouraged students (the costs to self-actualization).

The Consequences of Failing to Balance Divergent Categorical Logics

Given the importance of each of education's aims and the specific values, interests, and needs at play in any given educational setting, we do not believe that it's possible or even desirable to formulate a "correct" balance between these three logics. But we do believe that it's possible to see when school systems fail to establish a balance between self-actualization, solidarity, and efficiency logics. In this section, we discuss instances of this sort of educational imbalance, offering them as cautionary tales and highlighting what happens when educational systems overemphasize a particular logic at the expense of others. Our hope is that these accounts will help readers to identify when one educational logic is overwhelming others, to think about ways to recalibrate educational category construction processes to strike a better balance, and to build guardrails to protect against future educational imbalances.

When self-actualization overwhelms other logics. In early 2021, the Maria Montessori Academy of North Ogden, Utah, a public charter school, allowed families to have their children opt out of Black History Month activities. In response to the outcry about the school's initial approval and eventual revocation of this policy, the school's director, Micah Hirokawa, said, "It's been a tough road as we work to honor and follow each child's and each adult's personal journey."[4] This statement makes it clear that the school initially allowed parents' goals of self-actualization for their children to override the solidarity-oriented intent of the Black History Month activities. What's more, when such an exception is granted to families in a 70 percent White school with only three Black students, it becomes clear how easily the language of self-actualization can be harnessed by the powerful to avoid explicit attempts at solidarity with marginalized students and to ignore collective histories in ways that might contribute to the further marginalization and harm of others.[5]

One of the problems revealed by this example is that the self-actualization of some often comes at the expense of others, and privileged students often hoard opportunities to self-actualize at the expense of other students.[6] But an overemphasis on self-actualization can also affect solidarity (as at the Maria Montessori Academy) and efficiency (as occurs when self-actualization motivates cheating). As we discussed in chapter 7, many students resort to cheating in school because they do not agree with their erstwhile categorization. That is, they prioritize their self-actualization over the efficiency of the system. This trade-off was particularly salient in the Operation Varsity Blues scandal. In orchestrating the admission of students into elite colleges on behalf of parents, Rick Singer explicitly sold the plan to parents on the grounds that the students themselves would not know that their parents had paid somebody to take the test for them; the students would feel great about the scores they received and about being able to get into the schools they hoped to attend.[7] And although Singer and the parents involved in this scheme were prosecuted as criminals, it is legal for parents to make generous donations to elite universities that bolster their children's chances of being admitted. Indeed, Harvard maintains lists of applicants who are children of current and prospective donors for preferential admission, and universities routinely give preference to legacy applicants. In each of these examples, efficiency and arguably solidarity are sacrificed for the self-actualization of a few.

When efficiency overwhelms other logics. Ashley wanted to be a marine biologist. With images of pelicans and dolphins covered in oil slicks after the 2010 BP Deepwater Horizon spill firmly in her mind, Ashley decided that this was work that mattered. Plus, she had heard from a counselor that "marine biologists make mad money"—a prospect that appealed to her practical side.

But Ashley's vision of her future, infused with elements of self-actualization and solidarity logics, faced a major hurdle: because Ashley's family needed the financial support, she had long worked as many hours as she could. As a result, she graduated from high school with a years-long work history that started with independently managing a hot dog stand at age eleven and included a series of dead-end minimum-wage jobs. But all that time spent on paid work had major consequences for her high school grades; she finished high school with a GPA well below the minimum for enrolling in a state university and majoring in biology. As a high school senior, Ashley resolved not to follow her mother, a nurse's aide, into the health professions—"I'm not cleaning nobody's ass, Ima tell you that much."[8] But after struggling to juggle community college and minimum-wage work for a couple of years, Ashley took a job working with her mom at a retirement home for $12.50 an hour.

We see Ashley's story as an all-too-common example of our educational system's overdependence on an efficiency logic. Throughout her high school years, educators repeatedly told Ashley that education was the path to a career, a career was the path to dignity, and the only thing that could hold her back was laziness. So when career doors opened and educational doors closed, Ashley did exactly what the efficiency logic dictated: she chose the career. "Why finish college? To make money, right? So then why give up money in the first place 'cause I don't even know what job I will get [after graduating from college]."[9]

Ashley's story follows a pattern that has been repeatedly demonstrated in the sociology of education: an educational system focused on preparing students for the labor market manages to convince working-class kids that they belong in working-class jobs.[10] Education's overemphasis on an efficiency logic is partly to blame because it is often easy to sort students into positions that reflect their family resources, regardless of their own goals, needs, and capacities.

In much the same way that the self-actualization of some individuals can come at the expense of the self-actualization of others, focusing too much on certain aspects of efficiency can lead to inefficiencies when schools fail to recognize students' potential. The story of the famed choreographer Gillian Lynne also illustrates this point. Unable to focus or sit still, young Gillian (aka "Wiggle Bottom") struggled in elementary school and was eventually sent to a doctor to be tested for learning disabilities. When the doctor left the office with the radio on, Gillian started to do what she most loved to do: dance. Categorizing Gillian as a dancer rather than as a child with learning disabilities, the doctor suggested that Gillian attend a dance school. Once she was surrounded by others who "needed to move to think," Gillian thrived. Why did it take a doctor's intervention to recognize Gillian's gifts and get her to a learning environment that better met her needs? An important part of the answer is a narrowly focused efficiency logic.

When solidarity overwhelms other logics. An overemphasis on solidarity can become problematic both when it heightens boundaries at the expense of those who are defined as nonmembers and when it comes at the expense of those who are defined as members. Consider, for example, state laws that prohibit undocumented immigrants from receiving in-state tuition at public universities. In raising the salience of the boundary separating high school graduates whose parents are U.S. citizens or documented immigrants from those graduates who are undocumented, these policies reaffirm a sense of belonging among the documented at the expense of educational opportunities for the undocumented. But these policies may have much broader consequences from an efficiency perspective. By erecting educational barriers around a group of young people, these policies may lead talented young people to leave the state or discourage them from pursuing further education. If so, these exclusionary polices may hurt the economic prospects even of young people who received in-person tuition under the policy.

Solidarity-building practices do not need to be exclusionary to have profound costs for educational efficiency. To see an example, just turn on your television on a fall Saturday afternoon in the United States and flip through the channels until you find a college football game. You'll see thousands of students and alumni in the stands, dressed in school colors, singing a cherished school fight song, and feeling the "collective effervescence" of communal identification. The sense of solidarity that educational organizations forge on these Saturday afternoons is powerful, and it has consequences for all aspects of campus life from recruitment to donations from alumni. But college football also has profound consequences for educational efficiency and self-actualization. In nearly every play in every game, some of the twenty-two college students on the field violently collide, regularly resulting in concussions that have been linked to permanent brain damage. These collisions clearly do not build human capital, and recurring academic scandals regarding athletes point to the compromises that many campuses make in pursuit of athletic success.

Diagnosing our Current State

While it is safe to say that the three of us are not fans of college football, we do believe that the contemporary educational system in the United States overemphasizes efficiency and self-actualization at the expense of solidarity.[11] We attribute this overemphasis both to the profound role that the family plays in the U.S. education system and to a set of organizational practices that are deeply embedded in contemporary schools.

In the contemporary American educational system—particularly at the K-12 level, but also to some extent in higher education—families are understood to be governed by a self-actualization logic. Parents spend considerable time and energy getting to know their children's particular interests and capacities, and they invest resources in cultivating these interests. The contemporary musical prodigy can typically thank a parent who bought a violin, made time to oversee daily practice sessions, paid for private lessons, and drove to rehearsals, tryouts, and recitals. Likewise, the contemporary soccer star often owes some measure of their success to a parent who paid soccer club fees and drove to tryouts, soccer skills workshops, and games.

The school, meanwhile, largely plays a sorting function in contemporary societies, testing students regularly and then sorting them into hierarchically ranked learning environments in the name of educational efficiency. This elaborate educational tournament structure aims to match people to social positions with maximal efficiency. In accordance with the logic of efficiency, schools try to teach students the skills that most directly align with social needs and provide appropriate signals to the labor market in order to produce economically desirable matches between workers and jobs.

This structure has at least two dire consequences for contemporary social life. First, in a society marked by profound economic inequality, families differ dramatically in the resources that they can dedicate to securing their children's self-actualization. As a result, young people who grow up in relatively affluent families often have far more opportunities for self-actualization than children who grow up in poorer families. This difference is apparent in research documenting inequalities in the time and resources that families dedicate to enrichment activities for their children.[12] And the Operation Varsity Blues story underscores the lengths to which affluent parents will go in order to ensure the self-actualization of their children. Perhaps the most heartbreaking aspect of this widely publicized scandal was how hard these parents tried to protect their children from the knowledge that their seats in college had been bought rather than earned, an effort that reflected an understanding that belief in one's merit is a crucial component of the journey toward self-actualization.

Second, the way education in the contemporary United States is organized profoundly neglects solidarity. In an educational system characterized by individualization at the family level and hierarchical categorization at the organizational level, education's role in constructing and maintaining our larger shared identities has largely been left to wither. The result is an education system that is organized around the efficient development and delivery of private goods but that largely neglects public goods. Compounding this problem is that, outside of education, there simply is no other institution with influence in the contemporary United States that is focused on reinforcing our sense of collective belonging and mutual dependence.

This is not to say, of course, that there are no educational stakeholders who think about solidarity as an educational imperative. As we discussed in part I, educators and commentators on education regularly engage in fierce debates about the nature of civic education. Furthermore, contemporary discussions about the socioemotional learning of youth have recently attuned many educators to the importance of cultivating a sense among youth that they belong at school and are a valued part of school communities. But as our educational system is currently organized, efforts to build solidarity lack strong institutional bases. As a result, educational efforts that cultivate civic virtues and a sense of belonging often sit at the educational system's periphery. Students may build school spirit at football games or pep rallies, and they may connect to their communities more broadly via the occasional service-learning opportunity. But in a deeply individualistic society, solidarity is simply not central to the educational enterprise.

Where Do We Go from Here?

We believe that our current educational system's imbalance is a profound problem. Building on a sociological tradition documenting the harms of social alienation and the power of belonging, we view solidarity as a valuable good in and of itself.[13] Further, we believe that solidarity is essential for addressing the many challenges facing our planet at this moment. As the Covid-19 pandemic burned its way around the world, it clearly demonstrated our profound interconnectedness. Even as the pandemic sent many to socially distanced private spaces, it reminded us of how deeply we need community and social connection. Further, the effort to contain the pandemic serves as an object lesson in how important trust, generosity, and collective care are to our very survival. Although no society on earth has avoided the pandemic's impact, in the United States, institutional distrust and an unwillingness or inability to commit to the common good has caused hundreds of thousands of eminently preventable deaths.

As we face down global crises associated with climate change, totalitarianism, and institutional failure, the pandemic should serve as a warning. A society that neglects solidarity does so at its peril.

To state the obvious, education did not create these global crises. In fact, many educators have worked diligently to foster the bonding role of contemporary schools and build educational institutions that reinforce social solidarity, trust, and civic virtues. But solidarity has become an increasingly marginal concern in contemporary educational practice at the same time as the rest of our society's discourse has become increasingly individualistic and competitive. As we argue elsewhere in the book, schools, like other organizations, construct and maintain categories in ways that they think will promote institutional legitimacy.

However, education—and educational categories—will play a crucial role in any plausible strategy to build the social solidarity, institutional trust, and civic virtues that we need to band together and collectively address humanity's contemporary crises. Educational categories play a crucial role in how status, power, and resources are allocated across our society. Furthermore, these categories are continually constructed and reconstructed via practices enacted day after day in classrooms and other educational environments. As a result, careful, courageous, and self-reflexive educational practice has the potential to change the world.

We hope that our book has helped to convince you that an understanding of categorical inequality is a crucial tool in this self-reflexive educational practice. When those of us who work and learn in school settings learn to see the categories that we are helping to enact and begin to imagine the ways we could enact different categories, we gain the power to imagine new worlds and to chart paths from our world to those alternative futures.

This may feel like a grand promise for a teacher who is just thinking about how to teach reading to a bunch of second-graders, or how to allocate students among eighth-grade math courses, and indeed it is. But even the little, seemingly technical decisions that educators make in the course of the school day contribute to balancing education's categorical logics. Second-grade teachers who are interested in building solidarity even as they build students' reading skills might resist the urge to sort students into reading groups based on stratified reading levels. Instead, they might make the time to read carefully selected books to their entire class before shuffling students into rotating, heterogeneous groups to work on exercises that put their budding literacy skills to work on making strong interpersonal connections. Similarly, middle school math teachers might develop instructional systems that flexibly group students, providing environments for students to work together in diverse groups as well as opportunities for students to get instruction targeted at their demonstrated skills. These instructional innovations may sometimes make it harder for teachers to cover the material in an orderly fashion, and they may particularly slow the academic progress of high-flying students. But those compromises are not a given, and even if they occur, the benefits of such innovations for classroom community may be worth the costs.

When educators develop a critical sense of how educational practices build the categories that in turn forge persistent inequalities, and when they pair that critical sense with the imagination and agency to pursue alternative educational practices, they open up new social possibilities. Furthermore, we believe that bringing a categorical inequality lens to these day-to-day educational practices deepens our understanding of the origins and operations of other, bigger, deeper social inequalities. Thinking hard about even the most basic educational categorical process—say, elementary school classroom assignments—forces a confrontation with racial, gender, and class inequalities; questions about what we mean by "merit" or "ability" or "skills" or "capacity"; and deep dilemmas about the nature of justice. We believe that a categorical inequality perspective provides a framework for engaging with these big questions of day-to-day educational life. And we believe that engagement with these day-to-day questions builds the habits of mind and discursive practices that we need to drive fundamental social change.

A Cautionary Word

In the next chapter, we provide some thoughts about how we might bring a categorical inequality perspective to bear on educational policy and practice in order to build more equitable schools. These policy recommendations are based on the optimistic belief that a better world is possible. Even as we aim to cultivate that optimism, we also want to highlight reasons for caution. The scholarship that we have pulled together in writing this book speaks to both education's liberatory potential and to the political and technical challenges standing between us and that potential. The story of educational categories is a story full of opportunity hoarding, stigmatization, and studied indifference to the needs of the disenfranchised. Education is an institution, and its constituents enact its rules, norms, and rituals with an eye to legitimacy. The imperatives of institutional legitimacy typically favor the status quo, stifling educational change and prioritizing entrenched power.

Educational transformation requires an ability to view our schools and the categories they create, enact, and reproduce honestly, without nostalgia or animus. It requires identifying inequitable category-creation processes, imagining new and better educational practices, and implementing them with care. It also requires a willingness to experiment. Because institutional change is often iterative, we need to be prepared to learn from failures and to celebrate and build on small victories. Education has a weakness for silver bullet fixes, and the field is crowded with policies and practices that promise overnight improvements. We want to be clear: a categorical inequality perspective is no silver bullet. Rather, it is a conceptual tool kit that we hope can inform an intergenerational process of institutional change. From where we currently stand, it's unclear how we can create categories without creating inequality, or how we can create a world without categories (or even if such a world is desirable), so it is hard to know what our ideal educational system would look like. But it is relatively clear how we can make slightly better categories. This suggests that the completion of our generation's work will be defined not by the absence of further issues to resolve, but rather by passing the work of reimagining educational categories on to the next generation. Our job is thus not to find a silver bullet that will fix schools, but rather to persistently and incrementally create a school system that can give our students the resolve, understanding, and vision to engage with education in the pursuit of a more equitable society.

9 MAKING EQUITABLE SCHOOLS

It is possible to read this book as a bestiary of inequality-producing educational categories. In the preceding chapters, we have recounted a number of outrageous and stunningly misguided educational practices that have contributed to the construction and maintenance of social inequality by creating and maintaining educational categories.

We have told you about schools that sort students into castes based on their test scores, handing out goodies to high-flying "platinum-card" students and indignities to low-achieving "white-card" students. We have told you about towns that simply shut down their schools rather than allow Black students to learn alongside their White peers. We have told you about schools that echo Jim Crow segregation by creating separate and unequal lunch lines and school administrators who humiliate students who cannot afford to pay for their lunch. We have told you about classrooms in migrant detention camps, where students are forced to pledge allegiance to a country that separates them from their families. And at the other end of the spectrum, we have highlighted the matchmakers who work to guarantee kids access to the world's most illustrious and high-status educational organizations, regardless of their qualifications—just as long as their families are willing to pay.

In telling these stories, we have argued that every categorical boundary creates winners and losers. Our descriptions of educational categories often emphasize the costs that students and communities must pay when they fall on the losing side of categorical boundaries. By discussing the ways that complicity in systems of categorical inequality warps the sensibilities of and causes profound alienation among those at the top of the hierarchy, we have labored to make it clear that categorical inequalities also exact substantial costs from their ostensible winners.

Educational Categories Are Better Than the Alternatives

In light of these arguments, we are tempted to argue for the complete abolition of educational categories, and perhaps of educational institutions more broadly. On reflection, however, we are not convinced that the abolition of educational categories is possible or desirable. We see category construction—and thus categorical inequality—as a defining feature of human civilization.

Although it is difficult to imagine a society without categories, it is much easier to imagine a society without the institution of mass education. Schools are by no means the only institutions capable of constructing social categories; imbuing those categories with value and meaning; attributing varying degrees of merit to people based on the categories in which they are situated; and using those categories to produce, reproduce, and legitimate social inequalities. Even though schools and other institutions are key mechanisms of categorization in our society, various societies have relied on other institutions—families and extended kinship networks, workplaces and other economic organizations, religion, the state—to play this role. Before we lay out some ideas for improving education as an institution, let's first consider why it would be a mistake to allow other institutions to supplant education's central place in our society.

THE MARKET

Consider, for example, a society that gives employers more power over the construction of unequal categories, perhaps by reallocating some of the training that schools currently provide to on-the-job training. That's the sort of society that Byron Auguste, cofounder of the nonprofit Opportunity@Work, would like to see. Auguste describes many white-collar employers' assumption that a bachelor's degree is a necessary qualification for entry-level positions as "dysfunctional." Rather than relying on credentials and the assessments of college professors, Auguste is working with employers to develop alternative pathways to these middle-class positions—for example, by developing tests to capture candidates' abilities in the particular skills required by their jobs or by creating rubrics to review portfolios of job candidates' work.[1] The economist Bryan Caplan argues in his provocative book *The Case against Education* that such a system would be more efficient than our current system, in which educationally defined merit—a construct that is at best loosely connected to labor market requirements—plays an important role in sorting young adults into jobs. Caplan argues that our contemporary education system dedicates inordinate time and energy to teaching content that neither increases students' workforce productivity nor cultivates their unique talents. "When learning is neither useful nor inspirational," he asks, "how can we call it anything but wasteful?"[2]

We are unwilling to accept Caplan's premise that mass education fails to boost human productivity and flourishing. But more foundationally, we note that Caplan's critique of education entirely neglects the third goal of education: building social solidarity. And neglecting this educational goal, we fear, is the most profound social risk associated with efforts to grant employers some of the social roles that we currently grant to educational organizations. Education's role in the labor market not only creates a market for educational merit but also legitimizes the categorical inequality created by education as necessary for economic reasons. Unlinking educational merit from the labor market would thus be likely to substantially weaken the relationship between educational categories and durable economic inequalities. But at the same time, we fear that such a move would further atomize our society by replacing what is left of education's egalitarian ethos and community-building function with a harsh market discipline. Discriminatory practices in the labor market drive persistent workplace inequalities along gender, racial, ethnic, disability, and religious lines. What's more, while egalitarianism sits at the conflicted heart of contemporary educational ideologies, labor markets typically have little place for consideration of questions of equity. As such, unless efforts to build apprenticeship systems and give employers a larger role in providing workforce development and training coincided with a rise in the power of organized labor, we are skeptical about the prospect of creating more egalitarian outcomes by increasing the centrality of the labor market at the expense of education.

TECHNOLOGY

As internet technologies and social media platforms have claimed a larger and larger role in our lives, some have suggested that these technologies might supersede education's social role. For example, Google's Career Certificate program, which we discussed in chapter 6, claims to provide training that is more convenient, efficient, affordable, and closely tied to occupational success than traditional higher education. Other Silicon Valley players claim to outperform schools in other regards. If the Google Career Certificate program aims to replace direct classroom instruction, LinkedIn aims to provide the venue for professional networking that happens as students find their seats before class or grab a coffee elsewhere. Instagram positions itself as a vehicle for self-actualization, inviting people to develop an artistic vision and document their aesthetic development while also possibly monetizing their lifestyle and mundane daily events. Facebook and TikTok, meanwhile, promise a sense of connectedness and solidarity that can also help to build professional success through personal network connections and the chance to market undiscovered talent.

We don't deny technology's affordances in each of these areas. We have certainly learned valuable skills from online tutorials and have regularly partaken in the dopamine rushes and sense of community that social media provides. But we are skeptical about Big Tech's ability to replace education in these key areas. As we write these words, Facebook—once an almost untouchable Silicon Valley titan—is looking more and more like just another problematic company fighting for its hold on the marketplace. Furthermore, as scholarship on algorithmic biases makes clear, the logics that drive Big Tech often bake inequalities into technological systems, making technology a powerful force for the reproduction—rather than the disruption—of our deeply unequal status quo.[3]

THE FAMILY

The family is another institution that could take on many of the social roles that the school plays in contemporary society. Indeed, as the sociologist James Coleman points out, in many times and places, industrialization and mass education dramatically changed the political economy of childhood in much of the world in a way that circumscribed the influence of family and extended kin networks on youth development. In a world in which most economic activity happened in and around the home, children often effectively apprenticed in family workplaces. We can imagine a social reorganization that undoes some of the separation between adult work and child development that occurred over the course of the nineteenth and twentieth centuries. Indeed, the Covid-19 crisis forced many families to develop work, parenting, and schooling arrangements that in many ways paralleled preindustrial configurations.

Changes to the social order that increase the family's social salience may provide important correctives to some of the problems that we associate with a schooled society. Families typically build strong, loving collective identities that focus on the intrinsic value of each family member rather than on their instrumental value. However, family identities are often exclusive, and as a result, profound inequalities arise between families when some families hoard resources and opportunities. There is some evidence that, on net, the institution of education counteracts this tendency toward family-level opportunity hoarding.[4] Thus, we suspect that increasing the salience of family at the expense of education is likely to exacerbate rather than mitigate inequality.

RELIGION

Similarly, we might imagine religion and religious organizations supplanting the centrality of education and schools in maintaining social order. Religious beliefs and rituals often build strong ties among co-religionists, and religion, like the family, is an institution that is associated with high levels of in-group social solidarity. At its best, religion inculcates a deep respect and love for humanity. In chapter 7, we discussed Victor Tan Chen's notion of grace and its potential to contribute to a more equitable social world. Although grace is often conceptualized as having deeply Christian roots, we believe that a broad array of religious teachings and practices can provide individuals with ethical foundations and interpersonal dispositions toward social solidarity and belonging. We also believe that religion may provide helpful lessons for how to counterbalance the overwhelming power of efficiency and self-actualization logics in contemporary schooled societies. Consider, for example, the Norwegian Humanist Association and the secular, humanistic confirmation rituals that it has created as a rite of passage for young people. By providing a setting for ethical education, these services cultivate a vision of individuals as servants to a broader public, celebrating not their particular competencies but rather their commitment to the community. Such ceremonies position young people as cherished members of society with inherent value.

However, solidarity among co-religionists often has profound social costs. As illustrated by the history of sexual abuse scandals in the Catholic Church, religious identities often create social organizations that tolerate profoundly abusive behavior among the elect. Moreover, religious norms and social control often stigmatize and alienate lower-status religionists who cannot or do not comply with religious strictures. Consider, for example, the suffering experienced by many gay, lesbian, and gender-nonconforming youth who came of age in the American evangelical movement. Furthermore, religions often build deep boundaries that encourage strong internal identities as well as fierce antipathies across religious lines. As a result, religious societies are often corrupt, repressive, and fiercely opposed to one another.

Ten Guidelines for More Equitable Categories

Although each of these alternative institutions may have lessons for education, we are not convinced that any of them strike a more desirable balance between the goals of solidarity, self-actualization, and efficiency than schools do. Furthermore, as these institutions are less subject to public oversight, they have the potential to fail even more dramatically than we see schools fail. Thus, rather than abandoning education, we are inclined to focus our energies on reforming educational categorization systems to help build schools that more closely approximate education's utopian ambitions.

In the following discussion, we lay out ten guidelines that we hope can inform these reform efforts. These guidelines represent ideas about how to build more just and equitable schools. In laying them out, we seek to emphasize real-world examples of efforts to remake educational categories with an eye toward educational equity. These exemplars of real-world category creation processes are necessarily imperfect and are thus unlikely to be entirely satisfactory. Nonetheless, we hope that they can raise awareness of the possibilities for educational change and generate new ideas for building educational categories—and therefore educational systems—that better reflect our ideals of justice.

1. *Strike a balance between educational paradigms.* Every society has different educational priorities. As such, the balance between efficiency, solidarity, and self-actualization will likely differ across contexts. Nevertheless, we believe that self-actualization needs to be available to everybody. Efficiency requires responding to differences. And solidarity should be about wholeness rather than oneness.

In many contemporary American schools, self-actualization and efficiency are riding roughshod over collective, democratic identity. Given this, we think that contemporary schools need to cultivate educational rituals that emphasize shared identity and responsibility to a larger collective and create nonhierarchical, broadly shared communal categories. One policy that moves in this direction is the Community Eligibility Program (CEP) for school lunch, which allows schools to determine eligibility for school lunch at the school level instead of the individual level. As schools are often reluctant to sign up for CEP because it is not well funded, better funding of this program would help schools create more egalitarian and collective categories.

Curricular changes can also support an increased focus on solidarity. Schools should dedicate instructional time to the study of local cultures and community history, giving students the opportunity to celebrate their individual and collective identities. Professional training programs should not only focus on core content and procedural skills but also spend class time on related social issues. Medical school, for example, should teach doctors not only how vaccines work but also how to talk to people about vaccines and how to best communicate their collective benefits to society.

2. *Recognize that all categories and category allocation processes are political.* In this book, we have argued that schools create categories that are defined by both who (and what) they include and by who (and what) they exclude, and that these educational categories are not neutral. Sometimes educational categories contribute to making

society more egalitarian, but category boundaries are often redrawn to perpetuate privilege. Because categories have a strong tendency to reinforce existing privileges, school leaders and educators should reflect carefully on their use of categories in allocating educational resources and opportunities. Each sorting decision requires careful consideration of the impact on different students, and it is critical to interrogate and teach everyone in the educational community about the social and cultural context of existing categories and the power structures that created them. Many of the long-standing categorization processes we use today have deep roots in exclusionary political decisions. Even decision-making tools intended to level unequal playing fields can perpetuate preexisting inequities.

Some categories used by schools have overtly political roots. For example, decisions about the types of educational supports provided to students who speak a language other than English at home have been profoundly shaped and reshaped by broader political attitudes toward immigrants. Voters' overwhelming support for California's Proposition 227, which required "English-only" instruction for all students in 1998, was a direct result of anti-immigrant sentiment across the state. It categorized a certain class of students as "English learners," defining them not by the language(s) they could speak, but by the one they had not yet mastered. This relegation of other languages to second-class status in California schools was detrimental for many students and contradicted the extensive research that underscores the benefits of multilingualism and learning to read in a native language before doing so in a second language. For many students, this classification has had cascading impacts on the courses and school supports available to them for many years of their K-12 education, limiting their opportunities to learn advanced content as well as their ability to develop and maintain fluency in languages other than English. Although this law was recently overturned by voters, it continues to have consequences for bilingual instruction, illustrating the long-lasting exclusionary effects of politically rooted category systems.

The political origins of other educational categories may be less instantly recognizable. In fact, some are framed as mechanisms for leveling the playing field and providing opportunities to all. For example, many defend the fairness of high-stakes admissions exams like the SAT, arguing that anyone can get a perfect score, regardless of their background. But at the same time, as many others have highlighted, such assessments have roots in racist admissions policies and often reinforce existing inequities in educational access.[5] That said, the SAT is just one of the many aspects of the college admissions process that reinforce affluent students' advantages and, while problematic, might not be the most biased element in this process.[6]

3. Create inclusive processes for category construction and revision. People create and continuously re-create educational categories. They also give categories their meanings in ongoing negotiations that determine which categories matter and how. Opening these category creation processes to diverse voices is thus key to creating educational categories that equitably serve diverse interests. To be clear, these negotiations are rarely easy. Categories produce winners and losers; that's one of categorical inequality's central theoretical insights. The stakes can be high, and the tensions irresolvable. But when educational organizations give real voice to a wide range of stakeholders, they surface the tensions among educational goals and make space for open deliberations about local conceptions of educational justice.

So how can educators and educational leaders open up their deliberative processes and give educational stakeholders agency in sorting processes? First, they must recognize the distribution of power and status in order to identify, cultivate, and amplify previously marginalized voices. Second, educators and school leaders need to examine their own biases that might inadvertently lead them to construct categories that systematically exclude some or privilege some over others. Third, educators need to cultivate their own openness to criticism and the responsiveness of the educational systems in which they work. Inclusive deliberation requires a willingness to listen and a commitment to engage in continuous improvement processes based on stakeholder feedback.

When educators engage in these processes, they can make space for marginalized groups to articulate their needs and interests. This input can reveal the need for everything from broad systemic change to simple adjustments in how categories operate that can have substantial consequences for students. For example, many U.S. schools are deliberating over the demands for recognition and accommodation being made by transgender youth. Opening educational decision-making to this traditionally marginalized group has sensitized educators to transgender students' needs and driven changes like relabeling bathrooms to make it easier for students to take care of their most basic needs.[7]

4. Engage in the long, important process of redefining category meanings. The social meanings of categories can be changed, but it's hard work. Given the politics behind categories, those in power have a vested interest in maintaining the existing systems of privilege codified in them. Categories enable us to mentally justify privilege and also serve as organizational mechanisms for the reinforcement and reproduction of privilege. To confront privilege and construct more equitable educational systems, we must therefore confront educational categories. Indeed, any attempt to create a more equitable educational system is at its core a question of redefining our categories.

But exactly because we use categories to justify privilege and because categories underpin social systems, existing categories and their meanings are deeply entrenched in our thinking and organizations. Redefining categories thus requires extraordinary imagination, persistence, resources, and resolve. Category redefinition often requires generations of social movement building and mobilization.

An important goal in redefining categories is reducing the stigma associated with marginalized categories. One approach develops strategies targeted at the needs of marginalized groups in the service of helping all students attain a universal goal.[8] By placing groups that experience social neglect at the center of societal care, this approach seeks to communicate their value and better meet their needs.

One promising exemplar of category redefinition is the Oakland Unified School District's African American Male Achievement Program. This program attempts to rectify decades of inadequate support for African American male students by creating a series of courses and out-of-school community activities targeted at Black male students and taught by Black male teachers and community members. These learning opportunities focus on content from Black scholars and center the experiences of the students. This program explicitly rejects dominant, stigmatized conceptualizations of Black masculinity, replacing narratives of Black male failure with narratives of Black male excellence and thereby attaching new meanings to this marginalized category.[9] The program has had a transformative effect on Black male students' educational outcomes.[10] Further, the program's success has inspired the creation of similar programs focused on the needs of other historically marginalized groups, such as African American Female Excellence, Latino/a Student Achievement, and Asian Pacific Islander Student Achievement.[11]

5. *Redesign category assignment processes to change category meanings.* Although the meanings of educational categories are deeply embedded in culture and are therefore hard to change, we often treat questions about the structure and placement processes governing educational categories as merely technical considerations. Because they are often relatively flexible, these technical considerations can provide a powerful and underutilized lever for redefining categories.

Take, for example, the case of algebra instruction, the subject of much of the discussion in part II. Algebra has long acted as a crucial gatekeeper, since many secondary mathematics curricula treat an understanding of algebraic functions as a prerequisite for the study of geometry, trigonometry, calculus, and other advanced mathematics. As a result, the meaning of educational categories associated with algebra instruction in American schools has remained fairly stable since the 1950s at least. To be an "algebra student" is to be a student who is at the start of an academic secondary mathematics track.

But the structures of these educational categories have changed significantly over time and vary considerably across educational environments. It was once common for high school students with postsecondary ambitions to enroll in algebra courses as ninth-graders. With the rise of AP calculus course offerings, however, a growing number of students began taking algebra in the eighth, and even seventh, grades. This structural shift created new educational categorical inequalities, which ultimately led to an effort to enroll more students in early algebra courses. Although our research shows that educational inequalities persisted despite these shifts in the structure of educational categories around algebra, these efforts nonetheless fundamentally reshaped access to algebra and to more advanced mathematics.[12]

While the jury is out on algebra-for-all's effects on student learning and educational inequality, it highlights the malleability of educational categorical structures. These technical changes serve to redefine algebra's place in the hierarchy and the meaning of being categorized into algebra classes. Further, given arguments that learning algebra is a civil right and concerns over racial disparities in access to these courses, this work underscores the power of technical processes to redefine the relationship between racial categorizations and math course categorizations.

6. Lower the scope of educational categories. Education's outsized influence in contemporary societies has paradoxical consequences for social inequality. On the one hand, education's expansion has served to deeply entrench notions about universal human dignity and worth in contemporary discourse (if not contemporary practice.) On the other hand, as we discuss throughout this book, education produces, maintains, and legitimates inequality by creating winners and losers.

To dismantle this paradox, we believe that educational institutions must learn to cede power by creating what we call "low-scope" educational categories. In a system of low-scope educational categories, students may be sorted and re-sorted into different educational environments repeatedly over the course of a day, a school year, or an educational career. Low-scope sorting systems may sort students randomly into their core courses, by interest into electives courses, and by identity groups for targeted universalist learning opportunities. By pairing classroom instruction with technologically enabled social networking, such low-scope sorting systems can reach beyond the school walls, allowing students to work in small teams with far-flung students who share their interests and needs. By also allowing students to sort and re-sort themselves, such systems give them the chance to build diverse webs of social connections in the school. Successful low-scope sorting systems provide students with multiple pathways to educational success that respond to their diverse needs, interests, and abilities.

High-scope educational categories, by contrast, are high-stakes categories. Our research demonstrates, for example, that enrolling in eighth-grade algebra courses boosts students' English scores by as much as it boosts students' math scores. We believe that happens because middle schools have only so many sections of each eighth-grade course. As a result, students sorted into algebra in eighth grade often end up taking English language arts together. This is one sense in which eighth-grade algebra is a high-scope category. The path-dependency of math course-taking raises the stakes associated with this assignment, as students who are placed into eighth-grade algebra will typically progress to advanced math courses, preserving their advantage over time. These dynamics help explain why advantaged families see to it that their children receive desirable categorical assignments, creating an alignment between categorical hierarchies in the school and our society's racialized, economic, and gendered inequalities. These dynamics further help explain why students interpret their educational categorical assignments as statements on their broad social worth.

Low-scope educational categorization systems can dismantle this winner-take-all system by creating multiple pathways to (and definitions of) success.

7. Avoid manufacturing scarcity and creating bottlenecks. Selectivity is a crucial driver of status in contemporary American education.[13] To demonstrate, scroll through *U.S. News & World Report*'s rankings of the best colleges and universities. Harvard and Stanford (numbers two and six, respectively, in the 2021 rankings) each admit fewer than one in twenty undergraduate applicants. Selectivity does not perfectly predict a school's rankings—Princeton claimed the top spot in 2021 with a 6 percent admissions rate, and MIT and Yale each came out ahead of Stanford despite admitting 7 percent of applicants. But the correlation is reasonably strong, and selectivity is one of the factors contributing to a school's rank. One must scroll to a second screen on the website's "National Universities" ranking page to find a school that admits more than 10 percent of applicants—Vanderbilt University, at number fifteen with a 12 percent admissions rate.

This logic of selectivity pervades many of the educational categories most profoundly implicated in the production of social inequalities. Educators deserve some blame for perpetuating this logic. We have often heard teachers motivate students by positioning a class as a highly selective, elite offering. Conversely, we have talked to demoralized teachers who feel disrespected and undervalued when they are assigned to teach a class of lower-performing students.

Our tendency to equate selectivity with status is deeply nonsensical. Even if we accept the (dubious) proposition that Harvard and Stanford accept only the "very best" students, there is very little reason to equate the quality of an educational experience with the quality of the students allowed to access it.[14] But even more troublesome, equating selectivity with status often rewards educational organizations for doing nothing more than artificially maintaining category selectivity, thus creating social bottlenecks—points at which people compete fiercely over limited access to categories that yield outsized social benefits. As the philosopher and legal scholar Joseph Fishkin points out, these bottlenecks produce outsized inequality. Because these bottlenecks are well known, advantaged families often strategically use their status and resources to ensure that their children make it through.[15] As such, bottlenecks become prime sites for opportunity hoarding. This process creates a self-sustaining system for the intergenerational reproduction of inequality as the advantaged young people who make it through educational bottlenecks become the adults who shepherd their own children through the same bottlenecks.

The good news, however, is that opening bottlenecks is simply a matter of will. Rather than pulling out a handful of elementary school students for "gifted" educational opportunities, teachers can provide all students with the opportunity to engage in self-directed learning. Rather than asking families to lottery into popular high school magnet programs, we can make the collective investment in excellent programs that are available to all. Rather than rejecting 95 percent of its applicants, Harvard could invest its (enormous) endowment in capital and faculty employment efforts that would allow it to increase its enrollment many times over.[16]

8. Divest from positional educational goods and invest in absolute goods. Economists note that investing societal resources in positional goods is bad policy because increasing the societal stock of a positional good does not increase societal utility.[17]

The value of positional goods depends on their holder's position relative to others. Because positional goods often result from zero-sum status competitions, when an individual gains a positional advantage, another individual, by definition, must lose. Thus, it can be rational for individuals to invest in positional goods, because they can benefit by moving up in the hierarchy. However, we would collectively be better off if our society prioritized investments in absolute goods, which are equally valuable regardless of whether they are scarce or plentiful.

Consider, for example, the social returns to a hypothetical Rolex-watches-for-all initiative. While we might all enjoy our new timepieces, the pleasure of having a fancy and exclusive watch would rapidly disappear. To the extent that the benefit of a Rolex is positional, a societal investment in universal Rolexes would be likely to yield less benefit than a societal investment in Casio calculator watches. By contrast, consider the social returns to investments in healthy food. Since nutrition is an absolute good with benefits that do not depend on other people's diets, we would expect everybody to be much better off from this investment.

Too often in our contemporary society, education works more like an investment in Rolexes for some and less like an investment in nutritious food for all. Although many of the skills students learn in schools have absolute value (for example, literacy), other aspects of education are largely positional (for example, a law school's reputation).[18] We collectively invest disproportionate societal resources in creating positional educational categories that benefit some individuals at the expense of others. As investing in purely positional goods yields no ultimate benefit to society (insofar as it simply rearranges who is and is not celebrated), we argue that society should divert resources away from the positional aspects of education and toward its absolute aspects.[19]

Divesting from positional goods requires reconceptualizing how educational institutions contribute to the public good. In a world that celebrates selectivity and exclusivity, this reconceptualization can be hard to even imagine. But examples of the prioritization of positional goods over absolute goods are easy to find throughout our education system. To pick a trivial example, consider the spelling bee. A mastery of the basics of spelling is arguably an absolute good, since spelling facilitates communication via the written word. The spelling bee may be defensible from an absolute goods perspective to the extent that it encourages young people to pay attention to spelling. But at some point, as competitive spellers work with coaches, building spreadsheets and memorizing obscure words in order to advance competitively, the ritual becomes purely positional, particularly given the ubiquity of spell-checking software. And it is clear that investments in basic spelling instruction produce more social good than investments in competitive spelling.

To give a more substantive example, we as a society currently give all universities, including elite universities, subsidies via substantial tax exemptions and tuition support. We also subsidize private philanthropy to universities through tax deductions. But elite universities create goods that are more positional than absolute.[20] To divest from positional goods, we might limit these public subsidies to selective, positionally oriented educational institutions, or we might link subsidies more closely with their success in serving particular groups of historically marginalized students. Such a proposal might seem punitive, but it seems incontrovertible that society would be better off using public funds to instead subsidize educational institutions that democratize access and actually create public goods (for example, community colleges). Likewise, we might provide tax benefits only for donations to preschools and K-12 schools that are broadly accessible and permit tax savings only for parents paying tuition at these institutions.

Divesting from positional goods and investing in absolute goods also involves making choices about the sorts of instruction our schools provide and the sorts of skills they seek to convey. As a general rule, more basic skills—literacy, numeracy, life skills, and the dispositions required for citizenship—tend to have more absolute value than relatively advanced and specialized skills. As a result, investments in early education tend to yield more absolute goods and fewer positional goods than investments in higher education.[21]

But within each sector of education, it is also possible to prioritize investments in absolute goods. At the elementary school level, we can imagine creating reading groups that are less about positional categories and more about creating absolute goods by encouraging students who can read well to read books that produce absolute goods, like empathy, rather than trying to simply further boost their already advanced reading skills.[22] In higher education, we might invest in broad access to medical and social services education while moving resources away from more positional programs like high-status selective MBAs and law schools.[23]

9. Expand educational standards. Too often we evaluate educational policies and practice using a narrow set of standards: Did test scores go up? Did more students graduate? But we should expect more from our educational system. The pressing social and environmental challenges facing contemporary society underscore the importance of not only evaluating how well our schools train students to solve quadratic equations but also how well they equip students to tackle issues like climate change, vaccine hesitancy, and xenophobia. Schools must nurture the skills, values, and competencies required to address these and other social ills.

Evaluating policies based only on their impacts on a narrow range of educational outcomes distracts from education's broader social goals. Desegregation provides an illustrative example. Recent research suggests that desegregation policies have only small positive effects on average test scores. But that is only part of the story. Desegregation also impacts a range of outcomes from racial attitudes to openness to investments in other social programs (like preschool and child health care) to students' capacity to thrive in racially diverse settings as adults. Without taking account of the broader social impact of such policies, detractors' focus on narrow metrics such as test scores plays a disproportionate role in desegregation debates. A more comprehensive understanding of desegregation's broad academic, socioemotional, and social impacts would make it clear that desegregation is worthwhile, even if it does not substantially raise test scores.[24]

Conversely, we might also need to more frankly discuss the harm perpetrated by our educational system. By creating and celebrating identities that are primarily positional, contemporary schools feed unhealthy tendencies in our society. Educational categories that ensure the continued privilege of certain groups at the expense of others—including everything from the honor roll to the boundaries of neighborhood schools—create positional goods for elites at an absolute cost for society.[25]

Important educational categories also are likely to need to be revisited from time to time. For example, in many schools across the United States, students take a variety of Advanced Placement (AP) courses—which allow students to earn college credit while in high school—in the hopes of earning high scores on AP tests to impress college admissions committees. AP courses were intended to create absolute goods by providing students with access to advanced curricula and affordable college credit. However, these courses are now driving an academic arms race as students seek to signal their position relative to others by accumulating high-status scores on AP tests. In contrast to the artificial bottlenecks created by AP test scores, high schools could capitalize on the wide availability and content diversity of community college and remote college courses to provide opportunities for academic enrichment and skills acquisition without incurring positional costs.

10. Encourage the cultivation of caring, trusting relationships between all students and school personnel. Many of our guidelines for building a more equitable educational system focus on identifying the practices that generate the most harmful educational categories and redesigning how education and structures are organized to avoid these harmful categories. But as central as these design questions are, it is important to remember that education is a fundamentally human institution and educational categories are enacted and embedded in the context of human relationships.

The implication of this insight is that the responsibility for implementing educational categories ultimately lies with the people who work with students. When educators bring care to their interactions with students, students are more likely to flourish. Indeed, educator care can mitigate some of the harshest consequences associated with educational categories.

Recall, for example, Kenneth Payne's account of the two cafeteria workers in part II: The first took care to memorize students' lunch status so that she could allocate free or reduced-price lunch to students without drawing attention to their status. The second, lacking that knowledge, forced young Payne to confront his free or reduced-price lunch status and the stigma that came with it. The point of this contrast is not to blame the second cafeteria worker in this story so much as to celebrate and learn from the compassionate efforts of the first. By empathizing with students who received free or reduced-price lunch and acting on that empathy, she helped to protect young Payne (and presumably many of his classmates) from the sharp consequences of a stigmatized category.

A key takeaway from work by the sociologist Angela Valenzuela and others is that the unequal categories that schools create often send marginalized students into dehumanized and uncaring educational environments. Understanding categorical inequality can help educators reformulate school relations toward a stance of authentic caring that involves "a search for connection where trusting relationships constitute the cornerstone for all learning."[26] A culture of care can help build more just and humane educational categories and create learning environments in which students can thrive. As educators grapple with decisions about category construction, assignment, salience, and maintenance, strong and authentic relationships with students enable them to center students' needs and cultures.

Categorizing toward a More Equitable World

Education is a utopian project, but as this book makes clear, schools are at best failed utopias. As we have argued, because schools simultaneously pursue a range of diffuse goals that are at least occasionally mutually incompatible, educational failure of one sort or another is inevitable.

At the same time, we are committed to the institution of education and to learning from past failures to create schools with healthier categories. We believe that schooling, as currently practiced, is ultimately a force for good in the world. Further, we believe that better schools—by which we mean schools that more compassionately balance the goals of efficiency, self-actualization, and solidarity—are possible.

A categorical inequality perspective points the way toward these better schools. Because categorization is inevitable in the context of schooling, educational inequality is inevitable. However, because we see categorization and inequality as endemic to our schools and to our society, we believe that it is essential to build categories that better reflect our understandings of social justice. Viewing schools through the lens of categorical inequality draws our attention to the processes that continually create and re-create educational categories. This approach highlights several attributes of categories—their size, their shape, and the way they relate to one another and to resources, status, and other social goods both within and beyond the educational system—that are consequential and malleable. By consciously interrogating our category creation processes and the attributes of the resulting categories, we all have the opportunity to fundamentally transform the schools and educational systems in which we work, learn, and live.

NOTES

Chapter 1: Categorization: How Schools Enact Inequality

1. As with accountability test scores across the United States, the CST scores from Sitwell's students were categorized into a number of proficiency brackets—for example, advanced, proficient, basic, below basic, and far below basic. Schools were supposed to ensure that students' scores were proficient or higher. More information about the color-coded ID card program is available in Domina, Penner, and Penner (2016).
2. Sitwell's ID card program shares many elements with the Renaissance Card program created by the memorabilia manufacturer Jostens. In this program, schools provide color-coded "Renaissance Cards" to students for meeting academic or behavioral goals set by the school.
3. Peters 1971, 17.
4. Ibid., 21.
5. To be clear, we are not endorsing the brown eyes/blue eyes pedagogy. In her time, Elliott was praised as a pedagogical innovator. Today her exercise feels risky, manipulative, and even unethical (Bloom 2021).
6. We could use a wide array of words to describe the complex and myriad ways in which schools act on categories. "Adopt," "make relevant," "imbue with meaning," "reshape," "redirect," and "emulate" are terms that highlight some of the important ways in which schools act vis-à-vis categories, but schools act on categories in other ways as well. See Domina, Penner, and Penner (2017) for a more explicit typology of the roles that schools play in category construction and maintenance.
7. We use the term "citizen" to denote individuals who are viewed as full members in a society, rather than as signifying that somebody is a legally recognized member of a nation-state.
8. Meyer 1977.
9. Davison et al. 2022; Marmot 2004; Massoglia and Pridemore 2015; Mohai, Pellow, and Roberts 2009; Waite and Gallagher 2001.
10. We note that we use the word "inequality" in a purely descriptive sense here and throughout the book. That is, we use "inequality" to mean "not equal"; in doing so, we are not necessarily speaking about whether or not a difference is "unjust." Because

our ideological commitments are broadly egalitarian, we believe that all social inequalities deserve close scrutiny. But some inequalities are clearly more problematic than others, and some inequalities may even be justifiable. When we are focusing more specifically on the normative aspects of inequality, we use the words "inequitable" and "unjust." By making a distinction between these descriptive and normative concepts, we want to acknowledge diverse understandings of group differences and their implications for our visions of equity and justice (Jencks 1988; Powell 2012).

11. Tilly 1999; Massey 2007.
12. Rhodes et al. 2018. Philosophers going back to Aristotle have discussed the precise nature and origins of categories (Gelman 2003), and it is beyond the scope of this book to resolve these debates. Readers who are interested in the origin of categories might find recent work at the intersection of philosophy and developmental psychology of interest; see, for example, the work of the philosopher Sarah-Jane Leslie (2008) and the developmental psychologist Andrei Cimpian (Cimpian, Gelman, and Brandone 2010), among others. Our focus here is less on where categories come from and more on where categories are taking us and how we can construct categories that will help us create a more equitable society.
13. See Domina, Penner, and Penner (2016) for a review.
14. hooks 1994; Giroux 2007; Lewis and Diamond 2015.
15. Thorne 1993.
16. Fields 2008; Pascoe 2007.
17. Bowles and Gintis 1976.
18. Erevelles 2000.
19. Bell 2004.
20. Ramirez, Bromley, and Russell 2009.
21. Meyer 1977, 59.
22. Tyack and Cuban 1995; Tyack and Tobin 1994.
23. For reviews of the relevant research, see, for example, Card (1999) and Hout (2012).
24. Blau and Kahn 2017; England, Levine, and Mishel 2020; Penner et al. 2022.
25. For a recent review, see Riegle-Crumb 2019.
26. For discussions about the uses of Whiteness as a credential or form of property to preserve and withhold rights in institutions like education, see work by Victor Ray (2019), who builds on work by Cheryl Harris (1993).
27. We use the term "logics" to refer to a system of sensemaking. Logics are often taken for granted but determine what is and is not understood as plausible, relevant, and prioritized in any given context. For example, one might buy a rabbit at a pet store or at a butcher. But as the logics of pet stores and butchers are very different, one would not generally expect to find that a store sold rabbits for both of these purposes.
28. Some approaches (such as fundamental cause approaches or maintained inequality approaches) take the perspective that changing the system simply changes how inequality is produced. We argue that a categorical lens provides a foundation for hope that is not naive. Specifically, it recognizes that inequalities will adjust to changing categories and find new expressions, but also that we can nonetheless create categories that produce less problematic inequalities.

Part I: Sorting into School

1. Jones 2003.
2. Crawford 2015.
3. Sacchetti, Sieff, and Fisher 2018.

Chapter 2: Making Students Citizens

1. Webster 1787.
2. Shapiro 1999.
3. Ramirez and Boli 1987.
4. Almond and Verba 1963; Nie, Junn, and Stehlik-Barry 1996.
5. Milligan, Moretti, and Oreopoulos 2004.
6. Wiseman et al. 2011.
7. Porter 1952, 45.
8. Tyack and Cuban 1995.
9. Santos, Varnum, and Grossmann 2017.
10. Baker 2020.
11. Smith and Sikkink 1999.
12. Stevens 2003.
13. Ibid.
14. Apple 2013; Lubienski 2000.
15. Mann 1848.
16. Lee and Lee 2016.
17. Kaestle 1983; Tyack 1974.
18. Meyer, Bromley, and Ramirez 2010.
19. Boisjoly et al. 2006; Gamoran et al. 2016.
20. Brighouse 2006, 98.
21. This work both centered White Americans as the "norm" and maintained structural barriers and formal and informal social interaction patterns that sustained the social and economic privileges of White Americans.
22. Ladson-Billings 2016; Mills 2014; Omi and Winant 2014; Watkins, Lewis, and Chou 2001.
23. Moss 2010, 1313.
24. Douglass 2016, 527.
25. U.S. Department of Education 2023.
26. Olivas 2010.
27. *Plyler v. Doe*, 457 U.S. 207 (1981).
28. Ibid., at 203.
29. Suárez-Orozco 1996.
30. State of California 1994, 54, emphasis in original.
31. Mann (1848) argued that universalizing education "would do more than all things else to obliterate factitious distinctions in society." Seen through a categorical lens, this argument suggests an awareness of education's role in creating and legitimating categories and a recognition that creating different categories could fundamentally reshape society by altering the distinctions made by social categories.

32. Cottom 2017. The term was first coined by Grubb and Lazerson (2004).
33. Quoted in Kaestle 1983, 163.
34. Ibid.
35. Foley 1878.
36. Grande 2015, 13.
37. Ibid.; Stout 2012.
38. Quoted in Holliday 2020.
39. Dawson 2012; Stout 2012.
40. Adams 1995; Rotondaro 2015.
41. Adams 1995; Child 1998; Dawson 2012; Rotondaro 2015.
42. Dawson 2012; Stout 2012.
43. Adams 1995; Child 1998; Davis 2001; Hyer 1990.
44. Spring 2016.
45. Bauman 2009; Bell 1883; Harmon 2021.
46. Bauman 2009, 93.
47. Bauman 2009; Davis 2007; Dunn and Anderson 2019; Hill et al. 2020.
48. Nash and Dunn 1995, 5.
49. Quoted in Nash, Crabtree, and Dunn 2000, 5.
50. Nash 1997.
51. Kurtz 2021.
52. Dee and Penner 2017.
53. Bonilla, Dee, and Penner 2021.
54. Billeaud 2011.
55. Gordon and Reinhart 2011.
56. Planas 2017.
57. Goldstein 2019.
58. Bedzow 2020.
59. National Governors Association 2010a, 2010b.
60. Organization for Economic Cooperation and Development 2016.
61. Sturm et al. 1998.
62. Berner 2012.
63. Angrist, Pathak, and Walters 2013.
64. Center for Research on Education Outcomes 2009.
65. Egalite and Mills 2021; Waddington and Berends 2018.
66. Carlson, Chingos, and Campbell 2017; McEachin et al. 2020.
67. Valenzuela, Bellei, and de los Ríos 2014.
68. Ladd, Fiske, and Ruijs 2009.
69. Bifulco and Ladd 2007; Billingham and Hunt 2016.

Chapter 3: Contesting Citizenship Boundaries

1. Educational categories are also fundamentally political insofar as they are created in societies defined by power relations and as such reflect the power dynamics and politics of society more broadly.

2. These are far from the only axes of social identity that schools help to create, but they are the two we focus on in this chapter because of their salience to U.S. history and their largely contrasting trajectories. Gender coeducation and racial integration also interact in important ways that further contribute to categorical inequality, though this interaction is less the focus of our discussion here.
3. Indeed, in the United States and elsewhere, many politicians who oppose broadening the boundaries of citizenship denounce educational systems that deny opportunities on the basis of gender.
4. We view gender and racial hierarchies as locally constructed and maintained, in terms of both how individuals are categorized into groups within these hierarchies and how groups of individuals are positioned vis-à-vis each other. In other words, though race and gender are often seen as static, we understand them to be fundamentally fluid, and we interpret the lack of changes that we observe as a telling indication of the dynamics constraining this fluidity. See Roth (2016) for an overview of the multidimensionality of race and fluidity; Pickett, Saperstein, and Penner (2022) on the interactional forces shaping racial self-reporting; Saperstein and Penner (2012) for additional information on racial fluidity in how people are racially categorized by others; and Bailey, Saperstein, and Penner (2014) for a discussion of how selective migration can create relatively unusual contexts where darker-skinned individuals are relatively advantaged.
5. Rochmes, Penner, and Loeb 2017.
6. Billingham and Hunt 2016; Reardon and Owens 2014; Rich 2017.
7. Blau 1974.
8. Tyson 2011.
9. Bonilla-Silva 2006.
10. See, for example, Soares (2017) on the use of SAT scores for college admission.
11. Lewis 2003.
12. Feliciano 2009.
13. McDiarmid and Pratt 1971; Morning 2008; Sleeter and Grant 1991.
14. Steele and Aronson 1995.
15. Evans and Davies 2000.
16. Nehm and Young 2008.
17. Legewie and DiPrete 2012.
18. Douglass 1857.
19. Tyack and Hansot 1990.
20. Tyack, James, and Benavot 1991.
21. Tyack and Hansot 1990.
22. "Report on the Co-Education of the Sexe" (1855), by J. W. Brown, P. W. Gegembre, and W. V. Davis, quoted in ibid, 100.
23. Mann 1853, 1891.
24. Buckley 1885; Tyack and Hansot 1990.
25. Ramirez and Cha 1990.
26. Kendrick and Kendrick 2004.
27. *Sarah C. Roberts v. The City of Boston*, 59 Mass. 198 (1849).
28. Ficker 1999.

29. Quoted in Tischauser 2012.
30. *Plessy v. Ferguson*, 163 U.S. 537 (1896).
31. Orfield and Eaton 1996.
32. Tyack and Hansot 1990.
33. Following Gibson's (2019) discussion of the ongoing evolution of nomenclature, the complex origins of these labels, the potential for homogenization in their use, and the strong feelings many possess about the use of labels to refer to diverse ethnic communities, we adopt the term Latine to refer to individuals with origins in the Spanish- and Portuguese-speaking Americas. We use these terms rather than the term Hispanic, which has been criticized for neglecting the indigenous, African, and Asian origins of some in this community, and Latina or Latino, which have been criticized for their reinforcement of gender binaries, except in cases where a specific term is included in a direct quotation. We refer readers to *Keywords for Latina/o Studies* for more engagement with these fluidly used terms.
34. *Lum v. Rice*, 275 U.S. 78 (1927).
35. See *Tape v. Hurley* for an important case from San Francisco that nearly ended school segregation in California in 1885.
36. Wollenberg 1974.
37. Dudziak 2000, 2004.
38. *Brown v. Board of Education*, 347 U.S. 483 (1954); here Warren is quoting a finding from the Kansas district court.
39. Bell 1980, 523.
40. Quoted in Titus 2011, 15.
41. Boyd 2007.
42. Delmont 2016.
43. Orfield and Eaton 1996.
44. *Swann v. Charlotte Mecklenburg Board of Education*, 402 U.S. 1 (1971).
45. Delmont 2016.
46. Quinn 2020.
47. *Guey Heung Lee v. Johnson*, 404 U.S. 1215 (1971).
48. *San Antonio Independent School District v. Rodriguez*, 411 U.S. 1 (1973).
49. *Milliken v. Bradley*, 418 U.S. 717 (1974).
50. Murray 2009.
51. Hannah-Jones 2014.
52. Billingham and Hunt 2016; Hailey 2021.
53. Lewis and Diamond 2015.
54. Jackman 2018.
55. *Gary B. v. Snyder*, 329 F. Supp. 3d 344 (E.D. Mich. 2018).
56. Guinier 2004, 113.

Part II: Sorting within School

1. Harwell and LeBeau 2010.
2. Domina et al. 2017.
3. Poppendieck 2011, 153.

4. Ibid., 190, 160.
5. Payne 2017, 11.

Chapter 4: Making Courses, Classrooms, and Other Educational Categories

1. Hallinan 1994.
2. Oakes 1994.
3. Bassok, Latham, and Rorem 2016; Russell 2011.
4. Tyack and Cuban 1995.
5. Francis and Darity 2021; Knoester and Au 2017.
6. Finley 1984.
7. Oakes 2005; Yonezawa and Jones 2006.
8. Massey 2007.
9. Sherif 1956.
10. Eckel et al. 2001.
11. Chmielewski, Dumont, and Trautwein 2013.
12. Yonezawa and Jones 2006.
13. Oakes et al. 1997.
14. Worthy 2010.
15. Tyson 2011.
16. Grissom, Kalogrides, and Loeb 2017.
17. Bassok and Reardon 2013.
18. Argys, Rees, and Brewer 1996.
19. Gamoran 1987, 1992; Gamoran et al. 1995; Rosenbaum 1976.
20. McEachin, Domina, and Penner 2020.
21. It's worth noting that the phrase "to the degree that" is doing some heavy lifting here. As we noted earlier, a small but growing proportion of families opt to hold their children back an additional year before enrolling them in kindergarten. Likewise, births may be timed with cultural considerations in mind, such as auspicious years in the Chinese zodiac (Do and Phung 2010; Huang et al. 2020). Furthermore, assignment to kindergarten is a relatively simple case. Decisions about which students to place in later grades can be more complicated. Many U.S. elementary schools practice "social promotion": moving most students forward to the next grade annually regardless of their performance (Jimerson et al. 2006). But according to the National Center for Education Statistics (McFarland et al. 2019), approximately 2 percent of students in American public schools repeat one or more elementary school grades, and the rate is substantially higher for Black and Hispanic students. When educators are deciding whether to retain a student in a grade, they move away from the easy-to-measure and socially unbiased age assignment mechanism and toward a harder-to-measure assignment mechanism related to student academic performance. In other words, they start making the sorts of judgments that educators make when they assign students to academic tracks.
22. Fryer and Levitt 2004; Jencks 1972.
23. Tyson 2011.

24. Tyson, Darity, and Castellino 2005.
25. Domina et al. 2019.
26. Shavit and Blossfeld 1993.
27. Al Otaiba et al. 2011; Connor et al. 2013.
28. Cottom 2017.
29. Rivera 2012.
30. Hanselman, Domina, and Hwang 2022.
31. Domina et al. 2019.
32. Lucas 1999.
33. That said, we can also think about scope in two other ways that help us understand its relationship with inequality, both of which reveal differences between age-grading and tracking. First, we can think about mobility as a form of scope over time (for example, how closely linked categories are at different points in time). Second, we can think about scope beyond education, such as when assignment mechanisms are related to other categories, or when track placement is linked with getting a better-paying job.
34. Carbonaro 2005; Oakes, Hare, and Sirotnik 1986.
35. Tach and Farkas 2006. Schools and educators are emphatically not exempt from merit judgments associated with educational categories. Since the birth of the school accountability movement in the 1980s, policymakers have not hesitated to impose labels on schools, including schools that toil endlessly to improve student outcomes. These accountability policies construct status-laden categories and prizes for schools and teachers, conferring honor or shame on educators based on their students' performance. These status incentives are powerful. During the height of the school accountability period, Atlanta Public Schools held an annual districtwide event at the stadium of the city's NFL football team to recognize schools that made great improvements in student achievement (and to punish schools that failed to do so). At that event, the principals of the celebrated schools were invited to sit in a specially marked section on the field, while principals of schools that were failing sat in the stands. Recalling that event and others like it in the district, one principal compared the humiliation associated with leading a "failing" school to "having leprosy in the Bible" (Aviv 2014, 6). In another highly publicized case, a teacher committed suicide after being publicly identified as a "least effective teacher" in a newspaper article summarizing teacher effectiveness research (Felch, Song, and Smith 2010; Lovett 2010).
36. To this point, it's telling that despite the rich literature on school meals, child nutrition, and health outcomes, very little research exists about the effects of free school lunches on student achievement. One exception is recent work by Amy Ellen Schwartz and Michah Rothbart (2020), who find evidence that universalizing school lunch has positive effects on achievement for both poor and nonpoor children.

Chapter 5: Contesting School Structures

1. Dunn 1993.
2. For a summary of these normative questions, see, for example, Brighouse et al. 2016.
3. Baker 2014; Bowker 2014; Bowker and Star 1999; Meyer 1977; Timmermans and Epstein 2010.

4. Lipsky 1980.
5. Teachers are particularly important actors in the construction of classrooms and other consequential categories that operate within schools. Other important educational categorical distinctions decide which students attend which schools. In this case, other street-level bureaucrats—school and neighborhood planners, admissions officers, and experts in educational assessment—are likely to play more important roles than teachers.
6. Adelman 1999, 2006; Attewell and Domina 2008; Conger, Long, and Iatarola 2009; Rose and Betts 2004.
7. California Department of Education 1985, 1991; Fenwick 1987.
8. California Department of Education 1998, 13–14.
9. Rosin, Barondess, and Leichty 2009.
10. Hess and Petrilli 2006.
11. *California School Board Association v. California State Board of Education*, 186 Cal. App. 4th 1298 (2010).
12. National Governors Association 2010a.
13. Wurman and Evers 2010.
14. California Department of Education 2013.
15. Ibid. 2021.
16. Jencks 1988, 518.
17. Ibid.
18. Posselt 2016, 57.
19. Ibid., 154.
20. Hart et al. 2015.
21. Dougherty et al. 2015.
22. Urdan and Paris 1994.
23. Martínez, Stecher, and Borko 2009.
24. McEachin, Domina, and Penner 2020.
25. Meyer and Rowan 1975; Weick 1976.
26. Diamond 2012; Hallett 2010.
27. Park and Datnow 2017.
28. Lewis and Diamond 2015.
29. Bidwell 2001; Hoy and Sabo 1998; Hoy, Tarter, and Kottkamp 1991; Spillane, Parise, and Sherer 2011.
30. National Governors Association 2010a; Laitsch 2006.
31. Domina, Penner, and Penner 2016. While some districts—most notably Santa Ana Unified—seem to have ignored the state's algebra-for-all policy and continued to consistently enroll approximately half of their students in eighth-grade algebra, others—including Anaheim Union, Corona-Norco Unified, and Garden Grove Unified—seem to have complied with the policy by enrolling virtually every eighth-grader in algebra courses. We see further variation in instructional category construction at the school level: some schools offered just one or two different classes for eighth-graders—algebra for most, but pre-algebra for a handful of struggling students—and other schools offered a highly differentiated eighth-grade math course sequence—geometry, accelerated algebra, standard algebra, the first half of a two-year algebra course, pre-algebra, developmental math, and others.

32. Handsman, Farrell, and Coburn 2022.
33. Allensworth, Ponisciak, and Mazzeo 2009; Clotfelter, Ladd, and Vigdor 2015; Domina et al. 2015; Stein et al. 2011.
34. Nomi and Allensworth 2012; Nomi and Raudenbush 2016.

Part III: Sorting into the World

1. Elman 2000, 291. Here, as elsewhere in part III, our discussion of the Chinese civil service examination system draws heavily from the work of the historian Benjamin Elman, and in particular from Elman's comprehensive history of the examination system in *A Cultural History of Civil Examinations in Late Imperial China* (2000). The careful reader may note, however, that we do not adopt Elman's Romanization of names. We change the Romanization of names where we quote (or draw) from Elman to be consistent in our Romanization and to avoid confusion when we reference other work.
2. Ibid., 405; Hu 1984, 15.
3. Miyazaki 1981.
4. Hu 1984, 16.
5. Ibid., 23.
6. It is important to note, however, that individuals from certain backgrounds—the sons of criminals, for example—were not allowed to take the examinations, echoing other efforts to enforce status boundaries around who was considered a full member of society and who was not.
7. Ho 1962.
8. Elman 2000, 173.
9. Hu 1984, 18.
10. Ibid., 19.
11. Elman 2013.
12. It is important not to overstate their similarities; in particular, there are important differences between Imperial China and the United States today in individuals' likelihood of success. While success rates varied across time, the civil service exams in Late Imperial China were hypercompetitive (sometimes half a million men were vying for three hundred spots), with much lower rates of success than admission rates at even the most selective universities in the contemporary United States. Interestingly, as Wang Feng (2018) notes, when Deng Xiaoping reinstated a college entrance examination after Mao's death, the pass rate was 5 percent; by 2005, 83 percent of examinees passed the college entrance examination.

Chapter 6: Making Merit

1. Cookson and Persell 2008, 125.
2. Khan 2011.
3. Ibid., 46.
4. Ibid., 47.
5. Ibid., 125.

6. Ibid., 74.
7. Bowles and Gintis 1976.
8. Oakes 1983.
9. Golann 2021.
10. Rios 2017.
11. Our argument diverges from a credentialist perspective insofar as we believe that the content of the categories is important. That is, where credentialism argues that it is the form and not the substance of education that matters, so that the human capital accrued and the content taught pales in comparison to the power of the credential, we argue that category content is likewise important. Indeed, given the pivotal role of education in creating citizens, we view the debates over whose history should be taught, whether religious beliefs belong in science class, and whether algebra is a civil right as central to our common understanding of citizenship and how we as a society define merit. We believe that recognizing the political processes behind category creation, the historical compromises that our current categories represent, and the ongoing debates about the content of the categories and how individuals are sorted among them provides a powerful framework for unpacking and resisting existing inequalities.
12. Rivera 2015.
13. Rivera 2012, 1009.
14. Blair et al. 2005.
15. Loeb and Bassok 2012.
16. Engel, Claessens, and Finch 2013.
17. Brint and Karabel 1989.
18. Elman 2000.
19. Sandel 2020.
20. Karabel 2006, 131.
21. Ibid., 2.
22. Quoted in ibid., 62.
23. Quoted in Brief *Amicus Curiae* of the Louis D. Brandeis Center for Human Rights Under Law and the Silicon Valley Chinese Association in Support of Petitioner, *Students for Fair Admissions, Inc., Petitioner v. President and Fellows of Harvard College, Respondent*, no. 20-1199 (2021). https://www.supremecourt.gov/DocketPDF/20/20-1199/173420/20210331104529484_Amicus%20brief.pdf.
24. Stevens 2009.
25. Binder, Davis, and Bloom 2016.
26. Rivera 2015.
27. Binder, Davis, and Bloom 2016.
28. Long, Saenz, and Tienda 2010.
29. DiPrete and Eirich 2006.
30. Tilly 1999.
31. Elman 2000.
32. Case and Deaton 2015.
33. Lucas 2001.

Chapter 7: Contesting Definitions of Merit

1. Elman 2013.
2. Osterhammel 2015.
3. Elman 2000. Sometimes examinees were sealed in their cells for the length of the exam (three days and two nights) and not permitted to come out even if they became ill or died. In other instances, examiners discouraged bribing by transcribing the essays so that graders could not recognize the examinee's calligraphy. Dynastic authorities levied harsh punishments when cheating was discovered, including executing officials complicit in the cheating, exiling their kin, and confiscating their property (Elman 2000).
4. Buckner and Hodges 2016.
5. Guhin 2021.
6. Rafalow 2020.
7. Aspelund, n.d.; Freyer et al. 2013.
8. Jiang and Hanson 2017.
9. Plagiarism.org 2017; Yee 2012.
10. Jiang and Hanson 2017.
11. We might also understand this view as a corollary to Campbell's law, which holds that adopting a measure for decision-making changes the meaning of an indicator; this suggests that when a process becomes used to allocate merit, the process becomes an end in and of itself (or solely because of its link to status, irrespective of any other value). This point was recognized by Emperor Qianlong, who complained in 1740 that the civil service examination had eclipsed the wisdom it was supposedly testing (see the introduction to part 3).
12. Jiang and Hanson 2017.
13. Golden 2016.
14. Watson 2021.
15. India TV Education Desk 2021.
16. *Edex Live* 2021; Pandey 2021; *The Times of India* 2021.
17. Sharma 2021. This example highlights that, although test-based systems are often understood as legitimate owing to their transparency about the criteria used for sorting, this transparency creates a liability for legitimacy that does not exist for opaque holistic review processes. That is, by providing applicants from elite backgrounds whose academic credentials are underwhelming with opportunities to gain admission through other putatively sanctioned means (such as large donations to universities), resources that might be directed toward cheating are captured by institutions and crises of legitimacy are at least temporarily forestalled.
18. Buckner and Hodges 2016.
19. Ibid., 617.
20. Aviv 2014.
21. Vasquez 2015.
22. Waldman 2016.
23. Dunn 2017.

24. Ibid.; Walsh 2015.
25. Arenson 1999.
26. Attewell and Domina 2011.
27. Reese 2008.
28. Emery, Braselmann, and Gold 2004; Menkart and View, n.d.
29. Zinn 1997, 10.
30. Baronnet 2008.
31. Gahman 2017; Oikonomakis 2015.
32. Gahman 2016.
33. Barmeyer 2008.
34. Herszenhorn 2005.
35. De Blasio 2018.
36. Brody 2018.
37. Elman 2000. Quotas were used to address two very different threats to the legitimacy of China's examination system that are relevant for contemporary educational systems as well: (1) if a particular group comes to understand itself as largely excluded from success in a system, it has little incentive to participate and the system loses legitimacy; and (2) if a system of creating elites and social status does not align sufficiently with existing power structures, it may lose legitimacy as elites turn to other mechanisms to maintain their advantages.
38. It is important to note that in contrast to the earlier (and subsequent) examination systems, passing the examinations under the Mongol system was neither necessary nor sufficient to secure a political appointment. It thus provided legitimacy and status to those who passed but was less tied to tangible rewards.
39. Elman 2000, 93.
40. Ibid., 94.
41. Ibid.
42. Tellingly, the 60-40 split between the south and the north was amended a few years later to a 55-35-10 split between the south, the north, and a central region that was formed because of ambiguity in determining whether some border regions were northern or southern.
43. Elman 2000, 96.
44. Karabel 2006, 23.
45. Elman 2000, 168.
46. Ibid., 252.
47. Antman and Duncan 2015. Other contemporary research also highlights the difficulties of determining category membership: in a widely publicized case in Brazil, a university panel determined that an individual was not eligible for admission to university under a quota for Black students, while his identical twin brother was (Bailey 2008). As this example highlights, the use of quotas in category construction requires institutions to demarcate boundaries to delineate those to whom the quota applies from those to whom it does not.
48. Regents of the University of California 2010.
49. Quoted in Sleeter 1986, 48.

50. Smardon 2008.
51. Sleeter 1986, 52.
52. Chen 2015.

Part IV: Sorting toward a Better Future

1. Meyer 1977.
2. Meyer and Rowan 1975.

Chapter 8: Balancing Categorical Logics

1. Labaree 1997.
2. Open Culture 2017.
3. Labaree 1997, 41. Although our typology of categorical logics aligns closely with Labaree's typology of educational goals, we would call attention to a few notable differences. Labaree describes three key educational goals: democratic equality (which he describes as the goal that motivates citizen education), social efficiency (which motivates worker training), and social mobility (which aims to prepare individuals to compete for social positions.) Our typology is somewhat broader. In saying that schools value solidarity and aim to make citizens, we want to make space for debates about who should be trained for citizenship by schools and the nature of the citizenship that they pursue. Likewise, in saying that schools value efficiency and aim to make workers, we note that efficiency is just one of many criteria that determine what sort of work each student should prepare to pursue. And in noting that schools value self-actualization and aim to make protagonists, we note that promoting their social mobility is not the only reason that we might want to help a young person discover and reach their full human potential.
4. Quoted in Hauser 2021.
5. A similar tendency to prioritize young men's self-actualization underlies rape culture at many elite institutions. Brock Turner was expelled from Stanford after raping Chanel Miller at a fraternity party, but even though he was convicted of three counts of felony sexual assault, he served only three months in prison for the crime. In sentencing Turner, the judge departed from the statutory minimum, arguing, "I think you have to take the whole picture in terms of what impact imprisonment has on a specific individual's life." The lenient sentence sparked controversy in part, we argue, because it prioritized Turner's potential over the harm he did to Miller and the community (Levin 2016). We see similarly gendered behavior at Justice Brett Kavanaugh's Georgetown Prep and other elite institutions where administrative responses facilitate rape culture by protecting privileged individuals and thereby undermine rules and norms designed to protect their peers and foster solidarity.
6. Lovett 2020. In this sense, an overreliance on self-actualization is often self-defeating. When educational systems protect children of the elite from the consequences of their actions in the name of self-actualization, they fail to allow them to fully develop their sense of self and responsibility.

7. A perhaps similar impulse to celebrate students' academic achievements drives grade inflation, especially at many private universities.
8. R. Ray 2017, 114.
9. Ibid., 162.
10. Bowles and Gintis 1976; Golann 2021; Rios 2017; Willis 1981.
11. Labaree (1997) similarly argues that the discourse around education's potential to allow for social mobility has led to the creation of an educational system that overemphasizes the private goods that proceed from education and underemphasizes public goods. In particular, we agree with Labaree that American public education focuses far too little attention on the imperatives of preparing students for citizenship.
12. Guryan, Hurst, and Kearney 2008; Kornrich and Furstenberg 2013; Ramey and Ramey 2009.
13. Rosa 2019.

Chapter 9: Making Equitable Schools

1. Coy 2021.
2. Caplan 2018, 2.
3. Noble 2018.
4. Raudenbush and Eschmann 2015.
5. Boeckenstedt 2020; Soares 2017.
6. Alvero et al. 2021.
7. In a 2021 essay, Cara Jackson provides an excellent introduction to the growing body of scholarship on democratic deliberation in education. She outlines several steps that educational organizations can take to create more open and inclusive decision-making processes. Inclusion begins with the development of educational agendas, she argues, and continues through processes of accountability and evaluation (Jackson 2021).
8. Powell, Menendian, and Ake 2019.
9. Nasir, Givens and Chatmon 2019.
10. Dee and Penner 2021.
11. Chatmon 2019.
12. Domina and Saldana 2012; Domina, Penner, and Penner 2016.
13. The costs of bottlenecks are not unique to contemporary education. Ping-ti Ho (1962, 251) notes that many people failed the highest Chinese civil service exam, which was typically offered every three years, a dozen or more times; as a result, they devoted their whole adult lives to test taking. Ho argues that this happened partly because there was relatively little status in science, technology, and commerce, and that passing these exams was the only path to a high-status position. The exam system thus created a bottleneck by funneling people away from other fields where they might have been successful and made strong contributions to society. In other words, even an engine of social mobility can come at a high cost to both individuals and society if it creates bottlenecks.

14. Hanselman and Fiel 2017.
15. The story of the Varsity Blues scandal is again illustrative here.
16. Although some might argue that Harvard and other urban universities are constrained by the physical space available to them, there is no reason why such universities cannot move their campus (or pursue virtual opportunities) if expanding access is sufficiently important to them. New York University's creation of NYU Shanghai and NYU Abu Dhabi was clearly not primarily motivated by expanding access, but if expanding access is the motivator, we could imagine universities doing so in this manner.
17. Frank and Cook 2010.
18. We believe that in many ways the magic of education works because people invest in education for its positional payoff, but society still benefits from these investments because people also obtain some absolute skills when they engage in this status competition (Elman 2013). That said, in an era of growing inequality, the positional status dimensions of education now threaten to overwhelm and undermine the absolute benefits of education. We might even argue that absolute goods have been positionalized in the quest for status.
19. It is perhaps important to note that what is an absolute good is at some level context-dependent; for example, the value of literacy depends on others also being literate and having implements to record and distribute the materials created by literate people. So when we say something is an absolute or positional good, we think of this as a matter of degree—that is, the degree to which a good is absolute or positional can vary somewhat from one context to another.
20. It is important to distinguish between the research and teaching functions of universities. To the degree that elite universities are creating public goods in supporting research that is made broadly accessible, societal investments ought to support this goal. However, to the degree that their teaching creates primarily positional goods by maintaining their elite status through the selective admission of students, societal investments should not underwrite this goal. We might imagine collectively investing in researchers at elite universities who are working to cure cancer by providing grants to support such work, while at the same time limiting the provision of federal financial aid to students at these universities and taxing selective universities on their tuition income, endowment returns, and donations. To ensure that societal investments in schools are proportional to the public goods they create, we might set tax rates according to the degree of selectivity, as well as exempt schools with capacity constraints to the degree that they are willing to admit students based on a lottery (or otherwise make opportunities broadly accessible).
21. This is not to argue that society should not invest in advanced and specialized skills, as clearly some very advanced skills are of great benefit to society, such as the skills needed to cure various diseases. But as a rule, the more widespread a skill is in contemporary society, like basic literacy, the less likely its value is to be primarily positional, and the less common a skill is, the more likely it is that its absolute value is accompanied by a sizable positional value.

22. We view literacy as positional insofar as an individual's benefit from it depends on there being others who also read, but given current literacy levels, literacy is more of an absolute good. That said, there are some who benefit from their position in the hierarchy—for example, those who accrue status from being in honors courses. We suggest that society should try, not to create a literary hierarchy, but instead to invest in literacy as an absolute good and use it to invest in other absolute goods.
23. That said, we would argue that the focus of medical education should be less on (positional) weed-out courses and more on providing broad access to the skills needed to do important jobs in medicine. Likewise, as knowledge is built from those who have acquired these specialized skills, it is also important to democratize this information to the greatest extent possible through policies that make knowledge widely accessible.
24. Anderson 2010.
25. School sports tournaments, particularly sports that have a high risk of injury and negative health repercussions later in life, might be another example. Although encouraging students to work as a team and to be physically fit has great long-term benefits, it seems difficult to argue that training students for elite-level competition has more value than expanding access to intramural sports.
26. Valenzuela 1999, 5. In her watershed book *Subtractive Schooling,* Valenzuela describes the alienation of Mexican American youth and their disconnection from teachers and others who could advocate for their needs. Their distance from educators compounded the challenges that students faced in encounters with stratified, punitive school structures that divested them of their cultures, languages, and identities. Valenzuela's focus on creating trusting relationships in schools aligns with Black feminist scholarship that highlights how critical care work often performed by women of color promotes social transformation, community uplift, and liberation (Collins 2009; Flores 2017; Foster 1997; Irvine 2003; Ware 2006). In addition to simply improving student-staff relationships, authentic caring also centers students' cultures and needs (Flores 2017; Rivera Maulucci 2010; Valenzuela 1999) and promotes a "transformative resistance" to counter and redefine punitive school structures and practices (Beneke 2021; Nasir et al. 2013).

REFERENCES

Adams, David Wallace. 1995. *Education for Extinction: American Indians and the Boarding School Experience, 1875–1928.* Lawrence: University Press of Kansas.

Adelman, Clifford. 1999. *Answers in the Tool Box: Academic Intensity, Attendance Patterns, and Bachelor's Degree Attainment.* Washington: U.S. Department of Education, Office of Educational Research and Improvement (January).

———. 2006. *The Toolbox Revisited: Paths to Degree Completion from High School through College.* Washington: U.S. Department of Education, Office of Vocational and Adult Education (February).

Allensworth, Elaine, Stephen Ponisciak, and Christopher Mazzeo. 2009. "The Schools Teachers Leave: Teacher Mobility in Chicago Public Schools." Chicago: Consortium on Chicago School Research (June).

Almond, Gabriel A., and Sidney Verba. 1963. *The Civic Culture: Political Attitudes and Democracy in Five Nations.* Princeton, N.J.: Princeton University Press.

Al Otaiba, Stephanie, Carol M. Connor, Jessica S. Folsom, Luana Greulich, Jane Meadows, and Zhi Li. 2011. "Assessment Data–Informed Guidance to Individualize Kindergarten Reading Instruction: Findings from a Cluster-Randomized Control Field Trial." *Elementary School Journal* 111(4, June): 535–60.

Alvero, A. J., Sonia Giebel, Ben Gebre-Medhin, Anthony Lising Antonio, Mitchell L. Stevens, and Benjamin W. Domingue. 2021. "Essay Content and Style Are Strongly Related to Household Income and SAT Scores: Evidence from 60,000 Undergraduate Applications." *Science Advances* 7(42, October): eabi9031.

Anderson, Elizabeth. 2010. "The Imperative of Integration." In Anderson, *The Imperative of Integration.* Princeton, N.J.: Princeton University Press.

Angrist, Joshua D., Parag A. Pathak, and Christopher R. Walters. 2013. "Explaining Charter School Effectiveness." *American Economic Journal: Applied Economics* 5(4, October): 1–27.

Antman, Francisca, and Brian Duncan. 2015. "Incentives to Identify: Racial Identity in the Age of Affirmative Action." *Review of Economics and Statistics* 97(3, July): 710–13.

Apple, Michael W. 2013. "Gender, Religion, and the Work of Homeschooling." In *Gender, Religion, and Education in a Chaotic Postmodern World,* edited by Zehavit Gross, Lynn Davies, and Al-Khansaa Diab. Dordrecht: Springer.

Arenson, Karen W. 1999. "Recognizing Achievement, Adding Glitz." *New York Times*, May 31. https://www.nytimes.com/1999/05/31/nyregion/recognizing-achievement-adding-glitz.html.

Argys, Laura M., Daniel I. Rees, and Dominic J. Brewer. 1996. "Detracking America's Schools: Equity at Zero Cost?" *Journal of Policy Analysis and Management* 15(4, Autumn): 623–45.

Aspelund, Karl M. n.d. "The Harvard Crimson: Class of 2017 by the Numbers." *Harvard Crimson*, https://features.thecrimson.com/2017/senior-survey/academics-narrative/ (accessed November 23, 2021).

Attewell, Paul, and Thurston Domina. 2008. "Raising the Bar: Curricular Intensity and Academic Performance." *Educational Evaluation and Policy Analysis* 30(1, March): 51–71.

———. 2011. "Educational Imposters and Fake Degrees." *Research in Social Stratification and Mobility* 29(1, January): 57–69.

Aviv, Rachel. 2014. "Wrong Answer." *The New Yorker*, July 28, 54–65.

Bailey, Stanley R. 2008. "Unmixing for Race Making in Brazil." *American Journal of Sociology* 114(3, November): 577–614.

Bailey, Stanley R., Aliya Saperstein, and Andrew M. Penner. 2014. "Race, Color, and Income Inequality across the Americas." *Demographic Research* 31(1, September): 735–56.

Baker, Bruce D. 2014. "America's Most Financially Disadvantaged School Districts and How They Got That Way: How State and Local Governance Causes School Funding Disparities." Center for American Progress, July 9. https://www.americanprogress.org/article/americas-most-financially-disadvantaged-school-districts-and-how-they-got-that-way/.

Baker, David. 2020. *The Schooled Society: The Educational Transformation of Global Culture.* Stanford, Calif.: Stanford University Press.

Barmeyer, Niels. 2008. "Taking on the State: Resistance, Education, and Other Challenges Facing the Zapatista Autonomy Project." *Identities: Global Studies in Culture and Power* 15(5, September): 506–27.

Baronnet, Bruno. 2008. "Rebel Youth and Zapatista Autonomous Education." *Latin American Perspectives* 35(4, July): 112–24.

Bassok, Daphna, Scott Latham, and Anna Rorem. 2016. "Is Kindergarten the New First Grade?" *AERA Open* 2(1). DOI: 10.1177/2332858415616358.

Bassok, Daphna, and Sean F. Reardon. 2013. "'Academic Redshirting' in Kindergarten: Prevalence, Patterns, and Implications." *Educational Evaluation and Policy Analysis* 35(3, September): 283–97.

Bauman, H-Dirksen. 2009. "Postscript: Gallaudet Protests of 2006 and the Myths of In/Exclusion." *Sign Language Studies* 10(1): 90–104.

Bedzow, Ira. 2020. "How California's Ethnic Studies Model Curriculum Got It Wrong." *Forbes*, September 16. https://www.forbes.com/sites/irabedzow/2020/09/16/how-californias-ethnic-studies-model-curriculum-got-it-wrong/?sh=6f76cb037c1c.

Bell, Alexander Graham. 1883. "Upon a Method of Teaching Language to a Very Young Congenitally Deaf Child." *American Annals of the Deaf and Dumb* 28(2, April): 124–39.

Bell, Derrick A., Jr. 1980. "*Brown v. Board of Education* and the Interest-Convergence Dilemma." *Harvard Law Review* 93(3, January): 518–33.

———. 2004. *Silent Covenants:* Brown v. Board of Education *and the Unfulfilled Hopes for Racial Reform.* New York: Oxford University Press.

Beneke, Abigail J. 2021. "Caring in the Context of Discipline Reform: A Framework for Researchers and Policymakers." *Educational Researcher* 51(3, April): 223–30.

Berner, Ashley Rogers. 2012. "The Case for Educational Pluralism in the U.S." *First Things* 228(July 11): 39.

Bidwell, Charles E. 2001. "Analyzing Schools as Organizations: Long-Term Permanence and Short-Term Change." *Sociology of Education* 74: 100–114.

Bifulco, Robert, and Helen F. Ladd. 2007. "School Choice, Racial Segregation, and Test-Score Gaps: Evidence from North Carolina's Charter School Program." *Journal of Policy Analysis and Management* 26(1, Winter): 31–56.

Billeaud, Jacques. 2011. "Ariz Schools' Ethnic Studies Program Ruled Illegal." *Boston Globe*, December 27.

Billingham, Chase M., and Matthew O. Hunt. 2016. "School Racial Composition and Parental Choice: New Evidence on the Preferences of White Parents in the United States." *Sociology of Education* 89(2, April): 99–117.

Binder, Amy J., Daniel B. Davis, and Nick Bloom. 2016. "Career Funneling: How Elite Students Learn to Define and Desire 'Prestigious' Jobs." *Sociology of Education* 89(1, January): 20–39.

Blair, Clancy, David Gamson, Steven Thorne, and David Baker. 2005. "Rising Mean IQ: Cognitive Demand of Mathematics Education for Young Children, Population Exposure to Formal Schooling, and the Neurobiology of the Prefrontal Cortex." *Intelligence* 33(1, February): 93–106.

Blau, Francine D., and Lawrence M. Kahn. 2017. "The Gender Wage Gap: Extent, Trends, and Explanations." *Journal of Economic Literature* 55 (3, September): 789–865.

Blau, Peter M. 1974. "Presidential Address: Parameters of Social Structure." *American Sociological Review* 39(5, October): 615–35.

Bloom, Stephen G. 2021. *Blue Eyes, Brown Eyes: A Cautionary Tale of Race and Brutality.* Berkeley: University of California Press.

Boeckenstedt, Jon. 2020. "Some Final Thoughts on the SAT and ACT." Jon Boeckenstedt's Admissions Weblog, January 13. https://jonboeckenstedt.net/2020/01/10/some-final-thoughts-on-the-sat-and-act/.

Boisjoly, Johanne, Greg J. Duncan, Michael Kremer, Dan M. Levy, and Jacque Eccles. 2006. "Empathy or Antipathy? The Impact of Diversity." *American Economic Review* 96(5, December): 1890–1905.

Bonilla, Sade, Thomas S. Dee, and Emily K. Penner. 2021. "Ethnic Studies Increases Longer-Run Academic Engagement and Attainment." *Proceedings of the National Academy of Sciences* 118(37, September 14): e2026386118.

Bonilla-Silva, Eduardo. 2006. *Racism without Racists: Color-Blind Racism and the Persistence of Racial Inequality in the United States.* Lanham, Md.: Rowman & Littlefield.

Bowker, Geoffrey, and Susan Leigh Star. 1999. *Sorting Things Out: Classification and Its Consequences.* Cambridge, Mass.: MIT Press.

Bowker, Travis. 2014. *What Teaching Has Taught Me: Lessons from a Secondary Classroom.* Mustang, Okla.: Tate Publishing & Enterprises.

Bowles, Samuel, and Herbert Gintis. 1976. *Schooling in Capitalist America: Educational Reform and the Contradictions of Economic Life.* New York: Basic Books.

Boyd, Herb. 2007. "Little Rock Nine Paved the Way." *New York Amsterdam News,* September 18, 2007, 28.

Brighouse, Harry. 2006. "Justifying Patriotism." *Social Theory and Practice* 32(4, October): 547–58.

Brighouse, Harry, Helen F. Ladd, Susanna Loeb, and Adam Swift. 2016. "Educational Goods and Values: A Framework for Decision-Makers." *Theory and Research in Education* 14(1, March): 3–25.

Brint, Steven, and Jerome Karabel. 1989. *The Diverted Dream: Community Colleges and the Promise of Educational Opportunity in America, 1900–1985.* New York: Oxford University Press.

Brody, Leslie. 2018. "New York City Schools Chief Questions How Students Are Screened." *Wall Street Journal,* May 23. https://www.wsj.com/articles/new-york-city-schools-chief-questions-how-students-are-screened-1527115702.

Buckley, Arabella Burton. 1885. *The Fairy-land of Science.* New York: D. Appleton and Co.

Buckner, Elizabeth, and Rebecca Hodges. 2016. "Cheating or Cheated? Surviving Secondary Exit Exams in a Neoliberal Era." *Compare: A Journal of Comparative and International Education* 46(4, October): 603–23.

California Department of Education. 1985. *Mathematics Framework for California Schools.* Sacramento: California Department of Education.

———. 1991. *Mathematics Framework for California Schools.* Sacramento: California Department of Education.

———. 1998. *Mathematics Framework for California Schools.* Sacramento: California Department of Education.

———. 2013. *Mathematics Framework for California Schools.* Sacramento: California Department of Education. https://www.cde.ca.gov/ci/ma/cf/mathfwchapters.asp.

———. 2021. "Revision of the Mathematics Framework." Website of the California Department of Education, November 4. https://www.cde.ca.gov/ci/ma/cf/.

California State Board of Education. 1992. *Mathematics Framework for California Public Schools: Kindergarten through Grade Twelve.* New York: Hippocrene Books.

Caplan, Bryan. 2018. *The Case against Education: Why the Education System Is a Waste of Time and Money.* Princeton, N.J.: Princeton University Press.

Carbonaro, William. 2005. "Tracking, Students' Effort, and Academic Achievement." *Sociology of Education* 78(1, January): 27–49.

Card, David. 1999. "The Causal Effect of Education on Earnings." In *Handbook of Labor Economics,* vol. 3, edited by Orley Ashenfelter and Richard Layard. New York: Elsevier Science Publishing.

Carlson, Deven, Matthew M. Chingos, and David E. Campbell. 2017. "The Effect of Private School Vouchers on Political Participation: Experimental Evidence from New York City." *Journal of Research on Educational Effectiveness* 10(3, October): 545–69.

Case, Anne, and Angus Deaton. 2015. "Rising Morbidity and Mortality in Midlife among White Non-Hispanic Americans in the 21st Century." *Proceedings of the National Academy of Sciences* 112(49): 15078–83.

Center for Research on Education Outcomes (CREDO). 2009. *Multiple Choice: Charter School Performance in 16 States*. Stanford, Calif.: CREDO.

Chatmon, Christopher P. 2019. "A View from the Inside: Reflections on the Work." In *"We Dare Say Love": Supporting Achievement in the Educational Life of Black Boys*, edited by Na'ilah Suad Nasir, Jarvis R. Givens, and Christopher P. Chatmon. New York: Teachers College Press.

Chen, Victor Tan. 2015. *Cut Loose: Jobless and Hopeless in an Unfair Economy*. Berkeley: University of California Press.

Child, Brenda J. 1998. *Boarding School Seasons: American Indian Families, 1900–1940*. Lincoln: University of Nebraska Press.

Chmielewski, Anna K., Hanna Dumont, and Ulrich Trautwein. 2013. "Tracking Effects Depend on Tracking Type: An International Comparison of Students' Mathematics Self-Concept." *American Educational Research Journal* 50(5, October): 925–57.

Cimpian, Andrei, Susan A. Gelman, and Amanda C. Brandone. 2010. "Theory-Based Considerations Influence the Interpretation of Generic Sentences." *Language and Cognitive Processes* 25(2): 261–76.

Clotfelter, Charles T., Helen F. Ladd, and Jacob L. Vigdor. 2015. "The Aftermath of Accelerating Algebra: Evidence from District Policy Initiatives." *Journal of Human Resources* 50(1, Winter): 159–88.

Collins, Patricia Hill. 2009. *Black Feminist Thought: Knowledge, Consciousness, and the Politics of Empowerment*. New York: Routledge.

Conger, Dylan, Mark C. Long, and Patrice Iatarola. 2009. "Explaining Race, Poverty, and Gender Disparities in Advanced Course-Taking." *Journal of Policy Analysis and Management* 28(4, Autumn): 555–76.

Connor, Carol McDonald, Frederick J. Morrison, Barry Fishman, Elizabeth C. Crowe, Stephanie Al Otaiba, and Christopher Schatschneider. 2013. "A Longitudinal Cluster-Randomized Controlled Study on the Accumulating Effects of Individualized Literacy Instruction on Students' Reading from First Through Third Grade." *Psychological Science* 24(8): 1408–19.

Cookson, Peter W., Jr., and Caroline Hodges Persell. 2008. *Preparing for Power: America's Elite Boarding Schools*. Boulder, Colo.: Basic Books.

Cottom, Tressie McMillan. 2017. *Lower Ed: The Troubling Rise of For-Profit Colleges in the New Economy*. New York: New Press.

Coy, Peter. 2021. "College Degrees Are Overrated." *New York Times*, October 18. https://www.nytimes.com/2021/10/18/opinion/college-degrees-employers.html.

Crawford, Amy. 2015. "How the Pledge of Allegiance Went from PR Gimmick to Patriotic Vow." *Smithsonian* (September). https://www.smithsonianmag.com/history/pledge-allegiance-pr-gimmick-patriotic-vow-180956332/.

Davis, Julie. 2001. "American Indian Boarding School Experiences: Recent Studies from Native Perspectives." *OAH Magazine of History* 15(2, Winter): 20–22.

Davis, Lennard J. 2007. "Deafness and the Riddle of Identity." *Chronicle of Higher Education*, January 12.

Davison, Miles, Andrew M. Penner, Emily K. Penner, Nikolas Pharris-Ciurej, Sonya R. Porter, Evan K. Rose, Yotam Shem-Tov, and Paul Yoo. 2022. "School Discipline and Racial Disparities in Early Adulthood." *Educational Researcher* 51(3, April): 231–34.

Dawson, Alexander S. 2012. "Histories and Memories of the Indian Boarding Schools in Mexico, Canada, and the United States." *Latin American Perspectives* 39(5, September): 80–99.

De Blasio, Bill. 2018. "Our Specialized Schools Have a Diversity Problem: Let's Fix It." Chalkbeat, June 2. https://ny.chalkbeat.org/2018/6/2/21105076/mayor-bill-de-blasio-our-specialized-schools-have-a-diversity-problem-let-s-fix-it.

Dee, Thomas S., and Emily K. Penner. 2017. "The Causal Effects of Cultural Relevance: Evidence from an Ethnic Studies Curriculum." *American Educational Research Journal* 54(1, February): 127–66.

———. 2021. "My Brother's Keeper? The Impact of Targeted Educational Supports." *Journal of Policy Analysis and Management* 40(4, Autumn): 1171–96.

Delmont, Matthew F. 2016. *Why Busing Failed: Race, Media, and the National Resistance to School Desegregation*. Berkeley: University of California Press.

Diamond, John B. 2012. "Accountability Policy, School Organization, and Classroom Practice: Partial Recoupling and Educational Opportunity." *Education and Urban Society* 44(2, March): 151–82.

DiPrete, Thomas A., and Gregory M. Eirich. 2006. "Cumulative Advantage as a Mechanism for Inequality: A Review of Theoretical and Empirical Developments." *Annual Review of Sociology* 32: 271–97.

Do, Quy-Toan, and Tung D. Phung. 2010. "The Importance of Being Wanted." *American Economic Journal: Applied Economics* 2(4, October): 236–53.

Domina, Thurston, Andrew McEachin, Paul Hanselman, Priyanka Agarwal, NaYoung Hwang, and Ryan W. Lewis. 2019. "Beyond Tracking and Detracking: The Dimensions of Organizational Differentiation in Schools." *Sociology of Education* 92(3): 293–322.

Domina, Thurston, Andrew McEachin, Andrew Penner, and Emily Penner. 2015. "Aiming High and Falling Short: California's Eighth-Grade Algebra-for-All Effort." *Educational Evaluation and Policy Analysis* 37(3, September): 275–95.

Domina, Thurston, Andrew M. Penner, and Emily K. Penner. 2016. "'Membership Has Its Privileges': Status Incentives and Categorical Inequality in Education." *Sociological Science* 3: 264–95.

———. 2017. "Categorical Inequality: Schools as Sorting Machines." *Annual Review of Sociology* 43: 311–30.

Domina, Thurston, and Joshua Saldana. 2012. "Does Raising the Bar Level the Playing Field? Mathematics Curricular Intensification and Inequality in American High Schools, 1982–2004." *American Educational Research Journal* 49(4, August): 685–708.

Dougherty, Shaun M., Joshua S. Goodman, Darryl V. Hill, Erica G. Litke, and Lindsay C. Page. 2015. "Middle School Math Acceleration and Equitable Access to

Eighth-Grade Algebra: Evidence from the Wake County Public School System." *Educational Evaluation and Policy Analysis* 37(1, supp., May): 80S–101S.

Douglass, Frederick. 1857. *Two Speeches, by Frederick Douglass: One on West India Emancipation, Delivered at Canandaigua, Aug. 4th, and the Other on the Dred Scott Decision, Delivered in New York, on the Occasion of the Anniversary of the American Abolition Society, May, 1857.* Rochester, N.Y.: C. P. Dewey, Printer, American Office.

———. 2016. *Life and Times of Frederick Douglass: The Illustrated Edition.* Zenith Press.

Dudziak, Mary, L. 2000. *Cold War Civil Rights: Race and the Image of American Democracy.* Princeton, N.J.: Princeton University Press.

———. 2004. "*Brown* as a Cold War Case." *Journal of American History* 91(1, June): 32–42.

Dunn, Frederick. 1993. "The Educational Philosophies of Washington, DuBois, and Houston: Laying the Foundations for Afrocentrism and Multiculturalism." *Journal of Negro Education* 62(1, Winter): 24–34.

Dunn, Lindsay Moeletsi, and Glenn B. Anderson. 2019. "Examining the Intersectionality of Deaf Identity, Race/Ethnicity, and Diversity through a Black Deaf Lens." In *Deaf Identities: Exploring New Frontiers*, edited by Irene W. Leigh, and Catherine A. O'Brien. Oxford: Oxford University Press.

Dunn, Trevor. 2017. "'It's Like Counterfeit Money': Toronto Man Angry He Paid $8,100 for a Fake Master's Degree." *CBC News*, September 15. https://www.cbc.ca/news/canada/toronto/fake-degree-toronto-investigation-1.4287347.

Eckel, Catherine C., Sheryl B. Ball, Philip J. Grossman, and William R. Zame. 2001. "Status in Markets." *Quarterly Journal of Economics* 116(1, February): 161–88.

Edex Live. 2021. "Students Petition NTA, Modi, Pradhan to Reconduct NEET after Paper Leak, Cheating Scams Rock Country." *Edex Live*, September 15. https://www.edexlive.com/news/2021/sep/15/students-petition-nta-modi-pradhan-to-reconduct-neet-after-paper-leak-cheating-scams-rock-country-24023.html.

Egalite, Anna J., and Jonathan N. Mills. 2021. "Competitive Impacts of Means-Tested Vouchers on Public School Performance: Evidence from Louisiana." *Education Finance and Policy* 16(1, Winter): 66–91.

Elman, Benjamin A. 2000. *A Cultural History of Civil Examinations in Late Imperial China.* Berkeley: University of California Press.

———. 2013. *Civil Examinations and Meritocracy in Late Imperial China.* Cambridge, Mass.: Harvard University Press.

Emery, Kathy, Sylvia Braselmann, and Linda Reid Gold. 2004. "Introduction: Freedom Summer and the Freedom Schools." *Freedom School Curriculum: Mississippi Freedom Summer, 1964*, edited by Kathy Emery, Sylvia Braselmann, and Linda Reid Gold. Available at Internet Archive, https://archive.org/details/FreedomSchoolCurrWPhotoCopy/page/n5/mode/2up.

Engel, Mimi, Amy Claessens, and Maida A. Finch. 2013. "Teaching Students What They Already Know? The (Mis)Alignment between Mathematics Instructional Content and Student Knowledge in Kindergarten." *Educational Evaluation and Policy Analysis* 35(2, June): 157–78.

England, Paula, Andrew Levine, and Emma Mishel. 2020. "Progress toward Gender Equality in the United States Has Slowed or Stalled." *Proceedings of the National Academy of Sciences* 117 (13, March 31): 6990–97.

Erevelles, Nirmala. 2000. "Educating Unruly Bodies: Critical Pedagogy, Disability Studies, and the Politics of Schooling." *Educational Theory* 50(1, March): 25–47.

Evans, Lorraine, and Kimberly Davies. 2000. "No Sissy Boys Here: A Content Analysis of the Representation of Masculinity in Elementary School Reading Textbooks." *Sex Roles* 42(3, February): 255–70.

Felch, Jason, Jason Song, and Doug Smith. 2010. "Who's Teaching L.A.'s Kids?" *Los Angeles Times*, August 14.

Feliciano, Cynthia. 2009. "Education and Ethnic Identity Formation among Children of Latin American and Caribbean Immigrants." *Sociological Perspectives* 52(2, Summer): 135–58.

Fenwick, James J. 1987. *Caught in the Middle: Educational Reform for Young Adolescents in California Public School: Report of the Superintendent's Middle Grade Task Force.* Sacramento: California Department of Education, Bureau of Publications.

Ficker, Douglas J. 1999. "From *Roberts* to *Plessy*: Educational Segregation and the 'Separate but Equal' Doctrine." *Journal of Negro History* 84(4, Autumn): 301–14.

Fields, Jessica. 2008. *Risky Lessons: Sex Education and Social Inequality.* New Brunswick, N.J.: Rutgers University Press.

Finley, Merrilee K. 1984. "Teachers and Tracking in a Comprehensive High School." *Sociology of Education* 57(4, October): 233–43.

Flores, Cheryl. 2017. "Filmic Representations of Fannie Lou Hamer and Sakia Gunn in Contemporary Black Feminist Thought: Considering Zenzele Isoke's Theories about Intramural Conversations through Documentary Film." Annual meeting of the National Conference of Black Political Scientists (NCOBPS).

Foley, Henry. 1878. *Records of the English Province of the Society of Jesus.* London: Burns and Oates.

Foster, Michele. 1997. *Black Teachers on Teaching.* New York: New Press.

Francis, Dania V., and William A. Darity. 2021. "Separate and Unequal under One Roof: How the Legacy of Racialized Tracking Perpetuates Within-School Segregation." *RSF: The Russell Sage Foundation Journal of the Social Sciences* 7(1, February): 187–202. DOI: https://doi.org/10.7758/RSF.2021.7.1.11.

Frank, Robert H., and Philip J. Cook. 2010. *The Winner-Take-All Society: Why the Few at the Top Get So Much More than the Rest of Us.* New York: Random House.

Freyer, Jake, Gautam S. Kumar, Danielle E. O'Neil, Benjamin Samuels, Corley E. Stone, Zoe A. Y. Weinberg, and Julie M. Zauzmer. 2013. "Class of 2013 Senior Survey." *Harvard Crimson*, May 28. https://www.thecrimson.com/flash-graphic/2013/5/28/senior-survey-2013-graphic/.

Fryer, Roland G., Jr., and Steven D. Levitt. 2004. "Understanding the Black-White Test Score Gap in the First Two Years of School." *Review of Economics and Statistics* 86(2, June): 447–64.

Gahman, Levi. 2016. "Zapatismo versus the Neoliberal University: Towards a Pedagogy against Oblivion." In *The Radicalization of Pedagogy: Anarchism,*

Geography, and the Spirit of Revolt, edited by Simon Springer, Marcelo Lopes de Souza, and Richard J. White. Lanham, Md.: Rowman and Littlefield.

———. 2017. "Dismantling Neoliberal Education: A Lesson from the Zapatistas." *Medium*, April 12. https://medium.com/communityworksjournal/dismantling-neoliberal-education-a-lesson-from-the-zapatistas-2fa8f44961c9.

Gamoran, Adam. 1987. "The Stratification of High School Learning Opportunities." *Sociology of Education* 60(3, July): 135–55.

———. 1992. "Synthesis of Research: Is Ability Grouping Equitable?" *Educational Leadership* 50(2, October 1): 11–17.

Gamoran, Adam, Ana Cristina Collares, and Sarah Barfels. 2016. "Does Racial Isolation in School Lead to Long-Term Disadvantages? Labor Market Consequences of High School Racial Composition." *American Journal of Sociology* 121(4, January): 1116–67.

Gamoran, Adam, Martin Nystrand, Mark Berends, and Paul C. LePore. 1995. "An Organizational Analysis of the Effects of Ability Grouping." *American Educational Research Journal* 32(4, Winter): 687–715.

Gelman, Susan A. 2003. *The Essential Child: Origins of Essentialism in Everyday Thought.* New York: Oxford University Press.

Gibson, Carrie. 2019. *El Norte: The Epic and Forgotten Story of Hispanic North America.* New York: Atlantic Monthly Press.

Giroux, Henry A. 2007. *Border Crossings: Cultural Workers and the Politics of Education.* New York: Routledge.

Golann, Joanne W. 2021. *Scripting the Moves: Culture and Control in a "No-Excuses" Charter School.* Princeton, N.J.: Princeton University Press.

Golden, Daniel. 2016. "The Story behind Jared Kushner's Curious Acceptance into Harvard." *ProPublica*, November 18. https://www.propublica.org/article/the-story-behind-jared-kushners-curious-acceptance-into-harvard.

Goldstein, Dana. 2019. "Push for Ethnic Studies in Schools Faces a Dilemma: Whose Stories to Tell." *New York Times*, August 15. https://www.nytimes.com/2019/08/15/us/california-ethnic-studies.html.

Gordon, Megan, and Mary Reinhart. 2011. "Arizona Ethnic Studies Ban Goes into Effect." *Arizona Republic*, January 1.

Grande, Sandy. 2015. *Red Pedagogy: Native American Social and Political Thought.* Lanham, Md.: Rowman & Littlefield.

Grissom, Jason A., Demetra Kalogrides, and Susanna Loeb. 2017. "Strategic Staffing? How Performance Pressures Affect the Distribution of Teachers within Schools and Resulting Student Achievement." *American Educational Research Journal* 54(6, December): 1079–1116.

Grubb, W. Norton, and Marvin Lazerson. 2004. *The Education Gospel: The Economic Power of Schooling.* Cambridge, Mass.: Harvard University Press.

Guhin, Jeffrey. 2021. "Why Study Schools?" In *Handbook of Classical Sociological Theory* edited by Seth Abrutyn and Omar Lizardo. Cham, Switzerland: Springer.

Guinier, Lani. 2004. "From Racial Liberalism to Racial Literacy: *Brown v. Board of Education* and the Interest-Divergence Dilemma." *Journal of American History* 91(1, June): 92–118.

Guryan, Jonathan, Erik Hurst, and Melissa Kearney. 2008. "Parental Education and Parental Time with Children." *Journal of Economic Perspectives* 22(3, Summer): 23–46.

Hailey, Chantal A. 2021. "Racial Preferences for Schools: Evidence from an Experiment with White, Black, Latinx, and Asian Parents and Students." *Sociology of Education* 95(2, April): 110–32.

Hallett, Tim. 2010. "The Myth Incarnate: Recoupling Processes, Turmoil, and Inhabited Institutions in an Urban Elementary School." *American Sociological Review* 75(1, February): 52–74.

Hallinan, Maureen T. 1994. "Tracking: From Theory to Practice." *Sociology of Education* 67(2): 79–84.

Handsman, Emily, Caitlin Farrell, and Cynthia Coburn. 2022. "Solving for X: Constructing Algebra and Algebra Policy during a Time of Change." *Sociology of Education* 95(3, July): 00380407221087479.

Hannah-Jones, Nikole. 2014. "Segregation Now." *Atlantic* 313(4, May): 58–69.

Hanselman, Paul, Thurston Domina, and NaYoung Hwang. 2022. "Educational Inequality Regimes amid Algebra-for-All: The Provision and Allocation of Expanding Educational Opportunities." *Social Forces* 100(4, June): 1722–51.

Hanselman, Paul, and Jeremy E. Fiel. 2017. "School Opportunity Hoarding? Racial Segregation and Access to High Growth Schools." *Social Forces* 95(3, March): 1077–1104.

Harmon, Kristen. 2021. "Un-Telling 'The Eugenist's Tale': Early Twentieth-Century Deaf Writers on A. G. Bell and Eugenics." *Journal of Literary and Cultural Disability Studies* 15(2): 151–67.

Harris, Cheryl I. 1993. "Whiteness as Property.' *Harvard Law Review* (106)8: 1707–91.

Hart, Ray, Michael Casserly, Renata Uzzell, Moses Palacios, Amanda Corcoran, and Liz Spurgeon. 2015. *Student Testing in America's Great City Schools*. Washington, D.C.: Council of the Great City Schools.

Harwell, Michael, and Brandon LeBeau. 2010. "Student Eligibility for a Free Lunch as an SES Measure in Education Research." *Educational Researcher* 39(2, March): 120–31.

Hauser, Christine. 2021. "A Utah School Made Black History Month Optional. Then It Reversed Itself." *New York Times*, February 8. https://www.nytimes.com/2021/02/08/us/utah-school-black-history-month.html.

Herszenhorn, David M. 2005. "Admission Test's Scoring Quirk Throws Balance into Question." *New York Times*, November 12. https://www.nytimes.com/2005/11/12/nyregion/admission-tests-scoring-quirk-throws-balance-into-question.html.

Hess, Frederick M., and Michael J. Petrilli. 2006. *No Child Left Behind Primer*. New York: Peter Lang.

Hill, Joseph, Lynn Hou, Anna Lim, Dominic Harrison, and David Player. 2020. "Race, Racism, and Racialization in Sign Language Research and Deaf Studies: Introduction for the Panel." Presented at the fourteenth biennial conference of the High Desert Linguistics Society, Albuquerque, N.M., November 20–22, 5.

Ho, Ping-Ti. 1962. *The Ladder of Success in Imperial China: Aspects of Social Mobility, 1368–1911*. New York: Columbia University Press.

Holliday, Wendy. 2020. "Hopi History: The Story of the Alcatraz Prisoners." National Park Service, last updated June 22, 2020. https://www.nps.gov/articles/hopi-prisoners-on-the-rock.htm.

hooks, bell. 1994. *Teaching to Transgress*. New York: Routledge.

Hout, Michael. 2012. "Social and Economic Returns to College Education in the United States." *Annual Review of Sociology* 38: 379–400.

Hoy, Wayne K., and Dennis J. Sabo. 1998. *Quality Middle Schools. Open and Healthy.* Thousand Oaks, Calif.: Corwin Press.

Hoy, Wayne K., C. John Tarter, and Robert Kottkamp. 1991. *Open Schools/Healthy Schools: Measuring Organizational Climate.* Thousand Oaks, Calif.: Corwin Press.

Hu, C. T. 1984. "The Historical Background: Examinations and Control in Pre-Modern China." *Comparative Education* 20(1): 7–26.

Huang, Cheng, Xiaojing Ma, Shiying Zhang, and Qingguo Zhao. 2020. "Numerological Preferences, Timing of Births and the Long-Term Effect on Schooling." *Journal of Population Economics* 33(2, April): 531–54.

Hyer, Sally. 1990. *One House, One Voice, One Heart: Native American Education at the Santa Fe Indian School*. Santa Fe: Museum of New Mexico Press.

India TV Education Desk. 2021. "JEE Main Result 2021: 20 Students Debarred for Cheating in Engineering Entrance." *India TV*, September 16. https://www.indiatvnews.com/education/news-jee-main-result-2021-20-students-debarred-for-cheating-in-engineering-entrance-jeemain-nta-nic-in-734265.

Irvine, Jacqueline Jordan. 2003. *Educating Teachers for Diversity: Seeing with a Cultural Eye*. New York: Teachers College Press.

Jackman, Michael. 2018. "U.S. Court: Detroit Students Have No Right to Access to Literacy." *Detroit Metro Times*, July 2. https://www.metrotimes.com/news/us-court-detroit-students-have-no-right-to-access-to-literacy-13478316.

Jackson, Cara. 2021. "Democratizing the Development of Evidence." *Educational Researcher* 51(3, April): 0013189X211060357.

Jencks, Christopher. 1972. "Inequality: A Reassessment of the Effect of Family and Schooling in America." New York: Basic Books.

———. 1988. "Whom Must We Treat Equally for Educational Opportunity to Be Equal?" *Ethics* 98(3, April): 518–33.

Jiang, Wen Shan, and Chloe Hanson. 2017. "Academic Dishonesty: An Inherent Issue?" *The Spectator*, December 20. https://www.stuyspec.com/news/academic-dishonesty-an-inherent-issue.

Jimerson, Shane R., Sarah M. W. Pletcher, Kelly Graydon, Britton L. Schnurr, Amanda B. Nickerson, and Deborah K. Kundert. 2006. "Beyond Grade Retention and Social Promotion: Promoting the Social and Academic Competence of Students." *Psychology in the Schools* 43(1, January): 85–97.

Jones, Jeffrey Owen. 2003. "The Man Who Wrote the Pledge of Allegiance." *Smithsonian* (November). https://www.smithsonianmag.com/history/the-man-who-wrote-the-pledge-of-allegiance-93907224/.

Kaestle, Carl F. 1983. *Pillars of the Republic: Common Schools and American Society, 1780–1860*. New York: Hill and Wang.

Karabel, Jerome. 2006. *The Chosen: The Hidden History of Admission and Exclusion at Harvard, Yale, and Princeton.* Boston: Houghton Mifflin Harcourt.

Kendrick, Stephen, and Paul Kendrick. 2004. *Sarah's Long Walk: The Free Blacks of Boston and How Their Struggle for Equality Changed America.* Boston: Beacon Press.

Khan, Shamus Rahman. 2011. *Privilege: The Making of an Adolescent Elite at St. Paul's School.* Princeton, N.J.: Princeton University Press.

Knoester, Matthew, and Wayne Au. 2017. "Standardized Testing and School Segregation: Like Tinder for Fire?" *Race, Ethnicity, and Education* 20(1): 1–14.

Kornrich, Sabino, and Frank Furstenberg. 2013. "Investing in Children: Changes in Parental Spending on Children, 1972–2007." *Demography* 50(1, February): 1–23.

Kurtz, Stanley. 2021. "Consensus by Surrender." *National Review*, June 10. https://www.nationalreview.com/corner/consensus-by-surrender/.

Labaree, David F. 1997. "Public Goods, Private Goods: The American Struggle over Educational Goals." *American Educational Research Journal* 34(1): 39–81.

Ladd, Helen F., Edward B. Fiske, and Nienke Ruijs. 2009. "Parental Choice in the Netherlands: Growing Concerns about Segregation." Presented at National Conference on School Choice, Vanderbilt University, Nashville, Tenn., October 25–27.

Ladson-Billings, Gloria. 2016. "Just What Is CRT and What's It Doing in a Nice Field Like Education." *Foundations of CRT in Education*, 2nd ed., edited by Edward Taylor, David Gillborn, and Gloria Ladson-Billings. New York: Routledge.

Laitsch, Dan. 2006. "Student Behaviors and Teacher Use of Approval versus Disapproval." *Research Brief* 4(3).

Lee, Jong-Wha, and Hanol Lee. 2016. "Human Capital in the Long Run." *Journal of Development Economics* 122(September): 147–69.

Legewie, Joscha, and Thomas A. DiPrete. 2012. "School Context and the Gender Gap in Educational Achievement." *American Sociological Review* 77(3, June): 463–85.

Leslie, Sarah-Jane. 2008. "Generics: Cognition and Acquisition." *Philosophical Review* 117(1, January): 1–47.

Levin, Sam. 2016. "Stanford Sexual Assault: Read the Full Text of the Judge's Controversial Decision." *Guardian*, June 14. https://www.theguardian.com/us-news/2016/jun/14/stanford-sexual-assault-read-sentence-judge-aaron-persky.

Lewis, Amanda E. 2003. *Race in the Schoolyard: Negotiating the Color Line in Classrooms and Communities.* New Brunswick, N.J.: Rutgers University Press.

Lewis, Amanda E., and John B. Diamond. 2015. *Despite the Best Intentions: How Racial Inequality Thrives in Good Schools.* Oxford: Oxford University Press.

Lipsky, Michael. 1980. *Street-Level Bureaucracy: Dilemmas of the Individual in Public Service.* New York: Russell Sage Foundation.

Loeb, Susanna, and Daphna Bassok. 2012. "Early Childhood and the Achievement Gap." In *Handbook of Research in Education Finance and Policy*, edited by Helen F. Ladd and Margaret E. Goertz. New York: Routledge.

Long, Mark C., Victor Saenz, and Marta Tienda. 2010. "Policy Transparency and College Enrollment: Did the Texas Top Ten Percent Law Broaden Access to the Public Flagships?" *Annals of the American Academy of Political and Social Science* 627(1, January): 82–105.

Lovett, Benjamin J. 2020. "Disability Identification and Educational Accommodations: Lessons from the 2019 Admissions Scandal." *Educational Researcher* 49(2, March): 125–29.

Lovett, Ian. 2010. "Teacher's Death Exposes Tensions in Los Angeles." *New York Times*, November 9.

Lubienski, Chris. 2000. "Whither the Common Good? A Critique of Home Schooling." *Peabody Journal of Education* 75(1/2): 207–32. DOI: https://doi.org/10.1080/0161956X.2000.9681942.

Lucas, Samuel Roundfield. 1999. *Tracking Inequality: Stratification and Mobility in American High Schools*. New York: Teachers College Press.

———. 2001. "Effectively Maintained Inequality: Education Transitions, Track Mobility, and Social Background Effects." *American Journal of Sociology* 106(6, May): 1642–90.

Mann, Horace. 1848. "Twelfth Annual Report to the Massachusetts Board of Education." In *The Republic and the School: Horace Mann and the Education of Free Men*, edited by Lawrence A. Cremin. New York: Teachers College Press.

———. 1853. *A Few Thoughts on the Powers and Duties of Woman: Two Lectures*. Syracuse, N.Y.: Hall, Mills, and Co.

———. 1891. *Annual Reports of the Secretary of the Board of Education of Massachusetts for the Years 1839–1844*, vol. 3. Boston: Lee and Shepard.

Marmot, Michael. 2004. *The Status Syndrome: How Social Standing Affects Our Health and Longevity*. New York: Henry Holt.

Martínez, José Felipe, Brian Stecher, and Hilda Borko. 2009. "Classroom Assessment Practices, Teacher Judgments, and Student Achievement in Mathematics: Evidence from the ECLS." *Educational Assessment* 14(2): 78–102.

Massey, Douglas S. 2007. *Categorically Unequal: The American Stratification System*. New York: Russell Sage Foundation.

Massoglia, Michael, and William Alex Pridemore. 2015. "Incarceration and Health." *Annual Review of Sociology* 41: 291–310.

McDiarmid, Garnet, and David Pratt. 1971. *Teaching Prejudice: A Content Analysis of Social Studies Textbooks Authorized for Use in Ontario*. Toronto: Ontario Institute for Studies in Education.

McEachin, Andrew, Thurston Domina, and Andrew Penner. 2020. "Heterogeneous Effects of Early Algebra across California Middle Schools." *Journal of Policy Analysis and Management* 39(3): 772–800.

McEachin, Andrew, Douglas Lee Lauen, Sarah Crittenden Fuller, and Rachel M. Perera. 2020. "Social Returns to Private Choice? Effects of Charter Schools on Behavioral Outcomes, Arrests, and Civic Participation." *Economics of Education Review* 76(June): 101983.

McFarland, Joel, Bill Hussar, Jijun Zhang, Xiaolei Wang, Ke Wang, Sarah Hein, Melissa Diliberti, Emily Forrest Cataldi, Farrah Bullock Mann, and Amy Barmer. 2019. *The Condition of Education 2019*. NCES 2019-144. Washington, D.C.: National Center for Education Statistics (May). https://nces.ed.gov/pubs2019/2019144.pdf.

Menkart, Deborah, and Jenice L. View. n.d. "Exploring the History of Freedom Schools." Civil Rights Teaching. https://www.civilrightsteaching.org/exploring-history-freedom-schools (accessed November 23, 2021).

Meyer, John W. 1977. "The Effects of Education as an Institution." *American Journal of Sociology* 83(1, July): 55–77.

Meyer, John W., Patricia Bromley, and Francisco O. Ramirez. 2010. "Human Rights in Social Science Textbooks: Cross-National Analyses, 1970–2008." *Sociology of Education* 83(2, April): 111–34.

Meyer, John W., and Brian Rowan. 1975. *Notes on the Structure of Educational Organizations*. Stanford, Calif.: Stanford Center for Research and Development in Teaching.

Milligan, Kevin, Enrico Moretti, and Philip Oreopoulos. 2004. "Does Education Improve Citizenship? Evidence from the United States and the United Kingdom." *Journal of Public Economics* 88(9/10, August): 1667–95.

Mills, Charles W. 2014. *The Racial Contract*. Ithaca, N.Y.: Cornell University Press.

Miyazaki, Ichisada. 1981. *China's Examination Hell: The Civil Service Examinations of Imperial China*. New Haven, Conn.: Yale University Press.

Mohai, Paul, David Pellow, and J. Timmons Roberts. 2009. "Environmental Justice." *Annual Review of Environment and Resources* 34: 405–30.

Morning, Ann. 2008. "Reconstructing Race in Science and Society: Biology Textbooks, 1952–2002." *American Journal of Sociology* 114(supp. 1): S106–37.

Moss, Hilary J. 2010. *Schooling Citizens: The Struggle for African American Education in Antebellum America*. Chicago: University of Chicago Press.

Murray, Dale. 2009. "Presumptions against School District Secession." *Theory and Research in Education* 7(1): 47–63.

Nash, Gary B. 1997. "Reflections on the National History Standards." *National Forum* (Honor Society of Phi Kappa Phi) 77(3, Summer): 14.

Nash, Gary B., Charlotte Antoinette Crabtree, and Ross E. Dunn. 2000. *History on Trial: Culture Wars and the Teaching of the Past*. New York: Vintage.

Nash, Gary B., and Ross E. Dunn. 1995. "History Standards and Culture Wars." *Social Education* 59(1, Fall): 5–7.

Nasir, Na'ilah Suad, Jarvis R. Givens, and Christopher P. Chatmon, eds. 2019. *"We Dare Say Love": Supporting Achievement in the Educational Life of Black Boys*. New York: Teachers College Press.

Nasir, Na'ilah Suad, Kihana Miraya Ross, Maxine Mckinney de Royston, Jarvis Givens, and Jalessa Bryant. 2013. "Dirt on My Record: Rethinking Disciplinary Practices in an All-Black, All-Male Alternative Class." *Harvard Educational Review* 83(3, Fall): 489–512.

National Governors Association. 2010a. "Common Core State Standards for English Language Arts & Literacy in History/Social Studies, Science, and Technical Subjects." Washington, D.C.: National Governors Association Center for Best Practices, Council of Chief State School Officers. http://www.corestandards.org/.

———. 2010b. "Common Core State Standards for Mathematics." Washington, D.C.: National Governors Association Center for Best Practices, Council of Chief State School Officers. http://www.corestandards.org/.

Nehm, Ross H., and Rebecca Young. 2008. "'Sex Hormones' in Secondary School Biology Textbooks." *Science and Education* 17(10, November): 1175–90.

Nie, Norman H., Jane Junn, and Kenneth Stehlik-Barry. 1996. *Education and Democratic Citizenship in America*. Chicago: University of Chicago Press.

Noble, Safiya Umoja. 2018. *Algorithms of Oppression: How Search Engines Reinforce Racism*. New York: New York University Press.

Nomi, Takako, and Elaine Allensworth. 2012. "Sorting and Supporting: Why Double-Dose Algebra Led to Better Test Scores but More Course Failures." *American Educational Research Journal* 50(4, August): 756–88.

Nomi, Takako, and Stephen W. Raudenbush. 2016. "Making a Success of 'Algebra for All': The Impact of Extended Instructional Time and Classroom Peer Skill in Chicago." *Educational Evaluation and Policy Analysis* 38(2): 431–51.

Oakes, Jeannie. 1983. "Limiting Opportunity: Student Race and Curricular Differences in Secondary Vocational Education." *American Journal of Education* 91(3, May): 328–55.

———. 1994. "More than Misapplied Technology: A Normative and Political Response to Hallinan on Tracking." *Sociology of Education* 67(2, April): 84–91.

———. 2005. *Keeping Track: How Schools Structure Inequality*. New Haven, Conn.: Yale University Press.

Oakes, Jeannie, Sharon E. Hare, and Kenneth A. Sirotnik. 1986. "Collaborative Inquiry: A Congenial Paradigm in a Cantankerous World." *Teachers College Record: The Voice of Scholarship in Education* 87(4, Summer): 545–61. DOI: 10.1177/016146818608700402.

Oakes, Jeannie, Amy Wells, Makeba Jones, and Amanda Datnow. 1997. "Detracking: The Social Construction of Ability, Cultural Politics, and Resistance to Reform." *Teachers College Record* 98(3, March): 482–510.

Oikonomakis, Leonidas. 2015. "Why We Still Love the Zapatistas: The Construction of a New World Is Much More than an Academic Exercise." *ROAR* (December): 114–32 (accessed December 17, 2015).

Olivas, Michael A. 2010. "Plyler v. Doe: Still Guaranteeing Unauthorized Immigrant Children's Right to Attend U.S. Public Schools." Migration Policy Institute, September 9. https://www.migrationpolicy.org/article/plyler-v-doe-still-guaranteeing-unauthorized-immigrant-childrens-right-attend-us-public/.

Omi, Michael, and Howard Winant. 2014. *Racial Formation in the United States*, 3rd ed. New York: Routledge.

Open Culture. 2017. "Thelonious Monk's 25 Tips for Musicians." *Open Culture*, December 18. https://www.openculture.com/2017/12/thelonious-monks-25-tips-for-musicians-1960.html.

Orfield, Gary, and Susan E. Eaton. 1996. *Dismantling Desegregation: The Quiet Reversal of Brown v. Board of Education*. New York: New Press.

Organization for Economic Cooperation and Development (OECD). 2016. *Innovating Education and Educating for Innovation: The Power of Digital Technologies and Skills*. Paris: OECD Publishing. http://dx.doi.org/10.1787/9789264265097-en.

Osterhammel, Jürgen. 2015. "La transformación del mundo." In *Una historia global del siglo XIX*. Barcelona: Crítica.

Pandey, Munish Chandra. 2021. "Fraud in JEE Mains: 3 Sent to CBI Custody, Rahul Gandhi Alleges Cover-up by Govt." *India Today*, September 4. https://www.indiatoday.in/india/story/jee-mains-fraud-3-in-cbi-custody-rahul-gandhi-cover-up-by-govt-1849276-2021-09-04.

Park, Vicki, and Amanda Datnow. 2017. "Ability Grouping and Differentiated Instruction in an Era of Data-Driven Decision Making." *American Journal of Education* 123(2, February): 281–306.

Pascoe, C. J. 2007. *Dude, You're a Fag: Masculinity and Sexuality in High School*. Berkeley: University of California Press.

Payne, Keith. 2017. *The Broken Ladder: How Inequality Affects the Way We Think, Live, and Die*. New York: Penguin.

Penner, Andrew M., Trond Petersen, Are Skeie Hermansen, William Anthony Rainey, István Boza, Marta Elvira, Olivier Godechot, Martin Hällsten, Lasse Folke Henriksen, Feng Hou, Aleksandra Kanjuo-Mrčela, Joseph King, Naomi Kodama, Tali Kristal, Alena Křížková, Zoltán Lippényi, Silvia Melzer, Eunmi Mun, Paula Apascaritei, Dustin Avent-Holt, Nina Bandelj, Gergely Hajdu, Jiwook Jung, Andreja Poje, Halil Sabanci, Mirna Safi, Matthew Soener, Donald Tomaskovic-Devey, and Zaibu Tufail. 2022. "Within-Job Gender Pay Inequality in 15 Countries." *Nature Human Behaviour* (November 24). DOI: https://doi.org/10.1038/s41562-022-01470-z.

Peters, William. 1971. *A Class Divided*. Garden City, N.Y.: Doubleday.

Pickett, Robert E. M., Aliya Saperstein, and Andrew M. Penner. 2022. "Identification in Interaction: Racial Mirroring between Interviewers and Respondents." *Social Forces* (November 11). DOI: https://doi.org/10.1093/sf/soac115.

Plagiarism.org. 2017. "Plagiarism: Facts & Stats." June 7. https://www.plagiarism.org/article/plagiarism-facts-and-stats.

Planas, Roque. 2017. "A Judge Is about to Rule Whether Banning Mexican-American Studies Is Constitutional." Long Beach, Calif.: California-Mexico Studies Center (August 10). https://www.california-mexicocenter.org/a-judge-is-about-to-rule-whether-banning-mexican-american-studies-is-constitutional/.

Poppendieck, Janet. 2011. *Free for All: Fixing School Food in America*. Vol. 28. Berkeley: University of California Press.

Porter, Katherine Anne. 1952. "The Downward Path to Wisdom: Complete Short Story." In *Selections from Her Writings Read by the Author* (LP). New York: Caedmon Records.

Posselt, Julie R. 2016. *Inside Graduate Admissions: Merit, Diversity, and Faculty Gatekeeping*. Cambridge, Mass.: Harvard University Press.

powell, john a. 2012. *Racing to Justice: Transforming Our Conceptions of Self and Other to Build an Inclusive Society*. Bloomington: Indiana University Press.

powell, john a., Stephen Menendian, and Wendy Ake. 2019. *Targeted Universalism: Policy and Practice*. Berkeley: Haas Institute for a Fair and Inclusive Society.

Quinn, Rand. 2020. *Class Action: Desegregation and Diversity in San Francisco Schools*. Minneapolis: University of Minnesota Press.

Rafalow, Matthew H. 2020. "Schools as Socializing Agents for Digital Participation." In Rafalow, *Digital Divisions: How Schools Create Inequality in the Tech Era*. Chicago: University of Chicago Press.

Ramey, Garey, and Valerie A. Ramey. 2009. "The Rug Rat Race." Working paper 15284. National Bureau of Economic Research, August. DOI: 10.3386/w15284.

Ramirez, Francisco O., and John Boli. 1987. "The Political Construction of Mass Schooling: European Origins and Worldwide Institutionalization." *Sociology of Education* 60(1, January): 2–17.

Ramirez, Francisco O., Patricia Bromley, and Susan Garnett Russell. 2009. "The Valorization of Humanity and Diversity." *Multicultural Education Review* 1(1): 29–54.

Ramirez, Francisco O., and Yun-Kyung Cha. 1990. "Citizenship and Gender: Western Educational Developments in Comparative Perspective." In *Research in Sociology of Education and Socialization*, vol. 9, edited by Ronald G. Corwin. San Jose, Calif.: JAI Press.

Raudenbush, Stephen W., and Robert D. Eschmann. 2015. "Does Schooling Increase or Reduce Social Inequality?" *Annual Review of Sociology* 41: 443–70.

Ray, Ranita. 2017. *The Making of a Teenage Service Class: Poverty and Mobility in an American City*. Berkeley: University of California Press.

Ray, Victor. 2019. "A Theory of Racialized Organizations." *American Sociological Review* 84(1): 26–53.

Reardon, Sean F., and Ann Owens. 2014. "60 Years after Brown: Trends and Consequences of School Segregation." *Annual Review of Sociology* 40: 199–218.

Reese, Linda W. 2008. "Septima Poinsette Clark (1898–1987)." *Black Past*, February 6. https://www.blackpast.org/african-american-history/clark-septima-poinsette-1898-1987/.

Regents of the University of California. 2010. "Regents Policy 4400: Policy on University of California Diversity Statement." https://regents.universityofcalifornia.edu/governance/policies/4400.html.

Rhodes, Marjorie, Sarah-Jane Leslie, Katya Saunders, Yarrow Dunham, and Andrei Cimpian. 2018. "How Does Social Essentialism Affect the Development of Inter-group Relations?" *Developmental Science* 21(1, January): e12509.

Rich, Peter. 2017. "Race, Resources, and Test Scores: What Schooling Characteristics Motivate the Housing Choices of White Parents?" Presented at the meeting of the Population Association of America, Chicago, April 27–29.

Riegle-Crumb, Catherine. 2019. "Gender Inequality in Education: Outcomes and Experiences." In *Education and Society: An Introduction to Key Issues in the Sociology of Education*, edited by Thurston Domina, Benjamin Gibbs, Lisa Nunn, and Andrew Penner. Berkeley: University of California Press.

Rios, Victor M. 2017. *Human Targets: Schools, Police, and the Criminalization of Latino Youth*. Chicago: University of Chicago Press.

Rivera, Lauren A. 2012. "Hiring as Cultural Matching: The Case of Elite Professional Service Firms." *American Sociological Review* 77(6, December): 999–1022.

———. 2015. *Pedigree: How Elite Students Get Elite Jobs*. Princeton, N.J.: Princeton University Press.

Rivera Maulucci, Maria S. 2010. "Navigating Role Forces and the Aesthetic Authentic Caring Dialectic: A Novice Urban Science Teacher's Developmental Trajectory." *Cultural Studies of Science Education* 5(3, September): 625–47.

Rochmes, Jane, Emily Penner, and Susanna Loeb. 2017. "Educators as Equity Warriors." CEPA Working Paper 17-11. Stanford, Calif.: Stanford University, Center for Education Policy Analysis (November).

Rosa, Hartmut. 2019. *Resonance: A Sociology of Our Relationship to the World.* Cambridge: Polity Press.

Rose, Heather, and Julian R. Betts. 2004. "The Effect of High School Courses on Earnings." *Review of Economics and Statistics* 86(2, May): 497–513.

Rosenbaum, James E. 1976. *Making Inequality: The Hidden Curriculum of High School Tracking.* New York: John Wiley & Sons.

Rosin, Matthew S., Heather Barondess, and Julian Leichty. 2009. *Algebra Policy in California: Great Expectations and Serious Challenges.* Mountain View, Calif.: EdSource.

Roth, Wendy D. 2016. "The Multiple Dimensions of Race." *Ethnic and Racial Studies* 39(8): 1310–38.

Rotondaro, Vinnie. 2015. "Boarding Schools: A Black Hole of Native American History." *National Catholic Reporter*, September 1. https://www.ncronline.org/news/justice/boarding-schools-black-hole-native-american-history.

Ruggles, Steven, Sarah Flood, Sophia Foster, Ronald Goeken, Jose Pacas, Megan Schouweiler, and Matthew Sobek. 2021. IPUMS USA: Version 11.0 (data set). Minneapolis: IPUMS. DOI: https://doi.org/10.18128/D010.V11.0.

Russell, Jennifer Lin. 2011. "From Child's Garden to Academic Press: The Role of Shifting Institutional Logics in Redefining Kindergarten Education." *American Educational Research Journal* 48(2, April): 236–67.

Sacchetti, Maria, Kevin Sieff, and Marc Fisher. 2018. "Separated Immigrant Children Are All over the U.S. Now, Far from Parents Who Don't Know Where They Are." *Washington Post*, June 24.

Sandel, Michael J. 2020. *The Tyranny of Merit: What's Become of the Common Good?* New York: Farrar, Straus and Giroux.

Santos, Henri C., Michael E. W. Varnum, and Igor Grossmann. 2017. "Global Increases in Individualism." *Psychological Science* 28(9, September): 1228–39.

Saperstein, Aliya, and Andrew M. Penner. 2012. "Racial Fluidity and Inequality in the United States." *American Journal of Sociology* 118(3, November): 676–727.

Schwartz, Amy Ellen, and Michah W. Rothbart. 2020. "Let Them Eat Lunch: The Impact of Universal Free Meals on Student Performance." *Journal of Policy Analysis and Management* 39(2, Spring): 376–410.

Shapiro, Andrew L. 1999. "The Net That Binds." *The Nation* 268(23, June 3): 11–15.

Sharma, Kritika. 2021. "Why Tamil Nadu Has Tabled Bill Seeking Exemption from NEET." *The Print*, September 13. https://theprint.in/india/why-tamil-nadu-has-tabled-bill-seeking-exemption-from-neet/732632/.

Shavit, Yossi, and Hans-Peter Blossfeld, eds. 1993. *Persistent Inequality: Changing Educational Attainment in Thirteen Countries.* Boulder, Colo.: Westview Press.

Sherif, Muzafer. 1956. "Experiments in Group Conflict." *Scientific American* 195(5, November 1): 54–59.

Sleeter, Christine E. 1986. "Learning Disabilities: The Social Construction of a Special Education Category." *Exceptional Children* 53(1, September): 46–54.

Sleeter, Christine E., and Carl A. Grant. 1991. "Race, Class, Gender, and Disability in Current Textbooks." In *The Politics of the Textbook*, edited by Michael Apple and Linda Christian-Smith. New York: Routledge.

Smardon, Regina. 2008. "Broken Brains and Broken Homes: The Meaning of Special Education in an Appalachian Community." *Anthropology and Education Quarterly* 39(2, June): 161–80.

Smith, Christian, and David Sikkink. 1999. "Is Private Schooling Privatizing?" *First Things: A Monthly Journal of Religion and Public Life* (April): 16–17.

Soares, Joseph A. 2017. "Meritocracy Dismissed." *Ethnic and Racial Studies* 40(13): 2300–2307.

Spillane, James P., Leigh Mesler Parise, and Jennifer Zoltners Sherer. 2011. "Organizational Routines as Coupling Mechanisms: Policy, School Administration, and the Technical Core." *American Educational Research Journal* 48(3, June): 586–619.

Spring, Joel. 2016. *Deculturalization and the Struggle for Equality: A Brief History of the Education of Dominated Cultures in the United States.* New York: Routledge.

State of California. 1994. "Proposition 187. Illegal Aliens. Ineligibility for Public Services. Verification and Reporting. Initiative Status." https://repository.uchastings.edu/ca_ballot_props/1104/.

Steele, Claude M., and Joshua Aronson. 1995. "Stereotype Threat and the Intellectual Test Performance of African Americans." *Journal of Personality and Social Psychology* 69(5, November): 797.

Stein, Mary Kay, Julia Heath Kaufman, Milan Sherman, and Amy F. Hillen. 2011. "Algebra: A Challenge at the Crossroads of Policy and Practice." *Review of Educational Research* 81(4, December): 453–92.

Stevens, Mitchell L. 2003. "The Normalisation of Homeschooling in the USA." *Evaluation and Research in Education* 17(2/3, May): 90–100.

———. 2009. *Creating a Class: College Admissions and the Education of Elites.* Cambridge, Mass.: Harvard University Press.

Stout, Mary A. 2012. *Native American Boarding Schools.* Santa Barbara, Calif.: ABC-CLIO.

Sturm, Johan, Leendert Groenendijk, Bernard Kruithof, and Julialet Rens. 1998. "Educational Pluralism: A Historical Study of So-Called 'Pillarization' in the Netherlands, Including a Comparison with Some Developments in South African Education." *Comparative Education* 34(3, November): 281–97.

Suàrez-Orozco, Marcelo M. 1996. "California Dreaming: Proposition 187 and the Cultural Psychology of Racial and Ethnic Exclusion." *Anthropology and Education Quarterly* 27(2, June): 151–67.

Tach, Laura Marie, and George Farkas. 2006. "Learning-Related Behaviors, Cognitive Skills, and Ability Grouping When Schooling Begins." *Social Science Research* 35(4, December): 1048–79.

Thorne, Barrie. 1993. *Gender Play: Girls and Boys in School.* New Brunswick, N.J.: Rutgers University Press.

The Times of India. 2021. "SC Dismisses Plea Seeking Cancellation of NEET Undergraduate Exam." October 4. https://timesofindia.indiatimes.com/home

/education/news/sc-dismisses-plea-seeking-cancellation-of-neet-undergraduate-exam/articleshow/86751610.cms.

Tilly, Charles. 1999. *Durable Inequality.* Berkeley: University of California Press.

Timmermans, Stefan, and Steven Epstein. 2010. "A World of Standards but Not a Standard World: Toward a Sociology of Standards and Standardization." *Annual Review of Sociology* 36: 69–89.

Tischauser, Leslie Vincent. 2012. *Jim Crow Laws.* Santa Barbara, Calif.: ABC-CLIO.

Titus, Jill Ogline. 2011. *Brown's Battleground: Students, Segregationists, and the Struggle for Justice in Prince Edward County, Virginia.* Chapel Hill: University of North Carolina Press.

Tyack, David B. 1974. *The One Best System: A History of American Urban Education.* Cambridge, Mass.: Harvard University Press.

Tyack, David B., and Larry Cuban. 1995. *Tinkering toward Utopia: A Century of Public School Reform.* Cambridge, Mass.: Harvard University Press.

Tyack, David B., and Elisabeth Hansot. 1990. *Learning Together: A History of Coeducation in American Schools.* New Haven, Conn.: Yale University Press.

Tyack, David B., Thomas James, and Aaron Benavot. 1991. *Law and the Shaping of Public Education, 1785–1954.* Madison: University of Wisconsin Press.

Tyack, David, and William Tobin. 1994. "The 'Grammar' of Schooling: Why Has It Been So Hard to Change?" *American Educational Research Journal* 31(3, Fall): 453–79.

Tyson, Karolyn, ed. 2011. *Integration Interrupted: Tracking, Black Students, and Acting White after Brown.* New York: Oxford University Press.

Tyson, Karolyn, William Darity Jr., and Domini R. Castellino. 2005. "'It's Not "a Black Thing': Understanding the Burden of Acting White and Other Dilemmas of High Achievement." *American Sociological Review* 70(4): 582–605.

Urdan, Timothy C., and Scott G. Paris. 1994. "Teachers' Perceptions of Standardized Achievement Tests." *Educational Policy* 8(2, June): 137–56.

U.S. Department of Education. 2023. "A History of the Individuals with Disabilities Education Act." Individuals with Disabilities Education Act. January 11, 2023. https://sites.ed.gov/idea/IDEA-History/.

Valenzuela, Angela. 1999. *Subtractive Schooling: Issues of Caring in Education of U.S.-Mexican Youth.* Albany: State University of New York Press.

Valenzuela, Juan Pablo, Cristian Bellei, and Danae de los Ríos. 2014. "Socioeconomic School Segregation in a Market-Oriented Educational System: The Case of Chile." *Journal of Education Policy* 29(2): 217–41.

Vasquez, Michael. 2015. "Feds Say Florida College Chain FastTrain Scammed Taxpayers." *Miami Herald*, October 3, 8B.

Waddington, R. Joseph, and Mark Berends. 2018. "Impact of the Indiana Choice Scholarship Program: Achievement Effects for Students in Upper Elementary and Middle School." *Journal of Policy Analysis and Management* 37(4, Fall): 783–808.

Waite, Linda J., and Maggie Gallagher. 2001. *The Case for Marriage: Why Married People Are Happier, Healthier, and Better Off Financially.* New York: Random House.

Waldman, Annie. 2016. "How a For-Profit College Targeted the Homeless and Kids with Low Self-Esteem." *ProPublica*, March 18. https://www.propublica.org

/article/how-a-for-profit-college-targeted-homeless-and-kids-with-low-self-esteem.

Walsh, Declan. 2015. "Fake Diplomas, Real Cash: Pakistani Company Axact Reaps Millions." *New York Times*, May 17.

Wang Feng. 2018. "China's Uphill Battle against Inequality." In *Polarized Cities: Portraits of Rich and Poor in Urban China*, edited by Dorothy J. Solinger. Lanham, Md.: Rowman & Littlefield.

Ware, Franita. 2006. "Warm Demander Pedagogy: Culturally Responsive Teaching That Supports a Culture of Achievement for African American Students." *Urban Education* 41(4): 427–56.

Watkins, William H., James H. Lewis, and Victoria Chou. 2001. *Race and Education: The Roles of History and Society in Educating African American Students*. Boston: Allyn & Bacon.

Watson, Eleanor. 2021. "West Point Cadets Expelled over Worst Cheating Scandal in 40 Years." *CBS News*, April 18. https://www.cbsnews.com/news/west-point-cheating-scandal-cadets-expelled/.

Webster, Noah. 1787. "On the Education of Youth in America," *American Magazine*, December.

Weick, Karl E. 1976. "Educational Organizations as Loosely Coupled Systems." *Administrative Science Quarterly* 21(1, March): 1–19.

Willis, Paul. 1981. *Learning to Labor: How Working Class Kids Get Working Class Jobs*. New York: Columbia University Press.

Wiseman, Alexander W., M. Fernanda Astiz, Rodrigo Fabrega, and David P. Baker. 2011. "Making Citizens of the World: The Political Socialization of Youth in Formal Mass Education Systems." *Compare: A Journal of Comparative and International Education* 41(5): 561–77.

Wollenberg, Charles. 1974. "*Mendez v. Westminster*: Race, Nationality and Segregation in California Schools." *California Historical Quarterly* 53(4): 317–32.

Worthy, Jo. 2010. "Only the Names Have Been Changed: Ability Grouping Revisited." *Urban Review* 42(4, November): 271–95.

Wurman, Ze'ev, and Bill Evers. 2010. "National Standards Would Harm Math Curriculum." *San Francisco Chronicle*, July 30.

Yee, Vivian. 2012. "Stuyvesant Students Describe the How and the Why of Cheating." *New York Times*, September 25.

Yonezawa, Susan, and Makeba Jones. 2006. "Students Perspectives on Tracking and Detracking." *Theory into Practice* 45(1, Winter): 15–23.

Zinn, Howard. 1997. "Freedom Schools." In *The Zinn Reader: Writings on Disobedience and Democracy*. New York: Seven Stories Press. Originally published in *The Nation*, November 23, 1964.

INDEX

Tables and figures are listed in **boldface**.